LAW'S FRAGILE STA

MW01026531

How do a legal order and the rule of law develop in a war-torn state? Using his field research in Sudan, the author uncovers how colonial administrators, postcolonial governments, and international aid agencies have used legal tools, practices, and resources to promote stability and their own visions of the rule of law amid political violence and war in Sudan. Tracing the dramatic development of three forms of legal politics – colonial, authoritarian, and humanitarian – this book contributes to a growing body of scholarship on law in authoritarian regimes and on human rights and legal empowerment programs in the global South. Refuting the conventional wisdom of a legal vacuum in failed states, Mark Fathi Massoud reveals how law matters deeply even in the most extreme cases of states still fighting for political stability.

Mark Fathi Massoud is Assistant Professor in the Politics Department and Legal Studies Program at the University of California, Santa Cruz. He received the Law and Society Association Dissertation Prize and the American Political Science Association Edward S. Corwin Award for the best dissertation in public law.

CAMBRIDGE STUDIES IN LAW AND SOCIETY

Cambridge Studies in Law and Society aims to publish the best scholarly work on legal discourse and practice in its social and institutional contexts, combining theoretical insights and empirical research.

The fields that it covers are studies of law in action; the sociology of law; the anthropology of law; cultural studies of law, including the role of legal discourses in social formations; law and economics; law and politics; and studies of governance. The books consider all forms of legal discourse across societies, rather than being limited to lawyers' discourses alone.

The series editors work in a range of disciplines: academic law, socio-legal studies, sociology, and anthropology. All have been actively involved in teaching and writing about law in context.

Series Editors

Chris Arup
Monash University, Victoria

Martin Chanock
La Trobe University, Melbourne

Sally Engle Merry
New York University

Susan Silbey
Massachusetts Institute of Technology

Books in the Series

Diseases of the Will
Mariana Valverde

The Politics of Truth and Reconciliation in South Africa: Legitimizing the Post-Apartheid State
Richard A. Wilson

Modernism and the Grounds of Law
Peter Fitzpatrick

Unemployment and Government: Genealogies of the Social
William Walters

Autonomy and Ethnicity: Negotiating Competing Claims in Multi-Ethnic States
Yash Ghai

Constituting Democracy: Law, Globalism and South Africa's Political Reconstruction
Heinz Klug

The Ritual of Rights in Japan: Law, Society, and Health Policy
Eric A. Feldman

(*continued after index*)

LAW'S FRAGILE STATE

Colonial, Authoritarian, and Humanitarian Legacies in Sudan

Mark Fathi Massoud

University of California, Santa Cruz

CAMBRIDGE
UNIVERSITY PRESS

32 Avenue of the Americas, New York NY 10013-2473, USA

Cambridge University Press is part of the University of Cambridge.

It furthers the University's mission by disseminating knowledge in the pursuit of
education, learning and research at the highest international levels of excellence.

www.cambridge.org
Information on this title: www.cambridge.org/9781107440050

© Mark Fathi Massoud 2013

First published 2013
First paperback edition 2014

A catalogue record for this publication is available from the British Library

Library of Congress Cataloguing in Publication data
Massoud, Mark Fathi.
Law's fragile state: colonial, authoritarian, and humanitarian legacies in
Sudan / Mark Fathi Massoud.
pages cm. – (Cambridge studies in law and society)
Includes bibliographical references and index.
ISBN 978-1-107-02607-0 (hardback)
1. Rule of law – Sudan – History. 2. Law – Political aspects – Sudan – History.
3. Islamic law – Sudan – History. 4. Sudan – Politics and government – History.
5. Human rights – Sudan. 6. Authoritarianism – Sudan. I. Title.
KTQ1726.M37 2013
349.624–dc23   2012049887

ISBN 978-1-107-02607-0 Hardback
ISBN 978-1-107-44005-0 Paperback

Sudan has seen colonialism. It's tried communism. It's tried [democracy]. The people of Sudan have seen it all.

Senior judicial official in Sudan[1]

The world should give me my full rights. Help.

Displaced woman from Darfur, western Sudan[2]

[1] Interview with Mukhtar, senior judicial official, in Khartoum, Sudan (April 2007). With the exception of historical figures and the most prominent public officials, all names in this book have been changed to preserve confidentiality.

[2] Interview with Nisreen, internally displaced person, near Khartoum, Sudan (June 2005).

CONTENTS

FIGURES, TABLES, AND MAPS

FIGURES

TABLES

MAPS

PREFACE

July 9, 2005. Thousands of residents from the sweltering, dilapidated camps that surround Khartoum streamed into the city. So many poverty-stricken and war-weary Sudanese filled the streets that the city shut down. I remember seeing broad smiles and hopeful eyes. Beneath the smiles, one could still sense hunger and trepidation. But this was a day for rejoicing. After more than twenty-two years, southern Sudanese leaders were officially welcomed back to the capital city and into government. The civil war was finally over.

My family had fled Sudan when I was a boy in 1983, as war resumed after a decade of relative calm. I returned to Sudan for the first time in 2005 to spend the summer with the United Nations Development Programme (UNDP) as a graduate student from Berkeley. I hoped to learn more about my homeland and the people who had stayed behind. I also wanted to make better sense of the concept and functions of law – and lawlessness. I hoped that investigating the law in as little-studied and unstable a setting as Sudan would reveal insights into the basis of the law's instrumental and ideological malleability. I knew I was lucky to have been spared the devastation of war in the intervening decades until my return to Sudan. But I had no conception of the true price paid by the Sudanese people during periods of violence and repression.

In 2005, the government was putting the finishing touches on a historic peace accord and new national constitution. It seemed a time for celebration. During that summer and a year in 2006–7, when most of the research for this book took place, I attended fifteen "legal awareness workshops" conducted in the squatter camps by nongovernmental organization (NGO) employees and local consultants (described in Chapter 5). The international aid community, in coordination with Sudanese NGOs, funded and carried out these workshops to inform the nation's most destitute people of their legal and human rights. From the first meeting I attended at the United Nations offices in Khartoum and the first workshop I visited in the desert outside the city, it struck me how human rights law seemed to be promoted as a kind of carpet under which the dust and trauma of the war would be swept and left behind. "We are doing everything from scratch," a senior UN human rights official would later explain to me.[1]

Foreign aid workers in Sudan saw the immediate postwar period as a critical moment of transformation that separated the nation's violent past from what they hoped would be its peaceful future. Legal consultants arrived en masse to train new judges and build the strength of the judiciary. United Nations officers spoke publicly about the need for Sudan to adopt a constitution that respected human rights principles. The World Bank, UN agencies, and international NGOs sponsored major conferences in Sudan outlining the importance of the rule of law for political, economic, and social development. And foreign governments channeled millions of dollars to the United Nations and international and local aid groups to implement widespread education programs designed to empower war-displaced persons to learn about, and ultimately access, justice through these new laws. Though not always coordinated, these law-building efforts were extraordinary for their breadth and because they took place in Sudan, classified by Western think tanks as a failed, rogue state. Because hundreds of foreign organizations were involved in the rebuilding effort, aid workers privately labeled Sudan "NGOistan," a designation they had earlier given to Iraq and Afghanistan in the aftermath of U.S.-led interventions.

The sweeping attempts to build up Sudan's legal institutions and public trust in them beg some questions about the country's legal history, which led me to write this book. How did the Anglo-Egyptian colonial administration and the Abboud, Nimeiri, and Bashir military regimes shape how the Sudanese people have experienced, confronted, or resisted legal expansion efforts? What did law actually look like from the perspective of the Sudanese poor before they attended legal awareness workshops? How does the process of teaching and learning about human rights influence activists and those whom they represent, or does the discourse of rights do neither harm nor good in conflict settings? And in what visions of law and development are survivors of war being asked to put their faith?

The aid efforts I witnessed in Sudan were not the first attempts by foreigners or Sudanese to build up the state's legal capacity. The British colonial administration in Sudan drafted extensive legal codes, built

---

[1] Interview with Omera, United Nations official, in Juba, southern Sudan (June 2010).

courthouses, and trained and recruited Sudanese people to work in them as clerks and judges. Later democratic and authoritarian governments in Sudan used similar strategies to indoctrinate citizens into the state's narrow vision of the rule of law. Under both the colonial and Bashir regimes, new courts provided spaces for nonviolent dispute resolution, and new law schools and informal legal-training programs educated people to advance the state's legal norms, institutions, and systems. The case of Sudan reveals how a multitude of legal spaces flourish in conflict settings, however weak the political apparatus remains.

We live in an age in which the rule of law and human rights are touted as twin catalysts for reforming weak institutions and building civil society in fragile states. But it is increasingly an age in which legal efforts are vilified for adopting one-size-fits-all solutions disconnected from the local political realities of war-torn settings. For these reasons I have sought to illuminate through this case study of Sudan the complex environment in which legal order is promoted, constructed, and destroyed in order to achieve social, economic, or political (including humanitarian) objectives. To accomplish this goal, this book adopts a longitudinal approach to the study of legal politics, analyzing how colonial, authoritarian, and humanitarian actors at different times seek to build a legal order to achieve their goals and, ultimately, how their efforts influence the lived experiences of the poor.

The targets of contemporary legal empowerment programs are among six million Sudanese forced to flee their homes during the north-south civil war and related atrocities in Darfur, Kordofan, and eastern Sudan. They formed encampments in the rural areas surrounding Khartoum. Because so much of the fighting took place in the South, Khartoum filled with survivors displaced from southern Sudan. They were the world's largest population of internally displaced persons.[2] During the war, they could watch the planes taking off from Khartoum's airport, flying south to bomb their home villages. In a grisly repetition of history, new squatter camps emerged in the desert in 2003, when millions more were displaced by the eruption of another war in Darfur. Violent clashes surfaced again in 2012 along a disputed border between Sudan

[2] The Internal Displacement Monitoring Centre estimated about five million displaced persons in Sudan just before the secession of South Sudan. "Estimates for the total number of IDPs for all of Sudan (as of January 2011)." Available: http://www.internal-displacement.org/idmc/website/countries.nsf/%28httpEnvelopes%29/0026B2F86813855FC1257570006185A0?OpenDocument (accessed January 9, 2013).

and South Sudan, as interethnic rivalries and natural resource disputes resurfaced.

Displaced persons in Sudan have endured war; extreme heat; lack of electricity, clean water, or formal education; and frequent *haboobs* (powerful dust storms) that send walls of sand a thousand feet tall crashing over their homes. They have also endured surveillance by police and security officers searching out and eradicating potential threats to the government's power. To earn money to buy food to feed their children, some displaced women brew alcohol and sell it to the vast population of shell-shocked unemployed men. The activity is illegal, and women are punished with prison sentences or whiplashes across their backs. I met fifteen-year-old mothers and thirty-five-year-old grandmothers. According to the World Health Organization, average "healthy" life expectancy in Sudan is among the lowest on earth – forty-seven years for men and fifty years for women – but it is even lower in the squatter areas and shantytowns for war-displaced persons.

The trip from NGO offices in central Khartoum to the desert encampments where legal awareness workshops are held takes more than an hour by bus. Temperatures soar above 120 degrees Fahrenheit outside and get considerably higher inside the bus. Driving along bumpy and sandy desert roads, the bus passes thousands of small tent-like homes fashioned out of sandy earth and animal dung, the only natural resources in these areas. The tents in these desolate camps usually house multiple families. Sometimes more than a dozen people can be found cramped inside, taking shelter from the desert sun. There are no trees. The world is brown and covered in dust. For most of the year, the combination of wind and sand means that it is impossible to walk, talk, move, or eat without becoming covered in sand. During the rainy season, mud makes driving or walking impossible, so these areas are completely cut off from the cities. The desert encampments were meant to provide temporary shelter until the war ended. But many displaced persons have lived there for twenty years or more.

The signing of the 2005 peace accord, witnessed by multiple foreign heads of state and the then–U.S. secretary of state Colin Powell, represented an opportunity for Sudan's leadership and people to think about their fragile nation's future, the first such opportunity in a generation. The end of the war also created opportunities for foreign researchers to visit Sudan in relative safety. I was able to travel in Khartoum as well as in southern and central Sudan in 2005, in 2006–7, and again in 2010. But the window of peace that allowed me to conduct the research for this book is threatening to shut. With an ongoing humanitarian crisis in Darfur, recurrent clashes in eastern Sudan and in the oil-rich regions along the border with South Sudan, and the continued targeting of Sudanese and foreign aid workers, Sudan teeters once again on the brink of chaos.

Working in a nation so well acquainted with tyranny and terror, one could easily be overcome with grief. I met one displaced woman from Darfur who had managed to escape to a squatter area near Khartoum but had lost the rest of her family. In a remarkable display of humility, forgiving her adversaries and acknowledging the universality of human suffering, she said to me, "We are all Sudanese." This book does not presume to describe or comprehend the horrors experienced by the Sudanese people. My intention is to make sense of how the law operates in volatile, divided, and authoritarian states like Sudan and how it can be marshaled to promote peace rather than violence.

My legal training, intellectual endeavor, and Sudanese birth of mixed ancestry rather than a specific tribal background, I learned, helped me to transcend existing and deep political boundaries and build rapport among attorneys, judges, and local activists, who told me they were pleased to see a young man – whose family fled the country never to return – himself come home to the nation that delivered him into the world. This book forms part of my ongoing journey to make sense of Sudan and, more broadly, to discover what law does, and what it fails to do, in the world's most desperate environments.

ACKNOWLEDGMENTS

I have devoted nearly a decade to researching and writing this book, and I could not have completed the project alone. I extend my gratitude first to the many Sudanese people without whose genuine kindness this project could not have been completed. Specifically, I would like to thank Babiker Awadalla, former chief justice and prime minister of Sudan, as well as the current and former judges of the Sudanese courts, former government ministers, and Sudanese legal academics who took an interest in my research, made themselves available to me, and welcomed me with great hospitality. I thank the staff of the Sudan Judiciary library, Judiciary statistics department, and Sudan Bar Association Admissions Office for helping me find important historical and quantitative data, much of it locked in cabinets and covered with layers of sand and cobwebs. I also acknowledge the critical participation of many dozens of lawyers and activists who must go unnamed. Without these people this book would not be possible. *Ashkurukum 'ala musa'adatakum wa hikmatakum, khasatan i'ata'iy al-fursa al-'azhima li 'aml al-bahth. Amaani da'iman ma'akum.*

The preliminary study on which this book is based was incubated by the United Nations Development Programme's Rule of Law Unit in 2005. The United Nations Mission in Sudan, World Food Programme, Deutscher Entwicklungsdienst (German Development Service, since renamed the German Society for International Cooperation), British Foreign and Commonwealth Office, United Nations Office for the Coordination of Humanitarian Affairs, and the Salesian community of El Obeid provided logistical and travel support in Juba and El Obeid in 2007 and 2010. Special thanks to Bente Brandt, Omar Daair, Angela Grünert, Zaved Mahmood, Matthew Putorti, and Noah Salomon, who each provided friendship, support, and thoughtful engagement with me during my field research. Carolyn Fluehr-Lobban and Richard Lobban helped me to realize that studying law in Sudan would be possible and immensely rewarding.

I thank the staff of Ahfad University's Institute of Women, Gender, and Development Studies (since renamed the Regional Institute of

Gender, Diversity, Peace, and Rights) and its director, Dr. Balghis Badri, for providing me with a research affiliation, library, office, and intellectual base during my extended visits to Sudan. I owe particular thanks to Ali Suleiman Fadlalla and Mohamed Ibrahim Khalil of the University of Khartoum Faculty of Law for their valuable mentorship, wisdom, and advice.

The Sudan National Records Office, Egyptian National Records Office, and American University in Cairo each allowed me to study their texts on law in Sudan not available anywhere else. Thanks also to archivists at Durham University's Sudan Archive for making the document retrieval process so effortless.

I am grateful to the late Sir Donald Hawley for sharing with me his experiences as a high-ranking colonial administrator of the Anglo-Egyptian Sudan, and for graciously agreeing to answer my catalog of questions during a day-long interview at his country estate in Wiltshire. I express special gratitude to William Twining of University College London for his thoughtful conversation and to Sarah Spells and other library custodians at the School of Oriental and African Studies in London.

This book began as a dissertation in the Jurisprudence and Social Policy Program at the University of California, Berkeley. I acknowledge the support of my dissertation committee members: Malcolm Feeley, Martin Shapiro, and Kim Voss. From the first day I visited Malcolm Feeley in his office in 2002 to talk about religious influences on judicial decision making (a topic I have not abandoned), he has encouraged my intellectual and professional development. Other mentors at the UC Berkeley School of Law who undoubtedly also left their impressions on this book and deserve special thanks include David Caron, Lauren Edelman, Robert Kagan, Christopher Kutz, and Philip Selznick.

I received support for the research and writing of this book from a Fulbright-Hays fellowship; a University of California Institute on Global Conflict and Cooperation fellowship; grants from the UC Berkeley Center for African Studies and School of Law; a University of California, Santa Cruz, faculty research grant; a Hewlett postdoctoral fellowship at the Center on Democracy, Development, and the Rule of Law at Stanford University; and a visiting fellowship at the McGill University Centre for Human Rights and Legal Pluralism.

My colleagues in the Department of Politics at the University of California, Santa Cruz, have provided an idyllic scholarly environment in which to work. I am grateful to them for creating a supportive space for research and teaching. I completed many revisions to this book in 2011–12 at the McGill University Faculty of Law and Institute for Health and Social Policy. My colleagues over the years at UC Berkeley, Stanford, McGill, and UC Santa Cruz have blessed me with continued engagement and lasting friendship.

Some parts of the Preface and Chapters 5 and 6 appear in or draw from two previously published articles, "Do Victims of War Need International Law? Human Rights Education Programs in Authoritarian Sudan" (*Law & Society Review*, 2011) and "Rights in a Failed State: Internally Displaced Women in Sudan and Their Lawyers" (*Berkeley Journal of Gender, Law & Justice*, 2006). Some elements in Chapters 3 and 4 expand upon material found in "Lawyers and the Disintegration of the Legal Complex in Sudan," from *Fates of Political Liberalism in the British Post-Colony: The Politics of the Legal Complex* (Cambridge University Press, 2012). I am grateful to *Law & Society Review*, the *Berkeley Journal of Gender, Law and Justice*, and Cambridge University Press for permitting me to draw from these works.

I thank a number of individuals who gave helpful support to this project or feedback on the ideas presented in this book, including the anonymous reviewers, Adam Branch, Melissa Caldwell, Kent Eaton, Shelby Grossman, Edith Kinney, Lawrence Friedman, Shannon Gleeson, Robert Leckey, Larisa Mann, Khalid Mustafa Medani, Adam Millard-Ball, Eleonora Pasotti, David Pimentel, Benjamin Read, Brad Roth, Noah Salomon, Roger Schoenman, Rachel Stern, Heather Sharkey, and Juan Wang. Conversations with Clifford Bob, Richard Falk, Leila Kawar, and Helen Stacy helped me to refine my own thinking about human rights and the normative ordering of the law in politics. Adam Millard-Ball and Ramzi Ramey helped to design the maps in this book. Salma Gasim and Audrey Mocle provided valuable research assistance. I thank my editor at Cambridge University Press, John Berger, and the production team managed by Abidha Sulaiman, for their efficiency and responsiveness. Liz Goldberg and James Graham copyedited the manuscript. Julie Fontaine helped to organize the Bibliography. Any errors in the following pages are my own, of course.

Countless thanks to Adam, to my family and friends, and to God for being so strong and steady when I turned to them during my moments of need in Sudan and elsewhere. Finally, I extend my deepest gratitude to Fathi, Marola, Robert, Therese, Eddy, Galdino, and Muna, who at various times in Sudan gave me shelter from the sandstorms and safe places to laugh, to cry, to learn, and to write.

NOTE ON TRANSLATION AND TRANSLITERATION

All translations and transliterations from Arabic-language documents and interviews are mine. I provide English translations alongside Arabic words that appear in this book; terms that appear several times are translated after their first usage in each chapter, such as *shari'a* (roughly translated as Islamic law). Simple apostrophes are used to represent diacritical marks for the Arabic *'ayn*, as in *shari'a*, and for the Arabic *hamza*, as in *ara'id* (petitions). I maintain these diacritics for proper names and render nisba endings *-iyya*, as in *effendiyya*, per the *International Journal of Middle East Studies* transliteration system. I have strived to ensure that all Arabic transliterations into English would be accessible to those familiar with Modern Standard Arabic and non-Sudanese dialects, balanced with my intent to remain true to the Sudanese dialect in which much of the research was conducted. While standard transliterations do exist, some Arabic words, including names of persons, have several spellings when transliterated into foreign languages (for instance, Numairi/Numeyri, Omar/'Umr, and Awadalla/Awad-Allah). I have aimed for clarity and consistency in the transliterations that I use. Any mistakes in translation or transliteration are my own.

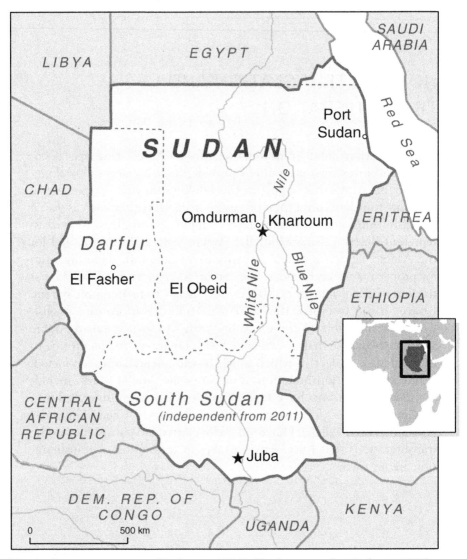

Map 1. Contemporary map of Sudan until 2011 (Darfur annexed to Sudan in 1917).
Source: Author, derived from ESRI base data.

INTRODUCTION

One of the first interviews I did for this book was with a well-respected Sudanese lawyer. We met outside the offices of the Sudan Bar Association in Khartoum and sipped sugary tea from miniature glass cups. Our movements were slow, weighted by the heavy Saharan heat. I told him that I was planning to write a book on the development of law in Sudan. "Law in Sudan?" he asked. "Really?" He gently put down his cup and turned his gaze away from me toward the stark emptiness of the desert beyond us. Then he fixed his eyes back on me. I held my pen over a fresh page, eagerly waiting to memorialize his words. "Your book," he said, "will be a very short one."

There is a common perception among both Sudanese and foreigners who know the country well that Sudan lacks any semblance of law or legal strictures. It is easy to see why, troubled as Sudan is by violence and political volatility. Sudan's national experience has been characterized by alternating horrors: the immediate suffering of war and the attenuated suffering of broken promises and dashed hopes. For sixty years, Sudan has been known around the world for the brutality perpetrated by its own people against one another and the trauma endured by the survivors. One of its many interconnected civil wars would become infamous as Africa's longest. It ignited in southern Sudan in 1983, and, by the time peace accords were signed in 2005, more than two million people had been killed and Sudan was left with the world's largest population of internally displaced persons. The resumption of violent conflict in Darfur in 2003, clashes along the border with South Sudan, and sporadic battles between the government army and splinter groups continue to typify the horrors of the region. Multiple wars are due in part to claims that the political leadership in Khartoum fails to represent Sudan's diverse population and to Khartoum's incessant drive to quell rather than to accommodate resistance.[1]

Because of Sudan's long history of political instability, legal scholars inside and outside the country perceive it as existing in a kind of legal vacuum. The view of Sudan as a nation without law is supported by its consistent ranking among the world's "failed" states.[2] Among scholars, there is also widespread acceptance of the idea that the law, where it exists to limit the actions of states, promotes peace and prosperity. Legal reform plays an important role in the efforts of humanitarian actors to consolidate democratic stability in war-torn areas and to res-cue weak states from their failures. Their efforts to promote the rule of law have largely centered on building up legal institutions responsive to the needs of citizens.

The rule of law, it has been argued, can counter a recalcitrant and repressive authority,[3] moderate state power and build capacity for good governance,[4] reduce the likelihood of violent conflict,[5] combat terror-ism, support stable and accountable institutions, enhance security, and

[1] Douglas H. Johnson, *The Root Causes of Sudan's Civil Wars* (Bloomington: Indiana University Press, 2003); Francis Deng, *War of Visions: Conflict of Identities in the Sudan* (New York: Brookings Institution Press, 1995).

[2] In the five-year period 2008–12, *Foreign Policy* and the Fund for Peace ranked Sudan as the second- or third-most "failed" state in the world, following two years (2006 and 2007) as the most failed state. Their *Failed States Index* (2012) ranks 177 coun-tries using twelve political and social indicators, including human-rights failures, human flight, uneven development, state delegitimization, factionalized elites, and economic decline. Sudan has also been ranked the second "most fragile" state in the world by the Center for Systemic Peace. Freedom House ranked Sudan among its "worst in the world" index in 2012, for a dearth of political rights and civil liberties. See http://www.foreignpolicy.com/failedstates2012 (accessed January 9, 2013); Monty G. Marshall and Benjamin R. Cole, *Global Report 2011: Conflict, Governance, and State Fragility* (Vienna, VA: Center for Systemic Peace); Freedom House, *Worst of the World 2012: The World's Most Repressive Societies* (Washington, DC, 2012).

[3] Philip Selznick, *The Moral Commonwealth: Social Theory and the Promise of Community* (Berkeley: University of California Press, 1992), 289.

[4] Susan Rose-Ackerman, "Establishing the Rule of Law," in *When States Fail: Causes and Consequences*, ed. Robert Rotberg (Princeton: Princeton University Press, 2004), 182–221.

[5] James Fearon, "Governance and Civil War Onset," *World Development Report 2011 Background Paper* (Washington, DC: World Bank, 2011).

pave the way for economic and social development. It is believed that the rule of law can end corruption, instability, and tyranny.[6] For this reason, a great deal of international aid is earmarked for programs that try to establish "law" as a step toward building a robust rule of law in countries wrestling with economic and political crisis or civil war. As important as direct provision of food, shelter, or health care can be in these dire situations, supporting the growth of legal institutions is seen as a way for aid donors to address the fundamental institutional needs of fragile states.[7]

By all accounts the rule-of-law enterprise is sweeping. Global legal and judicial development assistance from Organization for Economic Cooperation and Development (OECD) countries tripled between 2006 and 2008, from USD 841.5 million to USD 2.6 billion.[8] In addition to funding state legal development programs, OECD sources provide approximately USD 1 billion annually for grassroots human-rights projects and activities.[9] Some estimates also suggest nearly half of the World Bank's annual spending has some rule-of-law component.[10] Similarly, United Nations officials have called the rule of law the "driving force" behind the UN's work and the "very heart" of its mission to promote peace.[11] In 2006 the UN established a systemwide Rule of Law Unit under the direct authority of the secretary general, and UN agencies actively design and fund programs intended to construct legal institutions and to promote legal principles and awareness in high-conflict settings.[12]

---

[6] Thomas Carothers, "The Rule of Law Revival," in *Promoting the Rule of Law Abroad: In Search of Knowledge*, ed. Thomas Carothers (Washington, DC: Carnegie Endowment for International Peace, 2006), 3–14.

[7] *World Development Report: Conflict, Security, and Development* (Washington, DC: World Bank, 2011).

[8] See *Legal and Judicial Development Assistance Global Report 2010* (Rome, Italy: International Development Law Organization, 2010), 10–12.

[9] Ibid.

[10] "Briefing: Economics and the Rule of Law," *Economist* (March 15–21, 2008), 84.

[11] "Promoting Rule of Law 'Very Heart of the United Nations Mission,' Says Deputy Secretary-General, in Legal Committee Remarks," United Nations Department of Public Information, DSG/SM/346 GA/L/3327 (2007). Available: http://www.un.org/News/Press/docs/2007/dsgsm346.doc.htm (accessed January 9, 2013). See also "United Nations and the Rule of Law," http://www.un.org/en/ruleoflaw/index.shtml (accessed January 9, 2013).

[12] United Nations, *Report of the Secretary-General on The Rule of Law and Transitional Justice in Conflict and Post-Conflict Societies* 2004; UN Development Programme

Contemporary law-building programs in fragile states operate on two primary assumptions about the law. First, the law is either tarnished or entirely lacking in these places, and, second, through foreign assistance and "capacity building" states may build up a legal order rooted in the rule of law, to move from authoritarianism and war to democracy and peace. The mechanisms for introducing the rule of law are both top-down and bottom-up: providing advice and training to government staff to install a top-down political and economic order, and to civil society activists to promote a bottom-up social order that respects human rights. Ultimately the goal is to transform traditional or conflict-ridden societies into modern, liberal states.

This book challenges both of these assumptions: that a legal order does not exist in so-called failed states like Sudan and that legal tools and practices intrinsically serve to promote democracy and human rights. On the first assumption, I show that repressive regimes fighting civil wars may quite effectively use the law and legal resources to their own benefit just as they do their militaries in civil war. Where the law supplants violence, it can allow an illegitimate government to appear more moderate, thereby augmenting its authority. Civil society actors also adopt legal strategies of their own, by educating impoverished populations displaced by war to see human rights as an accessible set of legal tools and to adopt legal solutions to their oppression. On the second assumption, I argue that law's normative character is not inherent and should not be taken for granted. Different political actors insert

and UN Population Fund 2007:4; Louise Arbour (2008) "Foreword," in *Claiming the Millennium Development Goals: A Human Rights Approach*, Geneva: United Nations Office of the High Commissioner for Human Rights HR/PUB/08/3. Available: http://www.unhcr.org/refworld/docid/49fac1162.html (accessed January 9, 2013); UNICEF, "The Human Rights-Based Approach: Statement of Common Understanding," in *State of the World's Children (Annex B)*, 2004. Available: http://www.unicef.org/sowc04/sowc04_annexes.html (accessed January 9, 2013); Stephen Humphreys, *Theatre of the Rule of Law: Transnational Legal Intervention in Theory and Practice* (Cambridge: Cambridge University Press, 2010); Jane Stromseth, David Wippman, and Rosa Brooks, *Can Might Make Rights: Building the Rule of Law after Military Interventions* (Cambridge: Cambridge University Press, 2006); James J. Heckman, Robert L. Nelson, and Lee Cabatingan, eds., *Global Perspectives on the Rule of Law* (New York: Routledge, 2010); Amanda Perry-Kessaris, ed., *Law in the Pursuit of Development: Principles into Practice?* (New York: Routledge, 2010); Chandra Lekha-Sriram, Olga Martin-Ortega, and Johanna Herman, eds., *Peacebuilding and the Rule of Law in Africa* (New York: Routledge, 2011).

their own distinct moral predilections into the law to manufacture a range of tools to build up stability or security.

Law, then, cannot be detached from political systems and behaviors; it is, instead, inherent to politics. Determining which normative qualities are associated with law and legal practices involves investigating who uses the law, what their goals are, and how they implement their political agenda. The case of Sudan reveals this multifaceted nature of law and legal processes and, ultimately, how law is essential to, rather than missing from, unstable political environments.

Sudan serves as a useful case study for this type of inquiry into the multifaceted nature of law because the country's history exposes the variety of legal tools that elite actors use to achieve their aims in the battle for political influence over a diverse and divided population. Law in Sudan operates in a context marked by extreme human suffering, desperation, and a political structure perpetually on the edge of collapse. But contrary to conventional wisdom, law matters hugely in a nation as fragile as Sudan. Legal practices and ideas shape both the unstable bedrock of the state and the efforts to rescue it from future failure. The meaning of the law, then, emerges not only through struggles for national independence or democracy but also as law is incorporated into political violence and takes on new roles, articulations, and significance. (I define the central concepts used in this book, including law and legal politics, in detail in Chapter 1.)

Does it ask too much of the law to demand that it serve as a bulwark against tyranny or even genocide? After all, legal institutions in even the most democratically advanced nations are constrained entities.[13] Courts in the robust democracies of the United States, Canada, and nations in Western Europe have the power of neither sword nor purse,[14] and in many cases the poor face a range of complex social, legal, and financial obstacles to accessing the court system.[15] In

---

[13] Gerald Rosenberg, *The Hollow Hope: Can Courts Bring About Social Change?* 2nd ed. (Chicago: University of Chicago Press, 2008); Michael McCann, *Rights at Work: Pay Equity Reform and the Politics of Legal Mobilization* (Chicago: University of Chicago Press, 1994); Charles Epp, *The Rights Revolution: Lawyers, Activists, and Supreme Courts in Comparative Perspective* (Chicago: University of Chicago Press, 1998).

[14] See Alexander Hamilton, *Federalist* No. 78 (1788). Available: http://www.constitution.org/fed/federa78.htm (accessed January 9, 2013).

[15] Marc Galanter, "Why the 'Haves' Come Out Ahead: Speculations on the Limits of Legal Change," 9 *Law & Society Review* (1974): 95–160; Kristin Bumiller, "Victims

authoritarian states, legal institutions are susceptible to manipulation by elites seeking to monopolize power.[16] Nevertheless, the full force of the international aid community is now behind legal initiatives in the belief that building elaborated legal mechanisms and institutions in conflict settings will meaningfully alleviate the burdens of the poor and besieged.[17] Investigating these initiatives within the historical and political contexts in which they take place reveals the critical role of law and law-centered political strategies in the attempts to rescue states from their failures.

Sudan illustrates the ways legal tools and practices are used as political resources precisely because it is a weak state that has swung so wildly among the extremes of colonialism, socialism, authoritarianism, and democracy. During these regime shifts, court benches have been hastily emptied and refilled; legal systems have flip-flopped between common law, civil law, and Islamic law; and human-rights organizations have been shuttered and reopened. In this complex and troubled setting aid agencies inspired by a sense of humanitarianism have been trying to promote legal progress and develop the rule of law. In less volatile states, the range of legal toolkits is certainly more limited, as law is constitutive of a relatively orderly and more stable state infrastructure. In erratic or threatening environments, a wider array of legal tools and concepts can be adopted, manipulated, and discarded to build support for colonial administrators, authoritarian governments, and human-rights groups seeking to reach the war-displaced poor.

in the Shadow of the Law: A Critique of the Model of Legal Protection," 12 *Signs* (1987): 421–39; William L. F. Felstiner, Richard L. Abel, and Austin Sarat, "The Emergence and Transformation of Disputes: Naming, Blaming, Claiming …," 15 *Law & Society Review* (1980–81): 631–54.

[16] See Kathryn Hendly, *Trying to Make Law Matter: Legal Reform and Labor Law in the Soviet Union* (Ann Arbor: University of Michigan Press, 1996). See also Tom Ginsburg and Tamir Moustafa, eds., *Rule by Law: The Politics of Courts in Authoritarian Regimes* (Cambridge: Cambridge University Press, 2008); Gretchen Helmke and Frances Rosenbluth, "Regimes and the Rule of Law: Judicial Independence in Comparative Perspective," *Annual Review of Political Science* 12 (2009): 345–66.

[17] Mark Fathi Massoud, "Do Victims of War Need International Law? Human Rights Education Programs in Authoritarian Sudan," *Law & Society Review* 45 (2011): 1–32; *World Development Report: Conflict, Security, and Development* (Washington, DC: World Bank, 2011); *Report of the Secretary-General on the Rule of Law and Transitional Justice in Conflict and Post-Conflict Societies* S/2004/616 (United Nations Security Council, 2004).

How do colonial, authoritarian, and humanitarian actors use these legal toolkits to build stability in unstable places? In general, they seek to stabilize the political and economic order by constructing (or demolishing) key building blocks of the rule of law, including drafting constitutions, writing or reforming legal rules, and encouraging the development of courts and the creation of spaces for grievances to be heard. Colonial officials, for instance, set up a state-supervised legal infrastructure to civilize local subjects in their image. Authoritarian leaders calling for Islamic law similarly construct courts and law schools to extend social control, but also to provide state resources to those citizens who surrender to the regime's claims to authority. And civil society actors eager for foreign resources encourage impoverished persons to mobilize for peace and democracy under the shield of human-rights law. These three distinct actors have been among those most responsible for shaping Sudan's modern political history, and they create change through law-based reform and encourage the Sudanese people to follow their examples and turn toward the law. Table I.1 spotlights the primary law-based political strategies they have used in Sudan.

THE APPEAL OF LEGAL POLITICS

State and nonstate actors design, deploy, and destroy a variety of strategies and technologies to meet the goals of state building. States weakened by war or political violence, for instance, will seek to forestall the possibility of domestic revolution by providing resources to citizens. Building schools and providing subsidies for basic commodities, such as food and fuel, are obvious tactics. Less obvious are the protean legal strategies that states take, which include writing and enforcing laws that build social order, establishing law schools to train professionals, hiring judges to resolve citizen disputes, and improving the legal system's speed and effectiveness.

The process of achieving political, social, or economic objectives using legal mechanisms – or, *legal politics* – is complex, disordered, and often violent. For instance, some of the most democratically minded lawyers and judges in Sudan reversed course during military rule. When lured by the promise of political power, they imprisoned activists and colleagues in the legal profession. Paradoxically, the case of Sudan sheds light on the precarious path toward E. P. Thomson's vision of the rule-of-law ideal as an unqualified human good: the rule of law in action is stained by the blood of activists, nonviolent resisters, and the

Table I.1. The legal arsenal (law-based political strategies by elite actors in a fragile state)

Law-based Strategy	Actors		
	Colonial	Authoritarian	Humanitarian
Investing in courthouse construction and judicial training	X	X	X
Building law schools and the legal profession	X	X	X
Creating spaces for grievances against the government to be heard, managed, and processed	X	X	X
Encouraging citizens to use courts to seek redress of grievances and resolve private disputes	X	X	X
Training citizens to trust that knowledge of the law is valuable and righteous	X	X	X
Drafting constitutions, ordinances, and legal codes for domestic enforcement	X	X	X
Overhauling the legal system to leave an enduring legacy, facilitate economic development, or divert attention from political divisions or a collapsing economy	X	X	X
Devolving judicial power to local elites dispatched or co-opted by the central administration	X	X	
Appointing ideological supporters to the bench; dismissing nonaligned judges	X	X	
Monitoring and stifling dissent among legal academics and professionals	X	X	
Compartmentalizing religious (Islamic) law to private, family matters and limiting access to legal education	X		
Funding construction of religious institutions under a legal department, to attempt to enhance legitimacy and monitor activity among indigenous elites	X		
Ensuring the bar association is under the control of the dominant political party		X	
Increasing the number of criminal courts to promote social control, enforce the ability to punish, and dominate the legal order		X	
Adopting a sweeping vision of Islamic law to reinforce political control through claims to religious authority		X	
Shuttering human-rights organizations, overseeing ideologically supportive groups, and monitoring independent organizations		X	
Encouraging the belief among the poor that law – particularly international law – is an instrument of liberation from oppression			X

Source: Author.

poor. The *longue durée* of the Sudanese legal order may one day reveal that law ultimately protects and empowers the poor as much as it has also subjugated them. But it is precisely the poor who are left behind during a process captured by elite political actors carrying legal tools of their own.

The goals and ethical leanings of British colonial officials, postcolonial authoritarian leaders and their opponents, and contemporary civil society activists and their donors could hardly be more different. They range from the consolidation of territorial control and the expansion of state authority to the promotion of human-rights principles and human security. And yet, these actors all have similarly directed their limited resources toward drafting laws, constructing legal institutions, and training legal personnel – or, constructing a legal order. Why? By encouraging citizens to trust in and turn to formal legal institutions to resolve grievances with one another and with the government, law and legal institutions – particularly during periods of civil war and entrenched authoritarianism – become release valves for pressure that builds in civil society and spaces for anger to dissipate. Creating institutions like courts and grievance boards that purport to place limits on the regime's power helps those regimes swallow, digest, and discharge grievances against them, rather than allowing those grievances to fester and gain potency. By financing the expansion of courts, regimes institutionalize claims against them, paradoxically boosting the regime's legitimacy and authority by creating neutral spaces for dispute resolution. As civil society activists and aid donors encourage a similar expansion of legal institutions, authoritarian governments have been rewarded with more space to manufacture the image of legitimacy and social control.

But why would an unrepentantly nondemocratic regime like that of Sudan's President Bashir, or earlier President Nimeiri, use law instead of merely guns or buyouts to get what it wants? Law can be just as effective as an arsenal to manufacture and maintain authority: state actors see legal order as a public good they can deliver to help them hold on to power despite fueling catastrophic wars. Legal strategies are hidden behind the weak forms of legitimacy that otherwise illegitimate governments possess. But the results of these undertakings are in plain view – new courthouses and law schools, as well as the careers of lawyers and judges fulfilling the regime's vision of dispute resolution. When peace accords signed by the government also create openings for civil society interventions in the name of human rights (as occurred in Sudan in 2005), foreign aid actors and the local civil society groups they fund turn to international law to undermine authoritarianism and develop a grassroots legal culture of human rights. Legal resources, both domestic and international, are tools that elite actors use to achieve their political or moral ends. State actors turn to the law in order to consolidate top-down power and influence in moments of economic or political crisis, while civil society actors use it to promote human rights and political development from the ground up.

In times of political fumbling and crisis, elite actors turn to legal tools and resources to achieve twin goals: to expand their influence in society and to restrict the behavior and limit the power of adversaries. Nondemocratic states struggling to support themselves adopt legal innovations to prevent collapse, to monitor and control civil society, and to defuse tensions against the regime. Law becomes part of the technology they use to create stability and sow legitimacy in those areas where and among those populations over whom they seek control. Activists and nongovernmental groups use informal legal training practices to carve a space for grassroots social change, encouraging masses of war-displaced persons to see law as a mechanism to free themselves from the limits imposed upon them by states. From the perspective of states, law is an attractive tool to facilitate the management of civil society, and from the perspective of civil society, knowledge of the law is an advantageous start to contain the power of government. Connecting the behaviors of states and survivors reveals that state actors are not alone in their use of legal means to produce political change – civil society activists and aid workers are also deeply engaged in the project of building a legal order that supports their interests. Both political actors seeking to consolidate authority and those seeking to disrupt or challenge that rule employ legal toolkits to achieve their respective ends. In this way, law can serve tyranny and violence as easily as it can serve liberty and peacebuilding.

Legal tools and resources are inherent to the politics of both violence and peacebuilding precisely because law can be represented as distinct from politics. Its appeal as a social good and as an expression of a desired moral order gives meaning and rationale to everyday actions, even actions that heighten state violence. That law articulates a preferred moral order allows it to be used by scrupulous and unscrupulous elites who turn it into a weapon in their arsenal for change.[18]

---

[18] On law as an enterprise rather than "inert matter," see Lon Fuller, *The Morality of Law* (New Haven, CT: Yale University Press, 1969), 123. See also Martin

[handwritten margin note: law & culture are entertwined! can't to colonialize law too, won't make a successful system]

THE IMPERFECT NATURE OF LEGAL POLITICS

Certainly law becomes a resource for those seeking to build a functioning state out of a war zone. But legal strategies are imperfect at meeting the goals they are designed to achieve and may even backfire. Colonial officials in Sudan, for instance, attempted to build up a Sudanese common law rooted in British norms. They constructed an elite law school in Khartoum alongside sites outside the capital where grievances could be collected and discharged. Their efforts were intended to impose a single imperial authority over diverse populations, while inculcating rule-of-law values to confer a modicum of legitimacy upon their project. But law haunted them over time as young nationalists began to use courts that had been designed to monitor and subjugate them as key spaces to promote independence from British colonial rule.

Postcolonial authoritarian regimes responding to political or economic crisis also financed the expansion of legal institutions as a way to quell opposition, disempower opposition groups, maintain stability, and build authority. The Bashir regime in particular sought to undergird its rule by promoting a legal system based on political claims to Islamic authority – constructing new law faculties to educate future generations of Sudanese lawyers and judges and increasing the numbers of courthouses from 250 to more than 700 during the 1990s – to consolidate tenuous grips on power within and outside the capital city. But the 1964 and 1985 nonviolent revolutions in Khartoum that toppled earlier authoritarian governments demonstrate how citizens ultimately perceive legal maneuvering to be part of dirty politics. Fed up with the broader consequences of nondemocratic rule, they organized and took to the streets when political opportunities for engagement emerged.

Civil society and the aid community are also not immune to the attraction of the law and the imperfect nature of legal tools and resources. In the aftermath of civil war, a postconflict mindset takes hold. They reach into their legal toolkits to empower citizens with legal knowledge, relieve the burdens that impoverished populations face, and promote peace, stability, representative democracy, and economic growth. Providing education about standards of human rights to persons displaced by civil war, aid workers seek to persuade them that legal institutions will one day be trustworthy. But law haunts civil

Krygier, *Philip Selznick: Ideals in the World* (Stanford, CA: Stanford University Press, 2012), 108.

society, too: efforts focused on grassroots legal development alone are not the salvation of the poor.

THE CONSEQUENCES OF LEGAL POLITICS

My research in Sudan has uncovered the extraordinary measures political leaders have taken, including hastily supplanting one legal system with another, over and over again, in the name of state building. This repetitive process yields a layered and plural state legal order, and it exposes the diverse practices that elite actors adopt to stabilize the political environment. The attempts of both state and nonstate actors to build law in Sudan have succeeded largely in creating an elite class of Sudanese who possess fluency across multiple legal systems. Law ultimately provides a foundation for authorities to construct and legitimize illiberal government, but legal strategies are also tactics of elite resistance. These strategies can stymie change, and they can create space for change to occur.

Analyzing legal practices in a setting in which law is otherwise perceived to have failed or simply not to exist reveals connections between domestic and international approaches to legal development. Documenting a nation's struggle with the law particularly during periods of warfare and authoritarianism – scrutinizing who controls the legal system, at what points the legal order becomes salient to powerful and to weak actors, and how legal ideologies and arrangements are used to shape people's perceptions of the regime and aid actors – plays a central role in understanding how political order develops in deeply troubled nations. In this study, I examine the actual contexts in which law operates in Sudan, how it operates, and what it accomplishes. Ultimately, I ask whether the turn toward law has acted to lift people out of poverty and end the cycle of violence or has served to maintain an inequitable balance of power and enforce a subject-ruler dichotomy. I find that even in the extreme case that Sudan presents for legal scholars and political scientists, legal resources and tools have historically been used to bestow legitimacy on state institutions and leaders but have done little to alleviate poverty or bring lasting peace. Legal resources are just as likely to strengthen a dictatorship as they are to embolden people to overthrow it. In addition, contemporary activities to build legal and rights awareness among the poor may not be achieving their intended effects of legal empowerment and mobilization. These programs instead may be providing material and symbolic

law + society

benefits to war survivors who remain unlikely and unable to mobilize their rights against recalcitrant military regimes. These war-displaced persons seek out immediate forms of relief, tied to food and education (such as meals at a weeklong legal awareness workshop or graduation certificates bearing their names and emblematic of social status), rather than the intended benefits of legal mobilization.

My empirical observations of the work of advantaged and disadvantaged groups in Sudan suggest that law is neither static nor immutable: it is *lived* – simultaneously constituted by and shaping people's experience of and uses for it. In a setting overburdened by violence and exhausted from decades of warfare and political instability, legal tools and strategies become malleable resources in the arena in which state and nonstate actors compete for political influence among a shattered population.

AIMS OF THE BOOK

The widespread notion that law is an antidote to violence overlooks the ways that law and legal strategies are integral to political struggle. Scholars and practitioners focus attention on the undeniable problem of how to institutionalize the rule of law in states torn apart by war. But the guiding assumption about law's failures or absence during states of violence has stunted the development of theories on the diverse ways that legal tools matter as resources to political actors.

This book examines the institutionalization of the rule of law in a fragile state struggling with political violence and civil war. It links a growing body of literature on courts in authoritarian or nondemocratic states[19] with scholarship on rule-of-law and legal-empowerment activities.[20] To these studies Sudan adds the critical case of a fragile

[19] Tamir Moustafa, *The Struggle for Constitutional Power: Law, Politics, and Economic Development in Egypt* (Cambridge: Cambridge University Press, 2007); Tom Ginsburg and Tamir Moustafa, eds., *Rule by Law: The Politics of Courts in Authoritarian Regimes* (Cambridge: Cambridge University Press, 2008); Jens Meierhenrich, *The Legacies of Law: Long-Run Consequences of Legal Development in South Africa, 1652–2000* (Cambridge: Cambridge University Press, 2008).

[20] Stephen Humphreys, *Theatre of the Rule of Law: Transnational Legal Intervention in Theory and Practice* (Cambridge: Cambridge University Press, 2010); James J. Heckman, Robert L. Nelson, and Lee Cabatingan, eds., *Global Perspectives on the Rule of Law* (New York: Routledge, 2010); Amanda Perry-Kessaris, ed., *Law in the Pursuit of Development: Principles into Practice?* (New York: Routledge, 2010); Chandra

state devastated by decades of civil war. Studying how key actors in these settings use law is urgent for a fuller account of politics in authoritarian states and conflict settings.

The purpose of a case study such as this is to use details from the specific context to initiate debate on the role and development of law in unstable countries and conflict zones. It asks these underlying questions: How does the law operate in a chaotic setting with deep ethnic and religious divisions? And how do key actors – principally colonial, authoritarian, and humanitarian – use legal tools to achieve their goals in high-conflict settings? Ultimately, what are the circumstances under which law is manipulated, and the rule of law is advanced, in war-torn states with deep-rooted divisions? Domestic and foreign elites in Sudan have struggled to strengthen and stabilize an otherwise fragile state by reaching into their legal toolkits. This book investigates the legal efforts of three sets of elite actors: *colonial* (British colonial administrators), *authoritarian* (postcolonial autocratic governments), and *humanitarian* (contemporary civil society activists and the international donors that fund them).

This book also represents the first study of legal politics in a nation as battered and chaotic as modern-day Sudan. The major recent works in English on law in Sudan largely review case law or legal codes to document changes in jurisprudence over time in a specific area of law, particularly Islamic law. But none attempts a broader look at the Sudanese experience of building the rule of law, and none addresses in detail the status of the legal order after 1985.[21] Here, I demystify the legal order as a whole and specifically detail the ways that state and nonstate actors interact with legal institutions. Building an instrumental definition of law, I examine institutional practices, values, legal personnel, laws, and individual experiences with the legal system. I put my examination of law in a specific context, empirically

Lekha-Sriram, Olga Martin-Ortega, and Johanna Herman, eds., *Peacebuilding and the Rule of Law in Africa* (New York: Routledge, 2011).

[21] Abdullahi Ali Ibrahim, *Decolonizing the Judiciary and Islamic Renewal in the Sudan, 1898–1985* (Leiden: Brill, 2008); Zaki Mustafa, *Common Law in the Sudan: An Account of the Justice, Equity and Good Conscience Provision* (Oxford: Oxford University Press, 1971). See also Carolyn Fluehr-Lobban, *Islamic Law and Society in Sudan* (London: Frank Cass, 1987) and Aharon Layish and Gabriel R. Warburg, *The Reinstatement of Islamic Law in Sudan under Numayrī: An Evaluation of a Legal Experiment in the Light of Its Historical Context, Methodology, and Repercussions* (Leiden: Brill, 2002).

examining how legal resources and strategies have been used by public officials and nonstate activists in Sudan (from the British colonial administration and postcolonial rulers to civil society groups and aid organizations) at different times to augment and legitimize a desired social structure.

This book is aimed at an audience of interdisciplinary legal and sociolegal scholars, political scientists who study law in authoritarian and weak states, and policy practitioners. Africa specialists may also find the arguments and data presented helpful for assessing the state of political change and institutional development in Sudan. My goal has been to evaluate the role and proliferation of legal tools and remedies by colonial, authoritarian, and humanitarian actors in a society confronting a legacy of political violence. In fragile states like Sudan, the origins of state law are revealed through multiple ongoing projects of law promotion – elaborated endeavors emerging from an intricate web of colonial, criminal, and charitable enterprises. Promoting law is a deeply political undertaking, involving wanted war criminals, peace-minded humanitarians, and millions of war-weary poor standing between them. If there is one public-policy takeaway that this book proffers, it is this: scholars and rule-of-law practitioners must not be blindly optimistic about the force of law to create progressive social change in weak states; nor should we be overly skeptical about the ability of the world's most unreasonable dictators to use legal mechanisms for nefarious purposes without reproach. At root, law cannot be separated from the political practices that shape it. These processes involve the deployment and redeployment of legal tools (at times, malfunctioning tools) in an otherwise disordered battle between those holding national power and those striving to limit their authority.

ORGANIZATION OF THE BOOK

This book focuses on Sudan from the 1898 invasion by the British and Egyptian militaries to the 2011 secession of South Sudan. These two events bracket a volatile 114-year history of civil war and the pathologies of colonial and authoritarian rule. Between 1898 and 2011, Khartoum saw just ten years of independent democratic leadership. But even short-lived democracy in the capital city was not felt in every part of the country – southern Sudan, for instance, remained a security state and war zone during Khartoum's democratic periods, giving it the legacy of violence that continues to plague the nation.

Chapter 1, "Lawfare and Warfare in Sudan," frames the book's argument on legal politics in fragile states, defines central concepts and the literature to which this book contributes, and lays out the context of this study of Sudan and the methods I adopted.

The remainder of the book is divided into two parts. Chapters 2 through 4 collectively examine how state actors – primarily colonial and authoritarian – attempt to use legal change as a central strategy to solidify and extend their political authority, how the promotion of law serves their purposes, and how it does not (*colonial and authoritarian forms of legal politics*). Chapters 5 and 6 together illustrate how nonstate actors inspired by a sense of humanitarianism and progress use legal tools, specifically how the paradigm shift in rhetoric in international aid and development work from an economic to a human-rights focus has affected interventions in Sudan (*humanitarian forms of legal politics*). This organizing distinction shows how war-torn states, those who lead them, and those who seek to lift them out of their failures and crises continually seek out law's assistance.

Chapter 2, "The Colonial Path to the Rule of Law, 1898–1956," details how the British colonial administration took a legalistic approach to governance of a divided and pluralistic Sudan. They sought to impose a weak vision of the rule of law, which made them appear more moderate, but also helped them to manage people's grievances against the regime and to keep colonial subjects under surveillance. The habits and institutions implanted by the British to manufacture consent and stability still form the substrate of the current state.

Chapters 3 and 4 then examine the first fifty-five years of Sudanese independence, up to the secession of South Sudan in 2011, in order to scrutinize how different governmental administrations in Khartoum have consistently renewed the law to engineer their authority. Chapter 3, "Law in a State of Crisis, 1956–1989," analyzes how state leaders in the first generation following independence turned to legal resources – revising the legal system, passing ordinances, and building up legal institutions – to manage threats and ensure the survival of the state. Chapter 4, "Authoritarian Legal Politics and Islamic Law, 1989–2011," investigates firsthand Sudan's longest-lasting government under President Omar Hassan Al Bashir, who rose to power through a military coup and enjoyed little popular support. The Bashir government ruled *by* law to build a relatively stable legal order premised on what it portrayed as an immutable Islamic rule *of* law. Putting soldiers into war and lawyers and judges into courts were simultaneous strategies the regime used to meet the goal of maintaining political and economic dominance. Using the latest available and previously unreleased data from the government of Sudan, I examine the practical benefits and limitations for authoritarian states of using legal resources to consolidate power over an intensely divided population.

Chapter 5, "Law and Civil Society, 1956–2011," focuses on the behavior of nonstate actors promoting legal development. I detail the technical assistance, instructional strategies, and other practices undertaken by international actors in Sudan to reform government actors and convince the poor that law is a tool to uplift not just to oppress. I argue that different conceptions of law and rights exist for the Sudanese, who have experienced brutality under authoritarianism, and for the international aid community, which seeks to empower them using tools of law. Communication about these differences is strained because of hierarchical relationships induced by civil society's need for funding from and partnership with the international aid community.

Chapter 6, "Humanitarian Legal Politics in an Authoritarian State, 2005–2011," analyzes the effects of contemporary development programs in Sudan that view the promotion of human rights and the rule of law as a primary goal. Humanitarian legal politics, largely through rights-based development aid to governments and civil society organizations, creates unintended consequences, including increased reliance on legal strategies among nonlegal civil society groups. In the hands of an authoritarian government, rights-based programs can be used to support sympathetic groups and to restrain independent groups, ultimately leading to deeper splits in civil society.

Chapter 7, "Reflections on Legal Politics," discusses the functions of law promotion in authoritarian or war-torn contexts more broadly. From legitimizing colonial domination to harassing domestic opponents of a despotic regime, legal tools are consistently deployed to stabilize volatile environments, manufacture authority, and enhance governability. At the same time, international rule-of-law promoters and the local activists they fund carry with them a toolkit of legal resources to liberate marginalized populations from tyranny. In unstable political contexts, legal solutions are instruments of both oppression and liberation. Understanding this tension more fully may be a first step toward a more sustainable peace in weak states as historically volatile as Sudan.

The lawyer depicted at the start of this Introduction believed there would be little to communicate about law in Sudan and, thus, this book would be a very short one. But the chapters that follow carefully detail the meaningful ways that key actors in a fragile political environment promote legal institutions, personnel, and ordinances to achieve their goals. Whether attempting to maintain authority or to empower people to confront it, law and legal strategies feature as prominently as weapons in Sudan's turbulent and war-torn history.

CHAPTER 1

LAWFARE AND WARFARE IN SUDAN

THE LIVED EXPERIENCE OF THE LAW

At a dilapidated courthouse in the town of El Obeid, about three hundred miles southwest of Khartoum, I witnessed *ajaweed* (older persons, typically men who serve as mediators in community or family disputes) moonlighting as petition writers (called *kutaab al-'ara'id*). They sat on small iron chairs in a government-designated area under a tree by the courthouse. Women and men went to them to draft and file court petitions on their behalf, paying lower fees than what licensed attorneys would demand. Lawyers I met told me the practice was standard. While war was being fought just a few hundred miles away in Darfur and human rights and opposition activists were under surveillance or imprisoned in Khartoum, life seemed to go on as normal here. Women filed divorce petitions, workers demanded severance pay, and families stood in line to present their cases to judges enforcing the laws of the Bashir regime.

Sudan is not exactly a legal vacuum. Operating on the assumption that there is not enough law (or not enough "good" law) in high-conflict settings, international aid groups such as the World Bank, agencies of the United Nations, and major nongovernmental organizations arrive with the goal of promoting the construction of legal institutions and the legal empowerment of the poor. But as the example of the *kutaab al-'ara'id* drafting petitions under the trees outside the El Obeid courthouse reveals, a variety of laws, legal institutions, and legal personnel already exist in high-conflict settings, and state actors either create these resources or allow them to exist to benefit the state and its citizens.

19

The existence and use of courts, lawyers, and petition writers sig-
nifies the importance of studying legal arrangements and practices
and not just legal doctrine. Doing so reveals the political nature not
only of law but also of legal systems and the legal order as a whole.
A stable legal order matters to governments and their citizens: laws,
courts, law schools, and legal professionals are evidence that the state
uses legal strategies to maintain itself and to provide resources to citizens. Understanding how legal politics (see Table 1.1 later) builds a
state infrastructure and how citizens are encouraged to turn to the law
is critical to an examination of institutional development in fragile
states. An empirical approach to the study of legal politics captures the
functions of law in addition to structures of political and social power
that law supports, helpful to analyzing the ways that law matters and
fails to matter for those who seek its assistance.[1] Investigating these
broader legal practices entails stepping outside traditional analyses to
ask how and why courts or legal order come to exist in the first place,
divorced from the content of the cases judges hear and their doctrinal
or political consequences.

In this chapter, I first introduce the major legal concepts used in this
book. Second, I draw from sociolegal scholarship to analyze the politics
of law and courts in authoritarian states. Third, I provide an overview
of legal politics in the case of Sudan. Finally, I outline the methods I
adopted to study how colonial, authoritarian, and humanitarian actors
have used law and legal toolkits to achieve their goals in Sudan.

FROM LAW TO LEGAL POLITICS

Myriad concepts circulate in scholarship on law and legal practices,
and their meanings are contested among scholars and policy practitioners. In order to analyze the role of legal practices and tools in shaping Sudanese political history, I define a set of concepts – law, rule of
law, rule by law, legal system, legal order, and legal politics (Table 1.1).
These six concepts illuminate an instrumental view of law as a toolkit
of resources from which diverse political actors draw out principles and

---

[1] See Erik Jensen and Thomas Heller, *Beyond Common Knowledge: Empirical
Approaches to the Rule of Law* (Stanford, CA: Stanford University Press, 2005). On
law as a field of practice and ritual that exists beyond the scope of legal doctrine, see
Leila Kawar, *Defining Legal Frontiers: Immigrant Rights Adjudication in France and the
United States* (Ph.D. dissertation, New York University, 2009).

Table 1.1. *Six legal concepts and the multiple features of law*

Concept	Definition
Law	A set of norms, rationales, values, and techniques encouraged or imposed in order to manufacture social, economic, or political stability; ensure predictability and accountability in governance; and/ or promote social change for the benefit of the oppressed (e.g., norms prescribing rules of property transfer; contract; crime)
Legal system	A set of procedural and substantive rules for constructing and interpreting law (e.g., common law, civil law, customary law, canon law, and Islamic or Judaic law)
Rule of law	A structure of governance rooted in the normative belief that law exists to configure and constrain social, economic, and political relations and to resolve disputes peacefully; often (but not always) coexisting with contemporary values of human rights and democracy
Rule by law	A structure of governance in which law exists at the service of government officials, rather than as a force that constrains state behavior
Legal order	An interconnected web of formal and informal laws, legal systems (common law, religious law, customary law), personnel (judges, politicians, lawyers, civil society activists), institutions (courts, prisons, NGOs), and technologies that establish and maintain the state
Legal politics	The use and promotion of legal tools, practices, arrangements, and resources to achieve political, social, or economic objectives (e.g., constructing courts, teaching the poor about law, or altering a legal system or legal order)

Source: Author.

policies to achieve their aims. States use their legal capital to enforce political stability, while civil society and aid groups use it to empower poverty-stricken populations to access formal, state-controlled legal channels and resources.

Law can be a tool to impose order wielded by a repressive authority – law as the "command of the sovereign."[2] It can also be a mechanism to improve social relations and encourage predictability in governance.[3]

[2] Robert Campbell, *Lectures on Jurisprudence or the Philosophy of Positive Law by the Late John Austin of the Inner Temple, Barrister at Law*, 5th ed. (London: John Murray, 1885), 94–96.

[3] Ronald Dworkin, *Law's Empire* (Cambridge, MA: Harvard University Press, 1986), 252.

Law can protect private property, promote the resolution of disputes and state legitimacy,[4] and catalyze liberation movements.[5] In states facing a colonial or authoritarian legacy of jurisprudence, law can be a hybrid of all of these. For the purposes of this book, I define law as *a set of norms, rationales, values, and techniques encouraged or imposed in order to manufacture social, economic, and political stability; ensure predictability and accountability in governance; and/or promote social change for the benefit of the oppressed.* This definition interprets law as a lived experience; it certainly encompasses much more than what state law – including legislation, judicial pronouncements, and ministerial decrees – alone would reveal. While law's genealogy is traceable to the formation and maintenance of the state, its dimensions can be revealed through the practices of nonstate actors. Even in those settings where state institutions are weak, visions of law are carried across time and space through the activities of nonstate actors, including humanitarian activists.

A legal system is *a set of procedural and substantive rules for constructing and interpreting law.* A country may have its juridical roots largely in a single system – for instance, English common law. More typically, national law is derived from multiple systems blended into one. In Sudan, the state legal system is a plural and layered amalgamation of Islamic law, British and Sudanese common law, and civil law imported from Egypt. Each of these legal systems achieves prominence at different points in Sudan's history, depending upon the political leanings of state leaderships in Khartoum.[6]

The rule of law is *a structure of governance rooted in the normative view that law and legal systems exist to configure and constrain social, economic, and political relations and to resolve disputes peacefully.* Contemporary legal-development efforts advance a robust conception of the rule of law that coexists with values of human rights, democracy, and peace. But an absolute rule of law is a "rare achievement" and a force greater than the sum of those laws and institutions that constrain arbitrary state

---

[4] Martin Shapiro, *Courts: A Comparative and Political Analysis* (Chicago: University of Chicago Press, 1981).

[5] Costas Douzinas, *The End of Human Rights: Critical Legal Thought at the Turn of the Century* (Oxford: Hart, 2000).

[6] Mark Fathi Massoud, "Lawyers and the Disintegration of the Legal Complex in Sudan," in *Fates of Political Liberalism in the British Post Colony: The Politics of the Legal Complex*, ed. Halliday, Karpik, and Feeley (Cambridge: Cambridge University Press, 2012), 193–94.

power.[7] Like law and legal systems, the rule of law exists as a culture of ideas and norms; it is a layered phenomenon at the nexus of values, institutions, and political conditions.[8] Particularly in politically volatile or violent environments, the rule of law is a process of action. It emerges not organically but chaotically – it is never complete; nor is it ever perfect. The path toward the rule of law is not linear.[9] It is built up, torn apart, promoted by new actors, and then abused and manipulated for political profit. Within this disorganized process aid agencies create hope that a perfect rule of law will flourish as a result of their interventions. Their faith in the potential of the law to save a state from its political despondency is shared by governments – colonial, democratic, and authoritarian – that seek to consolidate power through their own legal visions and by amassing their own legal tools. In Sudan, these governments and their contemporary challengers or supporters in the aid community each labored to instill in a shattered Sudanese public the expectation that states and their courts will ultimately behave reasonably.

Rule by law is *a structure of governance, often associated with authoritarian rule, in which law exists at the service of government officials, rather than as a force that constrains their behavior*. State officials, particularly despotic leaders, may exercise political power using legal means, but they do so in a way that fails to live up to the values of the rule of law, democracy, and human rights.[10] Rule by law, then, connotes a kind of state-led abuse of the rule of law. In Sudan, the authoritarian leaderships of President Nimeiri during the 1970s and President Bashir from the 1990s onward both reflected a broad commitment to using legal means to undergird nondemocratic rule.

The legal order is *an interconnected web of formal and informal laws; legal systems (e.g., common law, religious law, customary law); personnel (e.g., judges, politicians, lawyers, civil society activists); institutions (e.g., courts, jails, NGOs); and technologies that establish and maintain the state*. In

---

[7] Martin Krygier, "Approaching the Rule of Law," in *The Rule of Law in Afghanistan: Missing in Inaction*, ed. Whit Mason (Cambridge: Cambridge University Press, 2011), 15.

[8] Martin Krygier, "Rule of Law," in *Oxford Handbook of Comparative Constitutional Law*, ed. Rosenfeld and Sajó (Oxford: Oxford University Press, 2012). Krygier discusses how the rule of law is concerned with social rather than merely legal outcomes.

[9] See Rebecca Bill Chavez, *The Rule of Law in Nascent Democracies: Judicial Politics in Argentina* (Stanford, CA: Stanford University Press, 2004).

[10] See Krygier (2012).

The Troubles

high-conflict settings a formal legal order is usually perceived to be absent or replaced by the rule of thugs. But constructing a legal order is an ongoing political project involving actors with diverse moral interests. The legal order captures the role and function of state judiciaries, where most important studies of law in authoritarian states have focused. But investigating the broad nature of the legal order entails walking in, and out of, courthouses. Looking beyond courts involves scrutinizing how law schools, the legal profession, administrative agencies, justice ministries, aid groups, and nongovernmental organizations serve as critical sites of transformation in which the politics of law is enacted.

Law students and graduates sitting for bar exams around the world learn to see legal doctrine as static, unchanging, and more generally reflective of a legal order. But legal doctrine is but one component of a more complex and layered order that states create to maintain stability. For instance, while the practical goals of colonial, authoritarian, or humanitarian legal strategies may be the construction of new courts and law schools, the passage of a new constitution, or the reformation of a legal system, the process can be benign and barbarous at different moments for different people. It involves police personnel, family connections, state institutional representatives and bureaucrats, foreign backers, and nonstate perpetrators and victims of violence (at times, one and the same). Repeated changes in legal systems and ultimately in the legal order open up spaces for elite maneuvering.

Legal politics is *the use and promotion of legal tools, practices, arrangements, and resources to achieve political, social, or economic objectives.* Legal politics is not unique to state actors. It can be elite-driven and top-down, or it can be bottom-up involving grassroots mobilization. Examples of top-down legal politics include various forms of law promotion by state elites, such as constructing courts, altering the legal system or legal order, financing a judicial administration, and planning legal education programs. Civil society and humanitarian elites also use legal tools and resources to create political, social, or economic change by attempting to deepen respect for human rights. At its core, the promotion of law by elite actors is a political process through which the legal tools, personnel, and arrangements of the state are revealed – constitutions, legislation, courthouses, judges, lawyers, prosecutors, law schools, and executive or judicial pronouncements.[11]

---

[11] Legal politics is largely consistent with the notion of "lawfare" articulated by anthropologists as "the use of law to achieve political or economic ends." Illuminating the

Types of legal politics

Legal politics may be either a top-down or a bottom-up process of using legal means to achieve various ends. This book investigates the top-down practices of law promotion among three sets of elite actors in Sudan – colonial, authoritarian, and humanitarian. *Colonial legal politics* takes shape as foreign administrators of a territory use tools of law and legal order to maintain control over a territory and its residents. As elsewhere across Africa, Latin America, and East and South Asia, in Sudan colonial law involved creating and co-opting different sets of competing elites to work under and promote the goals of the colonial administration. *Authoritarian legal politics* emerges through the legal tools that have helped nondemocratic regimes collect grievances and monitor social behavior. Institutionalizing claims against a regime paradoxically boosts the regime's legitimacy and authority. *Humanitarian legal politics* is a process through which elites in civil society and their international sponsors use legal concepts, such as human rights, and legal techniques, such as promoting the rule of law, to build up the capacities of state and society.

These three actors and their uses of legal tools to create stability in Sudan are historically distinct but interconnected. Each set of actors justifies its own legal politics and questions the moral worth of other varieties. Aid actors see authoritarian legal politics as a process they call a violation of human rights. Authoritarian governments see the promotion of international law by humanitarian actors as a violation of sovereign rights. Both actors decry colonialism and colonial legal politics as a past evil to which their efforts cannot justifiably be compared (though, of course, they often are so compared).

To understand the full panoply of legal practices, rituals, and behaviors in Sudan and its effects on the lived experience of the poor, it is critical to examine different political actors working to build state

---

features of legal politics involves analyzing the diverse legal tools, arrangements, and practices – law and legal doctrine, but also legal institutions, systems, and orders – that domestic and foreign political actors use to achieve their diverse goals. See John L. and Jean Comaroff, *Ethnicity, Inc.* (Chicago: University of Chicago Press, 2009). See also John L. and Jean Comaroff, "Law and Disorder in the Post-Colony: An Introduction," in *Law and Disorder in the Post-Colony,* ed. Comaroff and Comaroff (Chicago: University of Chicago Press, 2006). Legal politics also builds in part on earlier concepts of "legalism" in political theory, as a ritualized practice of using law or creating legal solutions to social ills. Judith Shklar first defined legalism in 1964 as a moral attitude and code of conduct, common to Western countries, related to rule following, orderliness, and formalism. See Judith N. Shklar, *Legalism: Law, Morals, and Political Trials* (Cambridge, MA: Harvard University Press, 1964).

order, and their different backgrounds and visions. Investigating government or courts alone is not enough because it fails to capture the broader landscape outside courts in which legal resources and strategies are located. Scholars typically have sought to illuminate one form of legal politics at a time – colonial,[12] authoritarian,[13] or humanitarian[14] legal politics. The longitudinal analysis in this book, instead, links these three forms of legal practice with the actors involved – revealing their emergence, connections, and positions in the politics of building a fragile state. For instance, colonial legal strategies reveal important details about a nation's legal history, while linking colonial practices with contemporary authoritarian and humanitarian approaches to state building uncovers how different actors turn to similar kinds of legal strategies. Law is not absent in fragile settings; it is, in fact, everywhere one turns.

New legal rules and doctrine are certainly one result of the elite promotion of law, but they are by no means the only result. Using legal tools for nonlegal ends is a risky strategy – it can yield a consolidation of ruling power or, if political opportunities allow it, create the conditions for the curtailment of that power. In this way, legal resources are part of a larger political toolkit. As processes with multiple facets and ends, instrumental uses of the law may be disordered or even savage. But they constitute the building blocks and processes – the DNA – that shape law, legal systems, and the legal order.

Legal politics has a variety of forms, and, as a project, it exposes the protean nature of law and the legal order. Colonial actors use legal tools to control and subjugate a vast and diverse population to an undersized foreign authority – for instance, by creating spaces for resolving private disputes or filing public grievances. Authoritarian actors similarly adopt legal strategies to consolidate their nondemocratic authority, or

---

[12] Lauren Benton, *Law and Colonial Cultures: Legal Regimes in World History, 1400–1900* (Cambridge: Cambridge University Press, 2002). See also Iza Hussin, "The Pursuit of the Perak Regalia: Islam, Law, and the Politics of Authority in the Colonial State," *Law & Social Inquiry* 32 (2007): 759–88.

[13] Jothie Rajah, *Authoritarian Rule of Law: Legislation, Discourse and Legitimacy in Singapore* (Cambridge: Cambridge University Press, 2012); Gordon Silverstein, "Singapore: The Exception That Proves Rules Matter," in *Rule by Law: The Politics of Courts in Authoritarian Regimes*, ed. Ginsburg and Moustafa (Cambridge: Cambridge University Press, 2008). See also Tamir Moustafa, *The Struggle for Constitutional Power: Law, Politics, and Economic Development in Egypt* (Cambridge: Cambridge University Press, 2007).

[14] Whit Mason, ed., *The Rule of Law in Afghanistan: Missing in Inaction* (Cambridge: Cambridge University Press, 2011).

to divert attention from economic or political crisis – for example, by impulsively removing the judges of a supreme court, converting the legal system from one rooted in Anglo-Sudanese common law to one based in Egyptian civil law or in Islamic law, and building a network of law schools to inculcate new legal norms. In these ways, law promotion as a form of top-down legal politics is not always overtly despotic, though it certainly contributes to "slow violence" that occurs "gradually and out of sight … dispersed across time and space [and] typically not viewed as violence at all."[15] Law promotion may also take seemingly benign forms – educating people about state law and human rights principles.

The actors who create and use legal institutions and resources to build a state or bolster their status in it can be democracy-minded, dictatorial, *power of law* or altruistic – or each at different moments in their political lives. But the central point of legal politics is that legal resources are instruments that political actors use to create moments of change or to maintain continuity against the threat of change. Investigating the processes that create law and legal order, and that ultimately shape the contours of the rule of law, reveals results more interesting than the rules of law themselves. It illuminates how legal practices reconfigure political relationships and hierarchies of power between governors, the governed, and their advocates. The tools of law promotion are akin to double-edged swords – while state actors use them to manufacture and maintain authority, civil society actors use them to undermine state authority and develop a culture of rights. Different aspects of law are used to punish both regime leaders and civil society activists as much as both sets of actors seek out new laws and legal resources for their own gain or salvation. Ultimately, the power of the law can be revealed even in states of chaos, violence, and deep-rooted conflict.

LAW AND AUTHORITY IN FRAGILE STATES

Law and legal strategies serve important functions in democracies. Creating and enforcing constitutions, for instance, is central to much of modern democratic governance. Scholars have also come to appreciate that law and legal institutions perform a variety of functions in authoritarian states, such as building legitimacy locally or abroad and

---

[15] Rob Nixon, *Slow Violence and the Environmentalism of the Poor* (Cambridge, MA: Harvard University Press, 2011), 2.

maintaining elite cohesion.[16] But what of the most chaotic of polities found in fragile or failed states? Law serves significant functions in these places as well. A modicum of legality, for instance, allows ordinary people to manage their affairs and social order to exist, even as despots use features of the legal order for exploitative purposes.

Legal politics has been studied in a variety of contexts from robust democracies to well-established authoritarian states. This study of a fragile state emerges out of a body of scholarship that seeks to understand legal strategies in their political contexts and how the rule of law can be constructed, enforced, and demolished. However, much scholarship has focused on philosophical debates on the meaning or inner morality of law[17] and on empirical studies of courts and litigation in democratic states.[18] Much contemporary scholarship on law in political science focuses on the relative power that judicial review provides to courts as an institution of government.[19] In this regard, great focus is placed on the role of constitutions and the politics of judicial oversight of constitutional law, including the countermajoritarian dilemma posed by judicial review.[20]

---

[16] Tamir Moustafa and Tom Ginsburg, "Introduction: The Functions of Courts in Authoritarian Politics," in *Rule by Law: The Politics of Courts in Authoritarian Regimes*, ed. Tom Ginsburg and Tamir Moustafa (Cambridge: Cambridge University Press, 2008).

[17] See Mathew H. Kramer, *Objectivity and the Rule of Law* (Cambridge: Cambridge University Press, 2007); H. L. A. Hart, *The Concept of Law* (Oxford: Oxford University Press, 1997); Lon Fuller, "The Forms and Limits of Adjudication." 92 *Harvard Law Review* (1978): 353–409; Martin Krygier, "Rule of Law," in *International Encyclopedia of the Social and Behavioral Sciences*, Vol. 20, ed. Neil J. Smelser and Paul B. Bates (Oxford: Elsevier Science, 2001), 13403–8.

[18] Rosenberg (2008). See also Michael McCann, *Rights at Work: Pay Equity Reform and the Politics of Legal Mobilization* (Chicago: University of Chicago Press, 1994); Rachel Cichowski, *The European Court and Civil Society: Litigation, Mobilization and Governance* (Cambridge: Cambridge University Press, 2007); A. James McAdams, ed., *Transitional Justice and the Rule of Law in New Democracies* (Notre Dame, IN: University of Notre Dame Press, 1997).

[19] Martin Shapiro coined the term "political jurisprudence" for this very reason: Courts are political actors. See Shapiro (1981).

[20] See, e.g., Kim Lane Scheppele, "Constitutional Ethnography: An Introduction," *Law & Society Review* 38(3) (2003): 389–406. See also Ronen Shamir, "'Landmark Cases' and the Reproduction of Legitimacy: The Case of Israel's High Court of Justice," *Law & Society Review* 24(3) (1990): 781–806. See also Alexander M. Bickel, *The Least Dangerous Branch: The Supreme Court at the Bar of Politics* (Indianapolis: Bobbs-Merrill, 1962). But see Robert Dahl, "Decision-making in

Legal politics exists within but also outside constitutional courts in robust democracies, and studying how law and legal institutions are used politically in different environments reveals deeper insight into the political nature of law and legal practice more broadly. For these reasons, scholars have sought to move beyond established democracies to study law and courts in nascent democracies in Eastern Europe,[21] Latin America,[22] East Asia,[23] and Africa (where judges have been particularly active in promoting judicial independence after the fall of colonial empires).[24] In weak and emerging democracies, elites adopt law-based political strategies. For example, aware that their days are numbered, state leaders may transfer some power to constitutional courts in order paradoxically to preserve their own. They promote independent constitutional courts as a kind of insurance policy; an independent court is more likely to affirm constitutional limits on the new government and to protect the old administration's interests than a court beholden to the new government or regime capturing power.[25]

This finding – that law plays an important role in the politics of both enduring and new democracies – left scholars with the recognition that many billions of people do not live in democracies, whether robust, transitional, or defective. The study of authoritarian states, then, arrived as a welcome addition to scholarship on law in established and new democracies. Early case studies of politically challenging settings such as the Soviet Union show how the law, despite its high level of detail, fails to matter when authoritarian leaders place judges under their control.[26] Later work has sought to explain the ways

---

Democracy: The Supreme Court as a National Policy-Maker. *Journal of Public Law* 6 (1957): 279–95.

[21] Maria Popova, *Politicized Justice in Emerging Democracies: A Study of Courts in Russia and Ukraine* (Cambridge: Cambridge University Press, 2012).

[22] See Chavez (2004). See also Gretchen Helmke and Julio Ríos-Figueroa, eds. *Courts in Latin America* (Cambridge: Cambridge University Press, 2011); Juan Méndez, Paulo Sergio Pinheiro, Guillermo O'Donnell, *The (Un)Rule of Law and New Democracies in Latin America* (Notre Dame, IN: University of Notre Dame Press, 1998).

[23] See Tom Ginsburg, *Judicial Review in New Democracies: Constitutional Courts in Asian Cases* (Cambridge: Cambridge University Press, 2003).

[24] Jennifer A. Widner, *Building the Rule of Law: Francis Nyali and the Road to Judicial Independence in Africa* (New York: W. W. Norton, 2001).

[25] Ran Hirschl, *Towards Juristocracy: The Origins and Consequences of the New Constitutionalism* (Cambridge, MA: Harvard University Press, 2004); Ginsburg (2003).

[26] Hendly (1996).

that law *does* matter, particularly the paradox of why otherwise recalcitrant regimes might instead allow or promote judicial autonomy. In China, for instance, judges enjoy independence in garden-variety cases that do not affect the interests of political and economic elites. They avoid political risk in nuanced ways, including by sending politically sensitive cases to administrative agencies more closely aligned with the Communist Party to resolve.[27] In Egypt, Hosni Mubarak ruled with an iron fist for three decades until his ouster in 2011, but he used an independent Supreme Constitutional Court to assure foreign investors that their interests would be protected by an independent Egyptian judiciary.[28] In so doing, Mubarak unexpectedly endowed courts in Egypt with independence to help secure an otherwise recalcitrant regime's long-term economic interests. However, as constitutional courts demonstrably protect regime interests, they simultaneously can undermine those interests by handing down decisions in favor of human rights and antistate activists, thus creating an institutional space for state-society contention.[29] In South Africa, a long-standing respect for legality and for the legal system during the otherwise savage era of apartheid helped to weaken tensions (and enhance the importance of the courts) during the nation's turbulent transition to democracy.[30] The case of apartheid South Africa suggests that, even under entrenched authoritarianism, a legal culture can be created and confidence in the legal system can be enhanced through reliable court decisions.

These important studies of law in authoritarian states have extended the literature in law and political science beyond studies of constitutional courts in democratic or emerging democratic contexts. Courts,

---

[27] Randall Peerenboom, ed., *Judicial Independence in China: Lessons for Global Rule of Law Promotion* (Cambridge: Cambridge University Press, 2010). See also Rachel E. Stern, *Environmental Litigation in China: A Study in Political Ambivalence* (Cambridge: Cambridge University Press, 2013); Randall Peerenboom, *China's Long March toward Rule of Law* (Cambridge: Cambridge University Press, 2002); Stanley Lubman, *Bird in a Cage: Legal Reform in China after Mao* (Stanford, CA: Stanford University Press, 1999).

[28] Moustafa (2007).

[29] Tamir Moustafa, "Law versus the State: The Judicialization of Politics in Egypt," 28 *Law and Social Inquiry* (2003): 883–930. See also Rachel A. Cichowski, *The European Court and Civil Society: Litigation, Mobilization and Governance* (Cambridge: Cambridge University Press, 2007).

[30] Jens Meierhenrich, *The Legacies of Law: Long-Run Consequences of Legal Development in South Africa, 1652–2000* (Cambridge: Cambridge University Press, 2008).

even in authoritarian states, are after all a visible manifestation of the legal order and can be good proxies of the general notion of the rule of law. But as useful as these studies are in assessing the long-term impact of judiciaries on rule-of-law reform, they typically use courts (and most often, constitutional courts) to generalize about the law or to investigate regions with some degree of political stability and civil peace. Moreover, comparative scholarship on law in non-Western or postcolonial states tends to examine either legal institutions such as courts[31] or legal professionals such as lawyers and judges and the extent to which they are champions of political liberalism or status-oriented elites.[32] But accounts that separate institutions from actors succeed in telling only half the story of the politics of law.[33]

By examining the paradox of independent courts and judicial review in weak democracies and authoritarian states, comparative studies of legal politics have been a welcome addition to sociolegal scholarship and comparative public law. But scholars have yet to examine critical cases of states struggling with entrenched political violence or long-lasting civil war. There exists little (and outdated) primary research on fragile states where the problem of institutionalizing the law is particularly acute. With minimal access to state-level institutions and political and judicial leaders in places like Sudan – or Congo, Chad, Belarus, Chechnya, Libya, and Somalia – scholars and practitioners have provided only minimal detail about how instrumental legal strategies exist and the rule of law might develop in the world's most fragile states. Expanding the frame set by studies that examine how constitutional courts or judges undermine or support democratization, I analyze the legal order as a whole. Courts are one visible manifestation of the legal order, but other indicators include basic legal awareness and street-level empowerment of the poor.[34]

---

[31] See, e.g., Tom Ginsburg and Tamir Moustafa, eds., *Rule by Law: The Politics of Courts in Authoritarian Regimes* (Cambridge: Cambridge University Press, 2008).

[32] See, e.g., Terence C. Halliday, Lucien Karpik, and Malcolm M. Feeley, eds., *Fates of Political Liberalism Freedom: The Legal Complex in the British Post-Colony: The Politics of the Legal Complex* (Cambridge: Cambridge University Press, 2012); Yves Dezalay and Bryant G. Garth, *Asian Legal Revivals: Lawyers in the Shadow of Empire* (Chicago: University of Chicago Press, 2010).

[33] For an account that links judges' roles as both institutional and ideological actors, see Lisa Hilbink, *Judges beyond Politics in Democracy and Dictatorship: Lessons from Chile* (Cambridge: Cambridge University Press, 2007).

[34] Commission on Legal Empowerment of the Poor, *Making the Law Work for Everyone*, Vol. 1 (New York: United Nations Development Programme, 2008).

SUDAN: EXTREME LEGAL PLURALISM IN A VOLATILE STATE

Sudan presents an important case for those who study legal politics. Our understanding of how law functions in high-conflict settings is minimal because of the practical challenges of site access, language acquisition, and researcher safety. Much of the research on law in these environments has been based on reports and press releases by organizations that document human rights abuses and have a vested interest in promoting the adoption of human rights treaties.[35] While calling attention to human rights abuses is vital work, these organizations are not properly positioned to analyze broader questions about how governments and nonstate actors use legal resources to achieve their goals.

Overview of the Conflict

Sudan is known throughout the world for its deep ethnic and religious divisions, interminable civil wars, widespread corruption, instability, and record-setting numbers of internally displaced people. The country launched itself into civil war in August 1955, just months before declaring independence from the British on January 1, 1956. Army officers from southern Sudan mutinied, demanding more representation in the Sudanese-led transitional government in Khartoum. The British had essentially handed power to a select group of Muslim families in the North who had been loyal servants of the colonial administration. The mutiny metamorphosed into a catastrophic seventeen-year civil war that destroyed towns and villages throughout southern Sudan, displacing surviving residents. A power-sharing agreement was signed in 1972 between the southern military rebels and the northern dictatorship of Jaafar Muhammad an-Nimeiri, a military leader who had seized control of Khartoum in 1969. President Nimeiri's socialist government ruled throughout the 1970s; inflation skyrocketed, breeding political and economic instability. In 1983, in a last-ditch effort to maintain some pretense of authority, Nimeiri imposed *shari'a* (Islamic law) throughout the country and dissolved the southern regional government,

---

[35] See Amnesty International, "Sudan," (2012), Available: http://www.amnesty.org/en/region/sudan (accessed January 9, 2013). See also Human Rights Watch, "Sudan," (2012), Available: http://www.hrw.org/africa/sudan (accessed January 9, 2013); International Crisis Group, "Sudan," (2011), Available: http://www.crisisgroup.org/en/regions/africa/horn-of-africa/sudan.aspx (accessed January 9, 2013).

overturning the peace accords he signed a decade earlier. This legal change enraged leaders in the predominantly non-Muslim South and added fuel to another eruption of civil war. Most of the fighting took place in the South, where many rebuilt towns and villages were once again utterly destroyed. In 2005, another power-sharing agreement ostensibly ended the civil war, although it certainly has not produced peace for many millions of displaced persons who remain in encampments and squatter areas, nor for those who live along the heavily militarized border between Sudan and South Sudan.

Even as the war between the North and South was drawing to a close, a new war started in Darfur, the western part of Sudan. The story is familiar: locals demanded better representation in the central government in Khartoum, and the government responded with military force, hoping to quell an insurgency that the regime believed was a threat to its authority. The conflict between armed tribal militias, splinter groups, and the Bashir regime swiftly spiraled out of control. Beginning in 2003, the violence in Darfur emerged as the first global humanitarian crisis of the twenty-first century. The United Nations and internationally respected criminologists estimated that from 2003 to 2006, the period of heaviest fighting in Darfur, hundreds of thousands of people were killed.[36] The ongoing crisis in Darfur and in oil zones – which international human rights groups, academics, and the U.S. Congress have at various times termed genocide – continues to roil the region and threatens to drag Sudan and South Sudan into renewed war. Such is Sudan's fate: every time the outlook seems to improve through the signing of an armistice or the arrival of UN peacekeepers, a new horror emerges in the form of war, political crisis, or famine. During the transitional years from 2005 to 2011 following a "comprehensive" peace agreement, millions of displaced persons living in the vast expanse of desert outside the capital continued to experience prolonged violence and destitution. Shocking as the brutality in Darfur had been, hostilities along the new and disputed border with South Sudan were no surprise to those familiar with Sudan's long and troubled history of violence and unstable politics.

---

[36] See John Hagan and Wenona Raymond-Richmond, *Darfur and the Crime of Genocide* (Cambridge: Cambridge University Press, 2008). See also Alex de Waal, *Famine That Kills: Darfur, Sudan* (Oxford: Oxford University Press, [1988] 2005); M. W. Daly, *Darfur's Sorrow: A History of Destruction and Genocide* (Cambridge: Cambridge University Press, 2008).

Geographic and Ethnocultural Makeup

To understand how the Sudanese people have endured a state of such extreme misery and chaos, one must begin with an appreciation of the nation's complex geographic and ethnocultural makeup. Before the secession of South Sudan in 2011, Sudan was the largest country in Africa, covering nearly 1 million square miles, roughly the size of the United States east of the Mississippi River. With a population of approximately 40 million people, many of whom live in a few urban areas, huge swaths of the country are sparsely inhabited. Sudan's landscapes range from arid deserts in the North, to savannas in the center, to lush forests and impassable swamplands in the South. Khartoum, the capital city, sits at the confluence of the Blue and White Nile rivers, the source of the region's water flow north to the Mediterranean. It is among the world's hottest cities, with daily summer temperatures typically rising above 50 degrees Celsius (122 Fahrenheit).

Sudan also exhibits tremendous cultural, ethnic, and religious diversity, having absorbed influences from the Middle East, South Asia, Europe, and sub-Saharan Africa. Sudan contains hundreds of tribes and ethnic groups that have their own customs, languages, and legal traditions. Some of these groups identify strongly as Arab, while others identify strongly as African. The majority of self-identified Arabs are also Muslim, and the majority of self-identified Africans are non-Muslim.[37] Particularly during the civil war, some Muslims in southern Sudan also attended Christian church services – in part to receive news about the conflict and warnings about ongoing threats and dangers. Considerable ethnic and religious mixing has certainly blurred the boundaries between these groups, rendering the distinction in many cases one of political identity. There are no reliable estimates of religious diversity; in the 1980s Sudan's population was estimated at 70 percent Muslim and 30 percent non-Muslim (Christian, animist, or a blend). However, the political influence of Christianity has grown tremendously in southern Sudan since that

---

[37] Christianity arrived in Sudan centuries prior to Islam. But as a result of efforts by Christian missionaries in the late 19th and early 20th centuries in southern Sudan to stabilize competing groups, southern Sudan has had a very different religious makeup from the Sudan north of the 12th parallel, which is predominantly Muslim – an unresolved tension of identity that has provided continued fuel for violence in Sudan through the present day. See also John O. Voll and Sarah P. Voll, *The Sudan: Unity and Diversity in a Multicultural State* (Boulder, CO: Westview Press, 1985).

time, further exacerbating tensions with northern Muslims holding political power.[38]

Colonial History and Independence

Sudan spent most of the nineteenth and twentieth centuries under the colonial control of foreign powers, first Turco-Egyptians (1821–84) and then an Anglo-Egyptian alliance (1898–1956). Decisions made by contemporary political leaders in Sudan regarding the state control of religion, repression of dissent, and use of law to support state authority are informed by and reminiscent of decisions made by ruling British authorities more than a half-century ago. The structures and strategies of governance deployed by British officials in Sudan have been maintained and reified by independent Sudanese leaders in such a way that Sudan's colonial history is replicated daily. In many ways, Sudan's colonization did not end when the British left. The territorial boundaries that have been a source of such strife in Sudan are themselves colonial constructions. During the first decade of the twentieth century, British administrators in Sudan and Egypt negotiated the country's boundaries with the European powers overseeing Sudan's neighboring territories. They finalized the southern boundary with Uganda in 1914[39] and annexed the previously independent sultanate of Darfur to Sudan in 1917.[40]

After nearly sixty years of British rule, in 1956 Sudan became the first sub-Saharan country to win independence from colonial control. In the decade following Sudan's independence, thirty-three other African nations saw the end of colonial rule; thirteen of these had been held as colonies by the British. (France and Britain had controlled most of the African continent for the better part of a century.) In the ensuing decades, Sudan was ruled by a series of unstable and weak governments.

---

[38] Since the time of Sudan's independence, many northern Muslims have regarded evangelical missionaries as "agents of British imperialism," leading to their formal expulsion from Sudan in 1964. See Heather J. Sharkey, "Missionary Legacies: Muslim-Christian Encounters in Egypt and Sudan during the Colonial and Postcolonial Periods," in *Muslim-Christian Encounters in Africa*, ed. Benjamin F. Soares (Brill: Leiden, 2006), 57–88.

[39] P. M. Holt and M. W. Daly, *A History of the Sudan: From the Coming of Islam to the Present Day*, 5th ed. (Essex, UK: Pearson Education, 2000), 114.

[40] While Sudan has experienced 120 years of foreign colonial rule since 1821 (1821–84 and 1898–1956), the Darfur region sustained 39 years of foreign-imposed colonial rule (1917–56).

The key state actors in postindependence Sudan have been the leaders of two rival Muslim families (and the sects they control) vying for dominance, authoritarian leaders gripping power in the face of these unresolved sectarian rivalries, and a range of lawyers and judges trained by the British colonial administration or by the authoritarian regimes themselves. Law has featured prominently in their actions to stabilize the country. But so too has violence: civil war has raged in some region of the country for forty-five of the first fifty-five years after independence, including two related wars between the North and South and a catastrophic war in Darfur. Sporadic conflict continues in eastern Sudan, though not so widely reported as the atrocities in Darfur or the South. These conflicts have their roots in the colonial past, which fostered toxic relationships between the central government in Khartoum and vast outlying rural areas, pathologies of authoritarian rule, and widespread sectarian and ethnic divisions.[41] The major wars Sudan fought against itself, and the millions of lives lost, confirm what was written forty years ago in Britain's *Daily Telegraph* about the folly of the colonial enterprise: Sudan "realistically ... is two countries [north and south]. About all they share in common is a boundary line drawn by Lord Kitchener after the [1898] battle of Omdurman."[42]

The Sudanese Legal Order

The Sudanese legal order can best be characterized as radically fragmented and unstable. It is often portrayed as dualistic (formal law and customary law). But even formal law is profoundly plural – a layered and evolving amalgam of British common law, Egyptian civil law (inherited from Napoleon), Islamic law, and Sudanese customary norms. In the first fifty-five years after colonial independence (1956–2011), the country experienced three military coups, three failed democratic regimes, six rewritten constitutions, and in 2011, a regional secession that split the country into two. As in other fragile states, many laws in Sudan are passed and ignored, revoked soon after their passage, or simply not enforced, depending on who wields political power at the time.[43] Through Sudan's colonial and postcolonial history, changes to

[41] Douglas Johnson, *The Root Causes of Sudan's Civil Wars* (Bloomington: Indiana University Press, 2003).

[42] John Ridley, Opinion, *Daily Telegraph* (May 27, 1969). K. D. D. Henderson Collection, Sudan Archive, Durham University 539/7/20.

[43] In perhaps the most extreme example, Mahmoud Mohammed Taha, a well-known 70-year-old civil society leader, was executed in 1985 by order of a presidential

the law have usually been the result of political engineering from above, undertaken without consulting the citizens below.[44] The application and enforcement of law also vary considerably across the nation. While political and judicial power is centralized in Khartoum, many regions simply are not governable by the central power – much of the Saharan desert in the north is inaccessible to all but camel-herding nomads, and, during periods of war, the forested areas of the south were policed by liberation armies and radical splinter groups. Consequently, numerous legal systems exist side by side, overlapping and uncoordinated.

In urban areas, where the regime has sought to extend its reach, people live under the formal law of the Bashir government, ostensibly rooted in Islam and enforced by agents usually sent or employed by the central authority in Khartoum. In rural areas, people live according to a set of localized, mutable, and often-unwritten legal customs sometimes influenced by Islam. This legal pluralism exists in the context of warfare. To some observers, the lack of a deep-rooted connection between state law, customary legal practices, and international law contributes to the disorder that has come to define modern Sudan, and to the lived experience of law among marginalized persons since the founding of the colonial administration in 1898. The boundaries between colonial, authoritarian, and humanitarian legal politics, as the remainder of this book reveals, are certainly more porous than conventionally assumed or expected.

Preliminary Remarks

A few preliminary remarks are apposite here. First, Sudan is a vast and diverse country, and I would do no service to it by attempting to describe the complex ways law functions, and legal politics is enacted, in every part of the country. As in other parts of the world, informal mediation by respected parties and diffuse customary laws and

---

military court for the crime of apostasy, which was not a crime in Sudan at the time. Apostasy was only listed in the criminal code in 1991, six years after Taha's execution, after two regime changes. And Sudan's 2005 constitution was in 2010 ranked among the world's most "sham" constitutions, because of the gap between its rights protections and reality. See David Law and Mila Versteeg, "Sham Constitutions" 101 *California Law Review* (August 2013).

[44] See also Ali Suleiman Fadlalla, "Law Reform in the Sudan: A Brief History," unpublished paper presented at United Nations Development Programme/Ahfad University for Women workshop on law reform, September 2006 (copy on file with author).

mechanisms have continued to thrive in local settings across Sudan even during its civil wars.[45] Law takes on this "everyday" nature as individuals resolve their disputes with one another or access local courts – to resolve property disputes,[46] family rivalries, or labor-related grievances, for example. But even seemingly benign legal schemes and institutions, I argue, have some measure of oversight and surveillance within the state. Chapter 2, for instance, reveals how customary dispute-resolution mechanisms materialized in their present form through colonial co-optation of local ethnic leaders and dispute processes incongruously labeled "native" or, in the contemporary context, "customary." The local is, then, inextricably tied to the national or even to the foreign, no matter how distant or peripheral. More generally, state and nonstate actors work to increase access to formal legal channels in a concerted effort to strengthen the state and maintain its stability in the face of political chaos.

Second, other important political actors exist in Sudan in addition to the three actors analyzed in this book, including insurgents or armed groups funded by or unaffiliated with the government, foreign embassies holding out carrots and sticks to the Sudanese regime, civil servants, opposition groups, and United Nations/African Union peacekeeping personnel. While important in the perpetuation of war or the maintenance of peace, they have not had the same lasting influence on the development of a state legal order in Sudan as the three major political actors – colonial, authoritarian, and humanitarian – analyzed in this book.

Third, in writing about the legal tools and resources that elite actors use, I do not reify law. Rather, I uncover a politics of advancing legal solutions to the ills that plague troubled settings and troubled leaders in these places. Each legal remedy, tool, and resource reveals a distinct component or fragment of the law, but not its entirety. My focus

---

[45] Because of access limitations, customary law, including that found in the "liberated areas" of southern Sudan during the civil war, though clearly important in many people's daily experiences in Sudan, is outside the scope of this study investigating formal law and legal institutions and legal-education programs in displaced-persons encampments and urban and squatter areas. The 2011 secession of South Sudan and the project between the Government of South Sudan and United Nations agencies to understand and document diverse customs and harmonize them with the new common-law legal system based in Juba is an ongoing and years-long effort.

[46] Ato Kwamena Onoma, *The Politics of Property Rights Institutions in Africa* (Cambridge: Cambridge University Press, 2010).

on elite legal tools recognizes and creates space for future research on bottom-up legal politics through grassroots mobilization in authoritarian regimes and conflict settings.

Finally, like the concept of law, the notion of development is an ideological vessel that political and social actors fill with their own goals and expectations. Development programs in Sudan created by international organizations such as the World Bank have historically focused on alleviating poverty. Promoting the rule of law has been viewed as a subordinate enterprise, necessary to create the conditions for economic growth. In contrast, donor groups and agencies of the United Nations have used the language of human rights to support and advance their development goals. These agencies, notably the United Nations Development Programme, have adopted a "rights-based approach to development," a concept examined more deeply in Chapters 5 and 6. Remarkably, the way that colonial administrators used legal strategies to promote their concept of development in Sudan is strikingly similar to the model being promoted by international aid agencies today. The actors and their intentions differ, but legal tools continue to be used as weapons meant to reinforce existing norms or to enhance political and social stability.

RESEARCH DESIGN: COMPARATIVE CASE METHOD

To understand the legal strategies, activities, and relationships of political actors in Sudan, I used three main data-collection strategies: in-depth personal interviews, archival research, and ethnographic observations. The book is based on fifteen months of field research in Sudan and archival research in England and Egypt, Sudan's twentieth-century colonial masters. I spent three extended periods of time in Sudan – in 2005, conducting preliminary research under the auspices of the United Nations, and in 2006–7 and in 2010 as a graduate student and, later, a professor at the University of California. To evaluate the functions of colonial and authoritarian legal politics, I secured entry into sensitive government archives and data repositories. I studied materials at the Sudan National Records Office in Khartoum and the libraries of the University of Khartoum Faculty of Law and Ahfad University for Women, in Omdurman. I accessed statistical data on growth in numbers of courts from the Ministry of Justice and the judicial administration. I also closely studied primary and secondary source material outside Sudan – in England at Durham University's Sudan Archive and the School of African and Oriental Studies of the University of London; and in Egypt at *Dar al-Watha'iq* (National Records Office) and the American University of Cairo. I also conducted in-depth interviews with surviving British and Sudanese personnel who worked in the colonial administration.

In addition to obtaining documentary evidence, I recorded, translated, and transcribed 175 personal interviews. Fifteen of these were follow-up interviews with relevant contacts. (I conducted a total of 205 interviews in Sudan and South Sudan, from which I draw on 175 most relevant to this book. The interview list is in Appendix B.) I gained unprecedented access to former top ministers of government, including prime ministers, ministers of foreign affairs, and ministers of justice; as well as chief justices of the judiciary, supreme-court and constitutional-court justices, business and political opposition leaders, and civil society activists. To understand the makeup and operation of the legal profession and civil society in contemporary Sudan, I conducted sixty-seven interviews with current or former workers from forty-four Sudanese nongovernmental organizations; twenty-one interviews with staff employed by international NGOs or UN agencies (most of these Sudanese staff); and fifteen interviews with independent human rights lawyers. The remaining seventy-two interviews involved current or former members of the Sudanese legal profession, comprising law students, law professors, private lawyers, chief justices, and at least two judges from each of Sudan's three highest courts: the Constitutional Court, the Supreme Court, and the Supreme Court of Southern Sudan, based in Juba. Interviewees ranged from nineteen to ninety-one years old. About 40 percent of them were women. (Best efforts were made to obtain gender balance, though in Sudan legal and policy professionals are predominantly men.)

In what was to become South Sudan, I met and interviewed seven of the first fifteen lawyers officially licensed by the transitional Government of Southern Sudan's Ministry of Legal Affairs and Constitutional Development (since renamed Ministry of Justice). Before it became dangerous for me, I also conducted extensive ethnographic fieldwork in desert encampments for displaced persons from the Sudanese civil war and the crisis in Darfur, areas normally off limits to foreign researchers. I conducted much of my field research in the local Arabic dialect, then digitized, coded, and analyzed more than two thousand pages of my data using qualitative analysis software.

The legal profession in Sudan, as in many unstable societies, is deeply fragmented on religious, educational, and ideological grounds, and legal professionals assume multiple and often competing roles during their careers.[47] Lawyers and judges fluidly shift between positions in government ministries and the private bar, depending in part on how the government (democratic or otherwise) perceives their support. A number of informants transitioned back and forth over the decades between private law offices, government service in the judiciary or ministries, and teaching in state law schools. An interview with a single person – for example, an early government minister who later was appointed a judge, then left the bench to open a private practice and subsequently to become attorney general – provides a contextualized and longitudinal perspective on the state's and the legal profession's historical relationship with law and politics. To analyze the effects of the Bashir regime's strategies of legal consolidation, I also conducted ethnographic observations of lower courts in Sudan's major cities by visiting these courts with lawyers, sitting in on cases, and meeting and interviewing lawyers who bring cases before the courts.

Similarly, the civil society activists I met had often transitioned from working for domestic NGOs to being employed through short-term contracts as "national staff" in international aid groups or in UN agencies carrying out legal-empowerment activities. A number of Sudanese NGO staff I had met in 2005–7 had, by my return to Sudan in 2010, left their NGOs to work with international NGOs or UN agencies in Khartoum or Juba. Some of the civil society activists I met were licensed lawyers who work for legal aid organizations, though the majority were nonlawyer activists doing some kind of legal work. Others moved between private practice and activism. An interview with a single person reveals the complex interactions between civil society groups and their donors, and the nature of their partnership. My field research in three metropolitan areas in present-day Sudan and South Sudan (Khartoum, El Obeid, and Juba) concentrated on Sudanese government activities and civil society activism and captured the behaviors and perceptions of the most important and active nongovernmental

---

[47] Mark Fathi Massoud, "Lawyers and the Disintegration of the Legal Complex in Sudan," in *Fates of Political Liberalism in the British Post-Colony: The Politics of the Legal Complex*, ed. Terence C. Halliday, Lucien Karpik, and Malcolm M. Feeley (Cambridge: Cambridge University Press, 2012).

actors, including their relationships to the international and national legal regimes within which they conduct their activities.

To gather information about national legal regimes in Sudan, I asked lawyers and members of the judiciary to discuss why they chose to work in the law, to give specific examples of obstacles or challenges they have faced, and to identify moments of change and times of continuity in the nation's legal history. Similarly, I asked civil society activists to describe why they sought to teach displaced persons in outlying areas to use legal resources, and what the outcomes of their efforts were. I asked persons who attended these legal-empowerment activities to tell me what they understood of human rights and law from the sessions they attended, and what – if anything – they have done with the information they learned, including changing their behaviors or sharing their knowledge with others. Interviews with these persons also enabled me to get a sense of the constraints and risks of learning or speaking about law and rights in authoritarian settings.

Educating poor people to be aware of legal and human rights is a strategy that NGOs with funding from international donors employ outside major cities, usually in the encampments for displaced persons or in villages where poor people have little access to electricity, clean water, news, educational facilities, justice, or the common amenities of urban life. I attended fifteen legal awareness workshops in five encampments and villages in Khartoum state and Blue Nile state between 2005 and 2010, in addition to meeting with displaced persons at their local "community-based organizations" in these encampments and squatter areas. I hypothesized that cultural norms and differences would play an important role in shaping the extent to which different groups of people adopted rights-based strategies to frame their grievances. Understanding these cultural codes helped me to interpret the variety of perceptions of rights and behaviors around the law in Sudan. I also observed internationally funded rule-of-law activities in Juba during the six-year transitional period prior to the city's emergence in 2011 as the national capital of South Sudan.

Using a methodology that combined qualitative, ethnographic, and archival research with descriptive quantitative indicators allowed me to do a comparative analysis of legal politics in Sudan over 113 years and across political regimes. It afforded the best chance of seeing deeply into the machinations of a fragile state always teetering on the edge of disintegration. This multimethod and longitudinal approach was a conscious "attempt to secure an in-depth understanding of the phenomenon in question … a strategy that adds rigor, breadth, and depth to any investigation."[48]

No prior work has established testable hypotheses to understand how law matters and fails to matter in high-conflict states, so this book sets out to generate such hypotheses. But theory-generating research often begins inductively; the conclusions in this book are based on specific observations of Sudan – a fragmented, uneven, and volatile state with hundreds of ethnic and linguistic groups, vast terrain, and only ten years without war since claiming independence in 1956. Because Sudan is an extreme and critical case, the desire to generalize my findings to other nations must be tempered with a careful attention to context. Where possible, I provide detailed – or "thick" – descriptions of my ethnographic observations for other researchers. Further methodological detail is set out in Appendix A.

While sitting in her new office in a United Nations compound, a Sudanese former judge told me that, through the legal cases over which she presided prior to joining the United Nations system, she learned that access to weapons increased the likelihood of violence. She encapsulated her thoughts in a sentence: "Once you have a gun, your behavior changes."[49] The following chapters uncover how access to law and legal resources similarly changes human behavior and human institutions. In the context of Sudan's deep-rooted civil war, both state and nonstate actors seek to build up the fragile state and to shape citizen conduct using diverse legal strategies and tools of law.

---

[48] Norman K. Denzin and Yvonna S. Lincoln, "Introduction: Entering the Field of Qualitative Research," in *Handbook of Qualitative Research* (Thousand Oaks: Sage Publications, 1994), 2.

[49] Interview with Suletra, former SPLA judge, in Juba, Sudan (April 2007).

CHAPTER 2

THE COLONIAL PATH TO THE
RULE OF LAW, 1898–1956

Law is the cutting edge of colonialism.

– Martin Chanock

INTRODUCTION

This chapter examines how the British put the Sudanese under colonial control by advancing a weak rule of law and seeking to create an independent judiciary. A close analysis of colonial legal politics in Sudan (the Anglo-Egyptian Condominium, 1898–1956) shows how nondemocratic regimes in general use legal strategies to perpetuate their authority. On the basis of original colonial records, interviews I conducted with colonial officials and local employees, and secondary resources gathered in Sudan, Egypt, and England, I argue that the British promotion of a weak form of the rule of law in colonial Sudan facilitated undemocratic governance – and helped to sow the seeds for its eventual overthrow. Colonial legal politics helped British authorities legitimize their illiberal project, but it also later created space for resistance and political change.

In 2007, I traveled to England to interview one of the last surviving members of the Sudan Political Service, the British political organization that ruled colonial Sudan during the first half of the twentieth century. Sir Donald Hawley, the former chief registrar charged with ensuring the colonial judiciary's independence, shared with me the story of a Sudanese man who petitioned his local district commissioner for an increase in grain rations. The man complained to the British colonial official that, according to the administration's regulations, a donkey received more rations of grain than an adult man. The Sudanese man then requested that he legally be considered a donkey. This man could have used a variety of methods to try to correct the perceived injustice. He could have taken the grain from a donkey or taken up arms against the officials who distributed grain. Instead, he petitioned the local legal representative of the colonial administration to amend its regulations. The commissioner reviewed and denied his petition.[1]

This story illustrates how subjects and rulers are in constant dialogue – on rulers' terms, using rulers' discourses, and in legal spaces created by rulers to perpetuate their authority. The colonial administration in Sudan was not required to hear this man's plea for additional grain for his family. But creating a space where he could air his grievance was part of the regime's effort to use legal resources to portray itself as a moderate, legitimate authority interested in ensuring an adequate living standard for all Sudanese people. That a Sudanese man with a complaint even approached the colonial administrator to review his petition suggests that he believed doing so might lead to an improvement in his life. Certainly, being encouraged to count on the rule of law was an important aspect of the Sudanese colonial experience.

Creating institutional spaces where Sudanese grievances against the colonial regime could be heard and addressed was just one of the strategies of legal politics used by the British in Sudan to maintain dominance. Since there were neither democratic institutions nor any national elections, the regime sought to secure legitimacy in the eyes of the Sudanese by promoting a legal system similar to the one followed by the British themselves. The colonial administration provided procedural and substantive guarantees to its subjects and created institutions in which the Sudanese people could interact directly with administrators. The British instituted courts, legal procedures, and standard methods of appeal in order to deter crime, resolve private disputes, address individual grievances, and moderate the exercise of state power. The provision of the rule of law was imperfect during Sudan's colonial period, but it was strong enough to be taken seriously (and later adopted wholesale) by *effendiyya* (urban elites and intellectuals) and major political and religious figures.

---

[1] Interview with Sir Donald Hawley, former chief registrar of Sudan Judiciary (1953–55), in Wiltshire, England (January 2007).

Sudanese acceptance of the British system of law helped to perpetuate the administration and its nondemocratic rule. The British used their laws, legal personnel, and legal institutions to promote colonial continuity by compartmentalizing and stifling dissent, manufacturing or reifying tribal or ethnic distinctions, and limiting the expression of nationalism. Colonial administrators also used legal strategies to try to stem the spread of the more populist forms of Islam and to monitor its adherents. In the long term, however, Sudanese understanding of British law formed the basis of indigenous claims for political freedom. Sudanese elites (including some tribal leaders and those working for the central administration) received a first-class education in the rule of law at the hands of colonial oppressors and ultimately used those laws and institutions to rid themselves of colonial authority.[2]

This chapter investigates how state actors and their subjects use legal tools and resources instrumentally and the extent to which the rule of law restrains those who impose it. In examining the rule of law in the context of colonial legal politics, I ask three related questions: First, why would a colonial administration seek to promote the rule of law? Second, how did the British create weak forms of the rule of law during their tenure in Sudan? And, third, to what extent did the strategy of promoting the rule of law succeed in securing control and consolidating British authority in Sudan? I conclude by using the answers to these questions to reflect upon the role of legal politics and the rule of law in the consolidation of colonial power.

WHY BUILD LAW?

Through colonialism, European authorities endeavored to transform "the savage into a civilized citizen of [the] empire."[3] The British experiment in Anglo-Egyptian Sudan was unusual, however, in that only a few British officers and even fewer European settlers immigrated to populate the region. When the British seized power in 1898, they placed a handful of officials in Khartoum and tasked them with overseeing a population of approximately five million Sudanese. In contrast, in

---

[2] See Heather J. Sharkey, *Living with Colonialism: Nationalism and Culture in the Anglo-Egyptian Sudan* (Berkeley: University of California Press, 2003).

[3] John Comaroff and Jean Comaroff, *Of Revelation and Revolution, Volume 2: The Dialectics of Modernity on a South African Frontier* (Chicago: University of Chicago Press, 1997), 366.

settler colonies like South Africa, Canada, and parts of India, large numbers of European immigrants also arrived to participate in the economic boom. Two sets of laws governed in settler colonies: a set of enhanced rights for British settlers and a circumscribed set of laws for local subjects of colonial rule. Colonial authorities used the law to maintain control and protect foreigners from the "natives." Anger over this double standard eventually led colonial subjects to fight for their independence and release from their subjugation. In Sudan, however, the presence of so few European inhabitants rendered a parallel system of law less meaningful. Britain simply did not invest the resources in Sudan to attempt complete cultural and religious domination.

Though the circumstances were different, the intention to advance the rule of law was a cornerstone of British governance in Sudan, India, and elsewhere in the empire's holdings.[4] In these places, ordinances were publicly promulgated by officials and enforced by judges independent of the administration. This form of governance created an image of legal certainty, supremacy of the law, and a benevolent and trustworthy legal system working autonomously, to counteract the concomitant nondemocratic regime. The British reliance on promoting aspects of the rule of law in Sudan was informed in part by the empire's experiences governing other colonies through law. British administrators in India co-opted and codified existing practices as "laws" in part to fulfill the empire's economic goals and to give the colonial administration the legitimizing force of the law.[5] In southern Nigeria, the British set up networks of local courts, partly to suit the purposes of local elites in northern Nigeria.[6] Gold Coast residents, according to British sources, were so impressed with measures to supply them with local courts that they "readily acquiesced in the payment of the Tribute Tax" imposed by the administration.[7]

As a political strategy, promoting the rule of law serves at least four purposes for a nondemocratic regime: it enhances social stability, oppresses local movements, facilitates economic development, and increases the likelihood of long-term legitimacy.

[4] See Mahmood Mamdani, *Citizen and Subject: Contemporary Africa and the Legacy of Late Colonialism* (Princeton, NJ: Princeton University Press, 1996).

[5] See Bernard S. Cohn, *Colonialism and Its Forms of Knowledge: The British in India* (Princeton, NJ: Princeton University Press, 1996).

[6] Lord Hailey, *Native Administration in the British African Territories*. Part 3. *West Africa: Nigeria, Gold Coast, Sierra Leone, Gambia* (London: Colonial Office, 1951), 172.

[7] Hailey (1951), 277.

Enhancement of Social Stability

To gain the consent of the conquered, a foreign authority must at the outset address the need for social stability. This raises the question – why do state officials ever rely on law instead of military might to enforce stability and order? Demonstrations of military prowess, after all, undermine and discourage local threats to authority and can potentially impose order more quickly than the courts, whose procedural guarantees are lengthy. Moreover, relying on the rule of law carries an inherent risk that the state's own exercise of power will be moderated. But the appearance of moderation is precisely what makes the rule of law – even weak forms of the rule of law – useful. The raw power of the military "offers handy tools for imposing order," but boots on the ground are less competent at securing long-term stability.[8] As an agent of a state's long-term policy, the rule of law can be used to win the tacit consent of the governed in a way that posing a credible threat of force may not.[9] A legal infrastructure lends legitimacy to the colonial project of state building and cultivates a sense of formal order, which promotes social stability. In this way, a legal system – like a religious system – starts to become a "foundational navigational aid in human society."[10] The need to impose legal structure was especially acute in Sudan, where the multiplicity of geographic, demographic, economic, linguistic, and religious allegiances posed a challenge to the regime in its maintenance of stability.

Promoting social stability is a primary goal of nondemocratic regimes. In different parts of Africa, British colonial administrators created legal institutions and integrated local elites into the processes of colonial power in pursuit of this goal. Courthouse oaths, lay panels with state adjudicatory power, and locally populated juries were meant to encourage a "public sense of duty," legitimize service to the colonial regime, and convince locals that they actually held some power.[11] Although

[8] Philippe Nonet and Philip Selznick, *Law and Society in Transition: Toward Responsive Law* (New Brunswick, NJ: Transaction, [1978] 2001), 52.

[9] See Alan Harding, *Medieval Law and the Foundations of the State* (Oxford: Oxford University Press, 2002). While not focusing on colonialism per se, Harding explains the legal foundations for the evolution of European states. Harding's earlier work shows the relationship between law and society in British history as monarchs attempted to expand power through law and order. See, e.g., Alan Harding, *A Social History of English Law* (London: Penguin Books, 1966).

[10] Simon Roberts, "After Government? On Representing Law without the State," 68(1) *Modern Law Review* 2005: 1–24, 7, citing Clifford Geertz.

[11] R. Knox-Mawer, "The Jury System in British Colonial Africa," 2(3) *Journal of African Law* (1958): 160–163, 163.

Africans could not make law, colonial administrators often accepted customary laws concerning matters of marriage to help promote social stability.[12]

Oppression of Local Movements

Law helps maintain a regime's power by criminalizing threats to order. Through the arrest, trial, and conviction of emergent political leaders, a regime can stymie or co-opt anticolonial agitation. Repression of domestic elites unwilling to join the regime also helps a regime consolidate its jurisdiction. Criminal legal procedures have a clear deterrent effect on challenges to state authority but are less inflammatory than direct violence or military action. While undertaking isolated violent repression of indigenous political leadership might have short-term success, employing a robust criminal code to prosecute agitators would produce more consistent and palatable repression.

Written requests, dated as early as 1910, from Sudan's governor-general to his superior in Cairo express the idea that British criminal law should be used to suppress the rise of threatening Sudanese social movements.

> I think you might confidentially [ask] Brunyate [the author of the Sudan Criminal Code] ... to help us in framing some Regulations by which we may cope with these insidious dealings on the part of our native officers. ... Our Foreign Office [should] take a strong line and deal firmly with this recrudescence of Nationalism.[13]

The colonial administration's first significant legislation was a criminal code, adopted in 1899 within months of the British takeover, and revised in 1924 after Sudanese intellectuals organized an unsuccessful rebellion against the British. A number of British officials were killed before the administration could quash the insurgency. The revolt prompted the administration to adopt a new set of criminal codes that levied penalties for petty crimes, thefts, and homicide but also curtailed the freedom to associate and prevented union organizing. The threat from the existing Sudanese leadership receded and emerging political forces were eradicated through the enforcement of these new criminal laws.

---

[12] James S. Read, "Studies in the Making of Colonial Laws: An Introduction," 23(1) *Journal of African Law* (1979): 1–9.

[13] Letter from Wingate to Asser, Acting Sirdar and Governor-General in Cairo, September 26, 1910, F. R. Wingate Collection, Sudan Archive, Durham University, 297/3/161.

Facilitation of Economic Development

In that law serves to create order, it also provides bedrock for economic development. Where stability and obedience coexist, resources are accessible, construction projects emerge, agricultural schemes evolve, and investment can be secured. In Hawai'i, for example, colonial law was used to conceal the discrimination and violence that had characterized the rulers' relationship with locals, in order to open the door to the lucrative tourism and trade industries.[14] In Sudan, social stability that the colonial regime won by promoting legal progress allowed for the development of the Gezira Scheme – a 2.1-million-acre human-made agricultural oasis that was built along a series of tributaries connecting the White and Blue Nile Rivers south of Khartoum. The irrigated farmland of the Gezira Scheme produced a variety of commodities for British consumption, including cotton, and was the world's largest agricultural center during the 1920s.[15] The scheme was a partnership of the British government, private enterprise (the Sudan Plantations Syndicate), and local farmers and lasted until 1950, six years before Sudan's independence.[16] As they did in other colonies, the British in Sudan also empowered local elites to collect taxes. But financial success in Gezira meant that the colonial administration did not have to rely as much on taxation for revenue as Britain did elsewhere.[17] This revenue source insulated the government from bothersome queries about taxation without representation.

Increase in Long-Term Legitimacy

Promoting the rule of law helps a nondemocratic authority secure a modicum of control and legitimacy.[18] Regardless of whether promoting

[14] Sally Engle Merry, *Colonizing Hawai'i: The Cultural Power of Law* (Chicago: University of Chicago Press, 1998).

[15] Robert Caputo, "Sudan: Arab-African Giant." *National Geographic* 161 (March 1982): 346–379.

[16] The colonial government paid rent to landowners, who had limited tenancy rights. Farmers were given plots of land and 40% of the cotton crop value. The government took another 40%, with landowners receiving the remaining profit. See James Robertson, *Transitions in Africa: From Direct Rule to Independence* (London: C. Hurst, 1974), 128–9.

[17] Tim Niblock, *Class and Power in Sudan: The Dynamics of Sudanese Politics 1898–1985* (London: MacMillan Press, 1987), 48.

[18] For a lucid interpretation of authority, see chapter 10, on authority and bureaucracy, of Philip Selznick, *The Moral Commonwealth: Social Theory and the Promise of Community* (Berkeley: University of California Press, 1992).

the rule of law actually achieves it (the colonial legal system was not rooted in a robust conception of justice), simply establishing regulations, institutions, and bureaucracy helps to substantiate a regime's existence and to foster a sense among citizen-subjects that the government might be trusted to act in a consistent fashion. Deploying judges and court officials as the face of the regime helps a nondemocratic regime cultivate its image as protector rather than oppressor. Criminalizing disruptive behavior can create a sense of order and enhance social stability. Delivering high-quality legal services in the form of an efficient judiciary increases the likelihood that a government will be trusted and accepted by its subjects. And having a relatively accessible and responsive judiciary makes it more likely that subjects will file their grievances through government channels, further supporting the regime's authority and stability.

LEGAL POLITICS IN CONDOMINIUM SUDAN

Prior to the nineteenth century, a series of kings, sultans, and tribal leaders ruled the lands that make up present-day Sudan.[19] Because of Sudan's geographic position along major trading routes that lead to Mecca, Islam began to take hold by the fifteenth century. Many tribes and kingdoms in Sudan started to follow Islamic laws based on *urf* (customs) of the Maliki school, one of the four schools of thought in Sunni Islam.[20] Maliki jurisprudence recognizes and builds on customary norms in local areas. By the eighteenth century, a more formal judicial system began to emerge in Sudan. Led by an Islamic qadirate (group of judges), it primarily served the interests of economic elites and traders.[21]

---

[19] These groupings were Christian (e.g., the Nubians until the 15th century) and Muslim (e.g., the Fur of what is today western Sudan). For an account of Sudan's 16th- to 19th-century history, see J. O. Udal, *The Nile in Darkness: Conquest and Exploration 1504–1862* (Norwich, UK: Michael Russell, 1998). *See also* J. O. Udal, *The Nile in Darkness: A Flawed Unity 1863–1899* (Norwich, UK: Michael Russel, 2005). For a comprehensive account of the development of a judiciary in Sudan from 980 to 1898, *see* Hussein Sir Ahmed Al-Mufti, *Tatowar Nizham al-Qadha Fi al-Sudan* [*The Development of the Judicial System in Sudan*] (Khartoum: Sudan Renaissance Library, 1959). Using historical accounts, Al-Mufti's book provides evidence for a judiciary with courts and court departments during the Funj kingdom. As early as the 11th century, judges in parts of Sudan used a combination of local custom and Quranic text to guide their decisions.

[20] These other three schools are Hanafi, Shafi'i, and Hanbali.

[21] Carolyn Fluehr-Lobban, *Islamic Law and Society in the Sudan* (London: Frank Cass, 1987), 24.

51

In 1821, Turco-Egyptian occupiers claimed Sudan for their own and began seizing taxes, land, minerals, and slaves to support the mighty Ottoman military.[22] As part of its strategy to centralize legal and political command and draw the divided Sudanese people under singular control, Egypt (itself occupied by Ottomans) tried to supplant Maliki customs in Sudan by imposing the Hanafi school of Islamic law.[23] Promoting components of the rule of law was a cornerstone of the Turco-Egyptian occupation: the administration aimed its first laws at itself, to prevent misconduct among government personnel.[24] These efforts by the occupiers to create and oversee a legal system based on the Hanafi rule of law achieved minimal success. Graft thrived in the central administration, and most Sudanese continued to follow diverse Maliki customs as they had done for centuries. According to one British observer, during the sixty-three years of Turco-Egyptian rule over Sudan, "nothing flourished except the slave trade and disease."[25] There was little social or economic development, and the Sudanese people remained impoverished.

In 1884, the Turco-Egyptian occupiers were toppled by a group of Sudanese tribes led by Muhammad Ahmad bin Abd Allah, a Sudanese religious figure who declared himself al-Mahdi (the expected one).[26] Al-Mahdi and his successor, al-Khalifa, held supreme executive and judicial authority from 1884 to 1898. Leadership during the Mahdiyya was repressive and austere, and many Sudanese and foreign residents fled to Egypt and elsewhere.[27]

---

[22] Muddathir Abd al-Rahim, Raphael Badal, Adlan Hardallo, & Peter Woodward, eds., *Sudan Since Independence* (Hunts, UK: Gower, 1986), ix.

[23] See Richard Hill, *Egypt in the Sudan, 1820–1881* (Oxford: Oxford University Press, 1959). See also Fluehr-Lobban (1987), 30.

[24] In one account of the rule of law in 19th-century Turco-Egyptian Sudan, the cabinet council is said to have pleaded to the governor-general to investigate alleged corruption by a governor of the Kordofan province in Sudan, insisting, "Do not permit injustices towards the people and do not overpass the law." See Hill (1959), 43–5.

[25] G. B. Crole, "Lecture on the Sudan." *Delivered at the General Meeting of the Elgin and District Branch of the Workers' Educational Association* (November 7, 1947). Crole papers, Sudan Archive, Durham University, SAD 748/12/1–8.

[26] Mahdi took on three titles: "successor of the Apostle of God," "Expected Mahdi," and "the Imam." See P. M. Holt and M. W. Daly, *A History of the Sudan: From the Coming of Islam to the Present Day*, 5th ed. (Essex. UK: Pearson Education, 2000).

[27] Mahdist rule, while not colonial, was based on a strict interpretation of Islamic law. One Muslim Sudanese lawyer I met referred to the Mahdiyya as Sudan's first "fundamentalist Islamic government." Interview with Sadiq, lawyer, in Khartoum,

In 1898, perceiving a political vacuum in Sudan, the British invaded Khartoum (with help from Egypt) and established a colonial outpost. The logic of the invasion was threefold. The British wanted to prevent other European powers, particularly France and Italy, from taking over Sudan's fertile Nile valleys and controlling Egypt's water supply,[28] to avenge the death of British General Charles George Gordon during the Mahdist rebellion of 1884 in Khartoum, and to protect the Red Sea coast of Sudan as a major trade port connecting Africa to India and the Far East.

In January 1899, Britain and Egypt signed the Condominium Agreement, which codified shared reign over what they called Anglo-Egyptian Sudan. Because Britain also controlled Egypt, the accord effectively allowed the British to siphon funds from Egypt – the sleeping partner – for use in the Sudan. Having taken over a political system in collapse, within a few months of the invasion the British sought to institutionalize important components of the rule of law through a centralized system of government based in Khartoum. Over the ensuing decades, the British designed a legal system that was strong enough to encourage trust and obedience, but weak enough to support nondemocratic rule. Discussed in the following sections are the key features of colonial legal politics in Sudan, which included:

- A professional class of "benevolent despots,"
- Limited social order and economic development,
- Administrative facilities and personnel to resolve grievances,
- Constraints on Islamic law and leadership,
- Devolution of legal authority to local elites, and
- Minimal and restricted access to education, particularly legal education.

"Benevolent Despotism"

For British foreign service officers, Sudan was a prestigious assignment. The ostensible power-sharing arrangement between Britain and Egypt

---

Sudan (February 2007). As with the Turco-Egyptian administration before it, cases revolved primarily around economic exchanges and trade. During the Mahdiyya, there existed a major Treasury Court and market courts in the then-capital city, Omdurman, as well as provincial courts in other areas of Sudan. See Fluehr-Lobban (1987).

[28] See "Newspaper Cuttings," K. D. D. Henderson Collection, Sudan Archive, Durham University, 539/7/4.

meant that Sudan fell under the jurisdiction of Britain's Foreign Office, rather than under the civil service of the Colonial Office that governed all other British holdings. British officers in Sudan did not answer to the Colonial Office nor did they generally rotate into colonial positions outside Sudan. This distinction afforded foreign service personnel in Sudan a greater degree of autonomy than those posted to other colonies.[29] Although the Union Jack and Egyptian flag flew side by side atop government buildings, the elite group employed by Britain's Sudan Political Service (SPS) controlled Anglo-Egyptian Sudan.

The SPS employed 393 officials between 1898 and 1956 – usually not more than 50 to 100 at any time. This small staff administered an area as large as Western Europe. They were a select group of young men, mostly recent graduates from Oxford or Cambridge Universities, who had successfully completed the civil service exam and, not uncommonly, earned a blue (similar to a varsity award or letter) in rugby.[30] Education and family background were used as proxies for ability to govern one of Sudan's districts or nine provinces, some of which were geographically larger than England. Athletic prowess was believed to demonstrate a capacity to withstand the harsh working conditions and oppressive temperatures common in Sudan. Those selected for the SPS spent a probationary year prior to their postings to study law and language, and they had to pass two exams in order to be confirmed or eligible for pay increases. The first exam covered civil and criminal codes; laws of evidence, torts, and contracts; and jurisprudence.[31] The second covered Arabic.[32]

Members of the SPS saw themselves as having a mandate to create institutions and train personnel as necessary for Sudan to join the "civilized" world. They believed themselves to be trustees of Sudan

---

[29] See A. H. M. Kirk-Greene, "The Sudan Political Service: A Profile in the Sociology of Imperialism," 15(1) *International Journal of African Historical Studies* (1982): 21–48.

[30] Of the 393 SPS officials between 1899 and 1952, three-quarters had graduated from Oxford (180) and Cambridge (103). See also A. H. M. Kirk-Greene, *The Sudan Political Service: A Preliminary Profile* (1982) [a 1982 paper from St. Antony's College, Oxford University, now on file at the Sudan Archive, Durham University].

[31] Hawley, Sir Donald, "Law in the Sudan under the Anglo-Egyptian Condominium," *Durham Sudan Historical Records Conference*, Durham University, April 14–16, 1982. Sudan Archive, Durham University, HAW 43/6/45.

[32] See, e.g., William Crocket McDowell, "Memoir of Work and Career," *McDowell Collection*, Sudan Archive, Durham University, 815/8/1–5.

protecting the region for the ultimate benefit of the Sudanese people.[33] In the words of one SPS official, they went "to do [their] best for the good of the Sudanese and to lead them to maturity."[34] This trustee mind-set and its concomitant paternalism fostered a particular approach to the law, one that regarded undemocratic rule by the conquering elite as a necessary evil to keep peace among Sudan's divided populations.[35] SPS officials candidly express this attitude in their correspondence and memoirs.

> It was the supreme example of benevolent despotism, which is a splendid system of administration so long as the despot remains benevolent and is seen to be just. The DO [District Officer] in the Sudan was a dedicated person, and his integrity was beyond question: consequently his benevolent despotism was accepted by the public in general and the system operated very efficiently.[36]

In 1898, the SPS began establishing its administration in Sudan by instituting a land registry system to resolve ownership disputes. The following year, the service drafted a set of ordinances; created a public service sector that employed judges, magistrates, and administrative staff; and built courts and other official spaces dedicated to resolving disputes. The SPS created three governmental departments – civil, financial, and legal – each led by a secretary who reported directly to the governor-general. In other British colonies, often only a single secretary of administration reported directly to the governor-general. In Sudan, each secretary presided over specific areas of government and acted as an advocate for his unit before the governor-general (see Table 2.1 later). The civil secretary handled health, education, agriculture and forests, local government and native administration, police and prisons, aviation, and labor. The financial secretary supervised audits, customs and excise taxes, the Gezira agricultural scheme, and the Sudan

---

[33] Crole (1947). See also Sir Harold Macmichael, *The Anglo-Egyptian Sudan* (London: Faber and Faber, 1934), 62.

[34] H. B. Arber, "The Typical Sudanese," Sudan Archive, Durham University (1944), 715/9/43–45.

[35] When William Luce, Anglo-Egyptian Sudan's last civil secretary prior to Sudan's independence, visited Darfur, he wrote of the local Fur people, "They are quiet and law-abiding by nature, do not move much outside their villages and prefer to be ruled than to rule." Sir William Luce, "Diary excerpts, February 20, 1934." William Luce Collection, Sudan Archive, Durham University, 829/12/42–43.

[36] A. J. V. Arthur (1982), "Memoir of a District Officer in the Sudan – 1949/54." A. J. V. Arthur Collection, Sudan Archive, Durham University.

Table 2.1. Departments in the Condominium and their functions

Post	Functions
Civil department	Health, education, agriculture, forests, local government, native administration, police and prisons, aviation, labor
Financial department	Audits, customs, revenue-generation projects, railways
Legal department	Supervision of judges of civil law and *shari'a* divisions, legal advice to government, drafting of legislation, registration of marriages and births, land policy, advocate licensing

Sources: Annual Reports 1902–1952, Robertson (1974), and Hawley (1982).

railways.[37] The legal secretary staffed and supervised both civil and Islamic courts, gave legal advice to the administration, drafted legislation, registered non-Muslim marriages and births, authenticated documents, oversaw land policy and registration, and licensed legal advocates. The legal department was "generally the insurer of strict legal standards in the country"[38] and the most public face of the colonial administration.

Among the most important projects of the legal department was the construction of a formal legal infrastructure capable of hearing and resolving local disputes among the Sudanese. In 1899, the legal secretary Edgar Bonham-Carter was assisted by "one clerk for the purposes of civil law and seven kadis [sic] of Mohammedan law and their staff of ten clerks." By Bonham-Carter's 1917 retirement, the Sudan judiciary consisted of "the Legal Secretary's Department, a High Court, Province Courts, District Courts, Moslem Courts, an Advocate-General's office, a system of land registration, and a department for the administration of government lands."[39] Notwithstanding its wide reach and docket of tens of thousands of cases annually (see Figure 2.4 later), the legal department staff remained small and elite. One new member was accepted every year or two.[40]

The legal department wanted to impose British common law but faced challenges because of the prominence of Islam in northern Sudan. Rather than outlaw or undermine Islamic law, the SPS integrated Islam into the legal system by splitting the legal department into civil law

[37] Robertson (1974), pp. 80–5.
[38] Hawley (1982), HAW 43/6/39.
[39] As cited in Hawley (1982), HAW 43/6/39.
[40] Ibid.

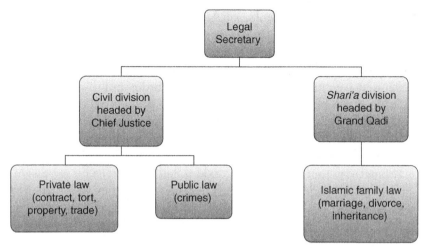

Figure 2.1. Hierarchical structure of the Legal Department.
Source: Author, using *Annual Reports* 1902–1952.

and *shari'a* (Islamic law) divisions. The civil division was led by a chief justice and the *shari'a* division was led by a grand *qadi* (an Egyptian judge until 1947, when the first Sudanese replacement was found). The civil division was itself divided into two departments, one handling private law (property, torts, contracts) and the other handling public law (crime) (see Figure 2.1).

The civil division of the legal department implemented and enforced British common law. Centuries in the making, the common law was used to consolidate control over subjects throughout the British Empire.[41] Section Four of the civil justice ordinance passed by the colonial administration in 1900 authorized courts to "act according to justice, equity and good conscience" when deciding cases or interpreting colonial legislation, effectively meaning that British common law would guide Sudan's district and appellate courts.[42] It was "the most important

---

[41] See Martin Shapiro, *Courts: A Comparative and Political Analysis* (Chicago: University of Chicago Press, 1981), pp. 65–125.

[42] For an historical account of the civil justice ordinance and the reception of British law in Sudan, see Zaki Mustafa, *Common Law in the Sudan: An Account of the Justice, Equity and Good Conscience Provision* (Oxford: Oxford University Press, 1971). The 1900 law lasted until its 1929 revision, which became the basis of tort, contract, and property jurisprudence in Sudan until the 1970s. See also Mohammed Abdel Khaliq Omer, *Qanoon al-Murafa'at al-Masri Fi al-Sudan [Egyptian Law of Pleadings in Sudan]* (Cairo: Modern Technical Press, 1986), 17.

single provision in the [colonial] law of the Sudan."[43] An individual could appeal a decision by a bench of lay magistrates to the district commissioner, the appellate courts, and high court of appeals based in Khartoum. According to Donald Hawley of the SPS, district commissioners were tasked with ensuring social order and were "conscious indeed" of the need to "work within a legal framework" or risk being reviewed and overturned by the courts.[44] The rule of law "was talked about the whole time in the administration. It was the basis, really, of the [colonial] government."[45]

"Sometimes [our superiors in London] said [we were] a bit too assiduous [in our application of] the law," he added. "But they never thought of challenging [us]."[46] Indeed, the SPS was widely respected, even if its actions were not universally endorsed in London. According to another British career diplomat:

> We in the British overseas services regarded the members of the SPS as the elite of British colonial administrators – and so did they. It was indeed a fine service, but [the SPS was] rather over-confident in its own authoritative administration.... We thought in fact that the SPS was insufficiently political.[47]

One example of the confidence that SPS officials had in their "benevolent despotism" is that judicial panels often consisted of one British judge or SPS official and two Sudanese laymen (often elders).[48] There were so few qualified judges that after 1930 panels of local magistrates decided many criminal cases, giving Sudanese laypersons considerable local judicial authority.[49] The fact that the Sudanese lay magistrates were empowered to overturn the rulings of a trained British judge is evidence both of SPS desire to win over local elites and SPS confidence that British common law could accommodate "native" influences and still protect the interests of the Crown.

[43] Mustafa (1971), 1–2.

[44] Interview with Sir Donald Hawley, former chief registrar of Sudan Judiciary (1953–5), in Wiltshire, England (January 2007).

[45] Ibid.

[46] Ibid.

[47] Lord Caradon, in the Introduction to Mohammed Ahmed Mahgoub, *Democracy on Trial: Reflections on Arab and African Politics* (London: Andre Deutsch, 1974).

[48] Judges were not appointed for life; provincial governors retained supervisory control over them, which helped to ensure that judges would not stray from the administration's needs.

[49] See Mustafa (1971), 231.

Promoting Social Order and Economic Development

Criminal law was the colonial regime's primary tool of legal politics, used to maintain authority and deter domestic opposition and disorder. It helped embed British norms in Sudanese daily life and culture; being judged in the courts by British standards of conduct gave the Sudanese incentives to adopt British ways of being. Sanctions serious enough to command respect – heavy fines, prison sentences, and capital punishment – were nonetheless credibly portrayed as the legitimate outcomes of a fair and effective justice system.

Criminal and tort procedures protected basic property rights and ensured that victims of serious crimes (or their families) were usually compensated. The Sudanese enjoyed procedural rights to appeal and protection from arbitrary decisions by local magistrates or commissioners. District commissioners "couldn't just try a case in any old way," recalled Donald Hawley, former chief registrar of the colonial judiciary. "There was the Sudan Penal Code and Code of Criminal Procedure, which had to be followed to the letter."[50] The criminal codes took effect almost immediately after the British invasion in 1899, after being drafted by Sir William (W. E.) Brunyate, a lawyer working in the Egypt service.[51] Having adapted them from similar codes that had been employed "with success in Zanzibar and the East African Protectorates,"[52] they employed common law concepts of reasonableness, probability, causation, forseeability, intent, act, and good faith.[53] The legal department began in 1904 to document offenses, including those committed by public servants, such as bribery, unlawful engagement in trade, or allowing a prisoner to escape.[54]

In order to establish a common rule of law, the British distributed court circulars and built local court centers. Circulars about the proper application of ordinances promulgated by the administration and about the scope of Islamic law were sent to Sudanese lay magistrates and shari'a courts (about one per year on average through independence)

---

[50] Interview with Sir Donald Hawley, former chief registrar of Sudan Judiciary (1953–5), in Wiltshire, England (January 2007).

[51] Richard Vogler, *A World View of Criminal Justice* (Aldershot, UK: Ashgate, 2005), 118.

[52] Hawley (1982), 40.

[53] Waktor Mohammed Al Din Awad, *Qanoon al-'Ouqoobat al-Sudani* [*Sudan Penal Code, Annotated*] (Cairo: World Press, 1970), 5.

[54] See *Annual Report of the Legal Secretary of the Sudan Government, 1903*. Sudan Archive, Durham University, Sud A PK 1561 GRE.

to help promote consistency from one court to another. And because district headquarters were widely dispersed, the British founded local court centers where the Sudanese could interact with an administrative representative and receive direct legal assistance.[55] In addition to larger district prisons, each local court had its own prison facility intended to deter threats to order.[56]

The extent to which the colonial administration used criminal law as a tool of political repression is difficult to measure, given the lack of reporting of most cases in the available *Annual Reports* from Sudan. But examining the political context during the years when summary convictions peaked (1927 and 1949) would suggest that the regime saw law as a means to enforce social and political order. Criminal convictions peaked for the first time after the first large-scale Sudanese revolt for independence in 1924, the subsequent passage of the "Unlawful Associations Act" that year, and the 1925 revision of the Sudan Criminal Code and Code of Criminal Procedure (see Figure 2.2). Facing opposition in Sudan, the British seem to have used their courts and magistrates to come down hard on any attempts by the Sudanese to disrupt the stability the British sought to institute. The nearly 50 percent drop in summary criminal convictions (from 33,000 in 1927 to fewer than 19,000 in 1928) and concomitant 14 percent increase in nonsummary convictions (from 3,157 in 1926 to 3,584 in 1928) also suggests that the British enlarged the repressive capacity of courts, using trials to maintain "legal" stability.

Reported criminal cases peaked again in 1949 following World War II and during the height of Sudan's independence struggle. Many Sudanese who had participated in the war effort in North Africa and southern Europe learned about independence movements in other colonies held by European empires. At the same time, *effendiyya* and political leaders in Khartoum began to pressure the colonial administration for Sudanese independence. The British adopted a variety of strategies to suppress opposition, including establishing an advisory council for the northern Sudanese. But courts were also active: summary convictions grew from

---

[55] Though I was unable to obtain the precise location of each of the colonial courts, their existence reveals an investment in courts by the colonial administration at least to promote a veneer of accessibility.

[56] A. H. Marshall, *The Position of Tribal Leaders in the Life of Sudan*, Report to the Foreign Office, PRO/150919 Public Records Branch Khartoum, July 16, 1953. Reprinted in *The British Documents on the Sudan: 1940–1956*, Volume 8, ed. Mahmoud Salih Omdurman (Sudan: Abdel Karim Mirghani Cultural Center), 100–101.

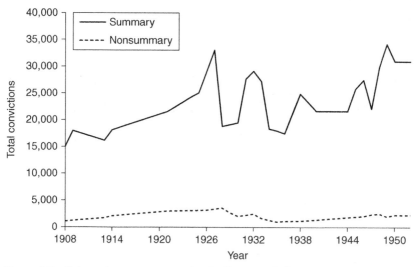

Figure 2.2. Criminal convictions in Anglo-Egyptian Sudan, 1908–1952.
Source: Compiled by the author using government data from each *Annual Report of the Finances, Administration and Condition of the Sudan*, 1910–52.

22,000 in 1947 to more than 34,000 by 1949 as the British sought to deter as quickly as possible perceived increasing threats to public order.

The use of the legal code to put down unrest was complicated by the fact that the uniquely autonomous SPS often found itself trying to serve two masters: the British Crown and the Sudanese people.[57] While clearly an arm of the metropole, many SPS officials also felt loyalty to the colonial subjects they ruled in Sudan. A former adminis-trator wrote that although he was a British citizen he was also a "loyal servant" of the Sudanese, "ready to disagree with or oppose the British government" policies in Sudan.[58]

---

[57] These primary allegiances may have been tainted by the drive for success. Because of the SPS's prestige among foreign officers, they were, predictably, preoccupied with career advancement. Sir James Robertson writes to a friend, "I am often asked why my name is not in "Who's Who" – as Civil Secretary [in Sudan] I should have thought it ought to be.... Perhaps I'm too young ... but I should like to know about it." Communication between Sir James Robertson, and R. C. Mayall, March 25, 1948. Mayall Collection, Sudan Archive, Durham University 521/11/17. Letters to their families highlight their simultaneous desire to reunite with their families in Britain; SPS officials were usually posted in Sudan for five or more years at a time because of the difficulty of traveling to and from the colony.

[58] Robertson (1974), 94.

Not only was the SPS striving to maintain independence from British oversight in Whitehall; the legal department was also constantly fending off meddling by the executive in Sudan. At one point, following debates over Governor-General Geoffrey Archer's plan to create a post of chief secretary to oversee the three main departments, as was common in Britain's colonial holdings elsewhere, the legal secretary forcefully rejected this plan as a threat to judicial independence. He famously argued, "I beseech you [Governor-General] from the bowels of Christ that you may think differently."[59] In another example, after receiving a personal note from an executive administration official about how to rule on a case, Police Magistrate James Watson returned "a blistering reply about the independence of judges."[60] While the legal department clamored for independence, in the end it was bound to a colonialist legal system. Judgments against the government "were not uncommon in the courts ... but there was ... some tendency for officers in the Administration to feel that they knew what sentence might be appropriate in a particular case with strong political connotations."[61] When faced with dueling legal systems and political mandates, one SPS judge wrote that he followed the dictum "Get the facts right and the law will look after itself."[62]

Protecting private property rights was another focus for the British because they felt ownership rights promoted social stability, encouraged investment and development, and buttressed their attempts to promote the rule of law. The British wanted to encourage the growth of a stable, pacified class of landowning Sudanese intelligentsia. After their 1898 takeover, the administration almost immediately turned its attention to resolving property disputes that had been created by the previous regime.

Many landowners had left Sudan after what the British called the "Dervish revolt" by al-Mahdi in 1884. After the colonial administration came to power, these economic refugees began to return to claim landownership rights.[63] In order to prevent the escalation of property disputes and ensure that "hungry European speculators did not buy up

---

[59] Sir Donald Hawley, *Sandtracks in the Sudan* (Wilby, UK: Michael Russell, 1995).

[60] Interview with Sir Donald Hawley, former chief registrar of Sudan Judiciary (1953–5), in Durham, England (October 2006).

[61] Hawley (1982), 42.

[62] McDowell, 815/8/30.

[63] *Annual Report on the Finances, Administration, and Condition of the Sudan* (1905).

native rights,"[64] the legal department established a land registry system to handle land titles, registration rights, and land rights among the Sudanese.[65] SPS annual reports support the assertion that property claims were among the first to be adjudicated by the British. SPS officers claimed, "The Sudan Land Registry System was frankly better than what we had in England."[66] Sudanese land claims certainly kept the administration busy. In 1906, three of the six British judges in Sudan were devoting all their time to land settlement and registry, while Sir Edgar Bonham-Carter, the first legal secretary, devoted "most of his time" to preventing and resolving land-related disputes.[67]

Once the land registry system was in place, the SPS turned its attention to other matters. It was not until the mid-1920s that the legal department once again began to focus on the design and application of new laws to protect private property rights in order to promote economic development. One in eight of the ordinances established during the fifty-eight years of colonial administration was passed in 1925 and 1926.[68] These policy changes included revisions to the criminal code following the unsuccessful bid for independence and sweeping changes to property and investment law. The British adopted a range of new ordinances meant to govern and formalize professional life in Sudan, including corporate and bankruptcy codes derived from British common law.

A New Space for Claim Making
In addition to an administrative role, district commissioners served a judicial function. They heard claims by Sudanese individuals against one another and against the colonial government. District offices were critical local spaces where people could file grievances and make their needs or the needs of their communities known to the administration. The purpose was clear: "Any person with a grievance

---

[64] Hawley (1982), 45.

[65] *Annual Report on the Finances, Administration, and Condition of the Sudan* (1904).

[66] Interview with Sir Donald Hawley, former chief registrar of Sudan Judiciary (1953–5), in Wiltshire, England (January 2007).

[67] *Annual Report on the Finances, Administration, and Condition of the Sudan* (1906), Legal Department Chapter, 347.

[68] Thirty nine of the total 323 new colonial ordinances reported in the Annual Reports for the 50-year period 1902–52 were passed in 1925 and 1926. Compiled by the author using government data from each *Annual Report of the Finances, Administration and Condition of the Sudan, 1902–1952*.

[against the administration] may go to his local court and state his complaint."[69] Even family members had standing with the administration. "Complaints against the course of justice are frequently made by a wife or relation [even] when the prisoner himself has not the slightest intention of appealing against his sentence."[70]

By opening its doors to receive complaints about everything from grain rations to dowries, the SPS claimed a position of authority, much like a monarch who receives individual grievances at court. By requesting the intercession of the SPS, the Sudanese were granting that the colonial administration had a legitimate claim to authority. The SPS placed itself in the role of the ruler, and the Sudanese went along as the ruled. Over time, these roles became entrenched, often without ever having been examined. This entrenchment facilitated a perception of benevolent rule. Allowing individuals to air their bad feelings also helped to prevent those feelings from festering and possibly inciting violent unrest. District commissioners' offices functioned as release valves that allowed antagonism against the administration to be vented in a formal and controlled setting.

A court building was intended to be the place where politics, kin, and tribal affiliation could be transcended, to become, according to the Sudanese, *mabna al-haqaniyya* ("the building of impartiality"). The perception that the judiciary was independent was not illusory and has remained among many lawyers in Sudan. Echoing these perceptions, one Sudanese former minister of justice said, "No one could interfere with the [colonial] judiciary. Not even the Governor-General of Sudan could tell the chief justice – also British – what to do. Just like in England."[71] In these ways, clear and fair procedures – seemingly irrelevant of whether a preferred outcome was achieved – were a bulwark of the rule of law and the grounds upon which the administration staked its claim to authority.[72]

Managing Islamic Law

One of the legal department's most important innovations was the creation of a two-tiered legal system – one for civil law and one for Islamic

---

[69] Marshall (1953), 100.

[70] Ibid., 101.

[71] Interview with Gasim, former government minister, in Khartoum, Sudan (November 2006).

[72] See Tom R. Tyler, *Why People Obey the Law* (Princeton, NJ: Princeton University Press, [1990] 2006).

law – guided by a single, overarching British authority. This allowed the administration to preserve its supremacy, while fostering an image of moderation and benevolence. The civil division (unfamiliar to most Sudanese) and the Islamic division (unfamiliar to the British) functioned side by side, each lending legitimacy to the other and serving as a bridge between the foreign government and its local subjects. The Islamic legal system served both to validate and to compartmentalize Islam in Sudan.

One Sudanese attorney said that the British accommodated *shari'a* "for the simple reason that they took over from [an] Islamic government – the *Mahdiyya* – and the people were very sensitive about … their religion."[73] When the British established a *shari'a* division within the legal department and began to hear cases in 1904, it did indeed serve to demonstrate British awareness of the importance of Islam. The British wanted to reduce the likelihood that Islam would become a political rallying point, particularly in the majority-Muslim regions of northern Sudan. (Christian missionaries were hard at work in southern Sudan, where few Muslims resided.) But creating the *shari'a* division also served to make Islamic law a subsidiary of the British common law system, helping to prevent Islamic law from becoming a viable alternative to the colonial project.[74] The scope of the Islamic courts was limited to matters of Islamic family law, personal relationships, divorce, and inheritance.[75] A former chief justice of the Sudan Judiciary said that the British effectively "imprisoned" Islamic law in the *shari'a* courts. He continued, "But Islam and *shari'a* [are] a way of life, [and because] the Islamic way of life [was] excluded … we had bars and alcohol just like western society."[76]

Trained *qadis* who spoke Arabic but were employed by the administration handled all the cases that passed through the intricate system of *shari'a* courts. Islamic law in Sudan allowed for appeals, which were heard by a provincial *mufti*.[77] The entire *shari'a* division was overseen

---

[73] Interview with Sadiq, lawyer, in Khartoum, Sudan (February 2007).

[74] See, e.g., Abdullahi Ali Ibrahim, *Manichaean Delirium: Decolonizing the Judiciary and Islamic Renewal in Sudan, 1898–1985* (Leiden: Brill, 2008).

[75] This compartmentalization of *shari'a* continued until the 1970s, when the judiciary's two divisions were joined for about three years and then re-separated. In 1983, then-President Nimeiri declared Islamic law the source of all law in Sudan, including crimes, tort, and property.

[76] Interview with senior judicial official 3, in Khartoum, Sudan (January 2007).

[77] Hussein Sir Ahmed Al-Mufti, *Tatowar Nizham al-Qadha Fi al-Sudan* [*The Development of the Judicial System in Sudan*] (Khartoum: Sudan Renaissance Library, 1959).

by the grand *qadi*, who reported directly to the British legal secretary. The British-controlled *shari'a* courts were among the busiest in Sudan and sometimes handled more than 10,000 cases a year (see Figure 2.4 later).

The *shari'a* division was just one of the resources that the legal department created in order to manage and compartmentalize Islam. The British in 1910 made Friday – the Islamic holy day – the official weekend holiday of northern Sudan. British officials also administered and tracked mosque construction on behalf of the Sudanese, as part of a broader effort to win over Muslim elites by promoting Islamic law. Similar to overseeing the *shari'a* courts' jurisdiction, this move also ensured the colonial administration's direct involvement in any new Islamic development. Since mosques were the one public place that British administrators did not visit, keeping track of the increase in the number of mosques may have been one strategy used to monitor the strength of anti-British sentiments and predict religious uprisings. Legal department records of mosque construction, kept from 1908 to 1913, reveal that the colonial administration oversaw the construction of fifty-five new mosques in those five years, increasing the prevalence of mosques in Sudan by 20 percent (Figure 2.3).

It is noteworthy that the legal department – and not the civil department – was responsible for the construction and management of religious institutions. The evidence suggests that the SPS saw the construction of mosques as a way to monitor Islamic activity and as a potential public relations boon, where the construction of mosques is a proxy for British support of Islam. To put it another way, the SPS's conscious supervision of mosques indicates a private surveillance posture and a simultaneous public display of the colonial administration's support for the Muslim Sudanese and their religious traditions. To the extent that the legal department took the lead on mosque construction, the British hoped it would foster positive attitudes toward the British legal structure and rule of law. Once again, law, not bureaucracy, was the basis of British control in Sudan. By issuing judicial circulars to the imams of the mosques, the legal department also reminded them "that they [were] in the employ of the colonial government."[78] The legal department sought to set rules for the administration of mosques, because, according to one judicial

---

[78] Fluehr-Lobban, C. and H. B. Hillawi "Circulars of the Shari'a Courts in the Sudan, 1902–1979," 27(2) *Journal of African Law* (1983): 79–140, p. 84.

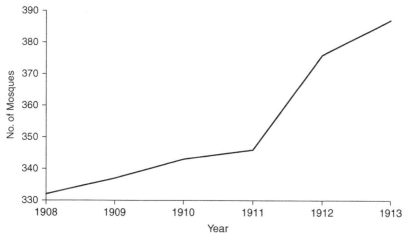

Figure 2.3. Number of mosques in Anglo-Egyptian Sudan, 1908–1913.
Source: Compiled by the author using government data from each *Annual Report of the Finances, Administration and Condition of the Sudan*, 1900–52.

circular directed to the imams in 1931, "mosques in Sudan are in need of supervision."[79]

Indirect Rule and the Co-optation of Customary Law

To be acceptable to a populace, an imposed legal system must integrate and accommodate, instead of supplant, existing practices. Rather than try to end Sudanese practices that were deeply ingrained as local custom (a strategy that the Turco-Egyptian occupiers in the nineteenth century had proved futile) the British simply integrated domestic and foreign legal norms to promote a unitary rule of law. In both civil and criminal law, the British aimed to accommodate traditional Sudanese methods of dispute resolution to enhance the government's image as a benevolent authority. The British purposefully looked for opportunities for the administration to serve as a moderator of disputes, while accommodating existing traditions and allowing elders to use the law to punish aberrant behavior among the Sudanese.

Qanoon al-maheliyya ("law of the locality") had been the operating system in most of Sudan, predating the British arrival by centuries. (For many Sudanese, particularly those outside major urban centers, customary law remains a salient aspect of the legal system in that social

[79] Ibid., 109.

norms are dictated by long-standing tradition.) To build legitimacy for the regime, colonial authorities wanted to coordinate the application of local customs with the use of formal judicial processes rooted in the British common law. Furthermore, because tribal chiefs and local elders were considered potential rivals, the British sought to buy their acquiescence through a process of devolution.[80] By inviting them to join the government and help administer SPS policy at the local level, the SPS used tribal leaders' personal ambition for the state's purposes.[81]

The shift to native or indirect rule came about after the First World War. Britain's Foreign Office commissioned a report on how to expand colonial authority beyond Khartoum without sparking resistance among Sudan's diverse population. The Milner Report, published in 1921, urged a policy of native rule or native administration. Finding that the centralized bureaucracy set up by the colonial administration was "wholly unsuitable for the Sudan," the authors deemed "a measure of devolution admirable."[82] A similar policy of native administration had been implemented in Nigeria in 1914 to great effect, helping to streamline colonial authority across a divided population.[83]

Legal reforms undertaken between 1927 and 1937, including the Powers of Sheikhs Ordinances, sought to "increase the prestige of tribalism" by promoting native authorities who agreed to implement colonial policies. Many of these leaders had scattered during the Mahdiyya or welcomed the British return.[84] Village sultans (in the South) and sheikhs (in the North) were given the authority to resolve certain types of disputes according to local laws and customs. The Local Government (Rural Areas) Ordinance of 1937 gave local officials the power to appoint and employ local staff, prevent crime and arrest offenders, and compel attendance before a local court. They were also empowered to collect taxes for the government, try petty crimes, and mete out punishments for specific crimes against individuals or

[80] Colonialism helped to create an administrative class to fill junior-level government positions. Most day-to-day administration was conducted by Sudanese junior staff – putting a local face on Britain's foreign rule. See J. Spencer Trimingham, *Islam in the Sudan* (Oxford: Oxford University Press, 1949). See also Peter Woodward, *Sudan, 1898–1989: The Unstable State* (Boulder, CO: L. Rienner, 1990), 30.
[81] Justin Willis, "Hukm: The Creolization of Authority in Condominium Sudan," 46(1) *Journal of African History* (2005): 29–50.
[82] Marshall (1953), 94.
[83] Nigeria Native Courts Ordinance, 1914, as cited in Hailey (1951), 172.
[84] Marshall (1953), 94.

families. Rather than go into hiding, tribal chiefs became local government administrators for the British colonial regime. The SPS retained authority by maintaining strict reporting requirements and establishing clear hierarchy. Chiefs were paid by the government and overseen by a regional *nazir* (principal chief) who was also paid by the administration and reported directly to the local SPS official or district commissioner. The *nazir* maintained village security, collected taxes, served summonses, reported health offenses, and "rall[ied] villagers for cooperative labor." The district commissioner, as a neutral outsider, still took the lead in resolving disputes between tribes. But without a Sudanese *nazir*, a British district commissioner was "seriously handicapped in the administration of his district."[85]

British recognition of customary law extended only so far as British views of "good conscience" would allow. In that way, similar to the compartmentalization of Islam, customary law was required to fit British normative sensibilities. Rather than allow retaliatory murder, for example, the British permitted a murder victim's family to petition a court for capital punishment or to have the accused's family pay *diyya* ("blood-price"), as is common in other majority-Muslim contexts.[86]

The pluralist approach the British adopted is nicely illustrated in a case described by one young district commissioner in a letter to his family.

> Dear Mum and Dad ... On Wednesday I tried my first murder case and it took the whole morning. In India, a DC [district commissioner] could not try a murder case, although he could give seven years imprisonment sitting alone. Here in the Sudan, a DC can only give two years imprisonment sitting by himself as a First Class Magistrate, but sitting as President of a Major Court with two third-class magistrates (just two local Sheikhs), he can try a man for murder and award the death sentence, though such sentence has to be confirmed by the Chief Justice.... We found the accused guilty of murder and sentenced him to death "to hang by the neck until he is dead." ... I felt sorry for the poor chap, but we all were unanimous that he must hang, although a *sulh* or compromise had been arranged between the relatives of the deceased and those of the accused.[87]

---

[85] Ibid., at 95–96.

[86] Hawley (1982), 40.

[87] Letter from A. J. V. Arthur to his parents, May 25, 1951. SAD 726/7/19, Sudan Archive, Durham University. He also writes that, spare the most wealthy defendants, rarely were the accused represented by advocates.

In this case, the British imposed the death penalty while the Sudanese constructed a monetary settlement between the families of the victim and the accused. British authorities accommodated local custom to ensure the ultimate punishment of hanging would also be viewed as just. In this way, legal pluralism became a tool used by the state to consolidate its authority while attempting to preserve and subordinate Sudanese culture.

Because of the enormous differences between northern and southern Sudan in geography, religion, ethnic composition, and economic structure, the British employed different approaches to native administration in each region. The two policies were similar in that local leaders or tribal chiefs were appointed as frontline dispute adjudicators and tax collectors, giving the systems an air of grassroots legitimacy.[88] But they differed in terms of which local authorities were vested with powers and the extent of those powers. By reifying a split between a politically dominant North and the peripheral South, the SPS exacerbated long-standing tensions between them that contributed to the eventual civil war.

Native administration in the North began in 1922 with the passage of the Powers of Nomad Sheikhs Ordinance. Rather than expand the judicial power of the sheikhs, this ordinance placed the sheikhs under central regulation. By 1923, 300 sheikhs across northern Sudan were empowered to act as local judicial representatives of the colonial administration.[89] As the number of criminal cases increased over time, so did sheikhs' powers – a 1927 ordinance allowed sheikhs to impose sentences of up to two years in prison and 100-pound fines (equivalent to about ten months' income for the average worker).[90] Homicide cases, however, remained under the purview of British district commissioners and government courts.

The colonial administration was slower to introduce native rule to the South because governance in these more rural provinces had been largely left to Christian missionaries teaching the Bible and providing English-language education. In 1931, the colonial administration passed the Chiefs' Courts Ordinance, introducing the policy of native administration to Sudan's southern provinces. Local chiefs or elders

---

[88] See, e.g., Hut and Poll Tax Order of 1938, *Annual Reports of the Finances, Administration and Condition of the Sudan*. Sudan Archive, Durham University.

[89] See, e.g., Muddathir Abd al-Rahim, *Imperialism and Nationalism in the Sudan* (Oxford: Clarendon Press, 1969), 67.

[90] Ibid., at p. 68.

were empowered to try minor cases. Provincial governors and district commissioners continued to serve as judges in major criminal cases, to which they applied the Sudan Penal Code and Code of Criminal Procedure. While customary law in southern Sudan did not generally distinguish between civil and criminal cases, "civil cases were rare and were usually tried by District Commissioners (DCs) acting as District Judges.... There were no Court buildings and the cases were usually tried in the District Commissioner's office, the DC presiding with two members who were usually Chiefs and Magistrates of the tribe or tribes of the accused and/or the victim."[91]

By implementing different legal systems in North and South Sudan, the SPS fostered inequity and mistrust between the two regions. British investment in the North led to educational and social development in Khartoum and neighboring areas, while the South remained, according to a former civil secretary, on a "care and maintenance basis, administration consisting chiefly of keeping law and order and trying to win the confidence of the backward, frightened and suspicious people."[92] Over time, the SPS grew concerned (prophetically) that the northern Sudanese it had educated and empowered would "ill-use" the South in any national government.[93]

By 1950, administration annual reports reveal that civil, *shari'a*, and customary courts combined were handling more than 100,000 cases a year and that almost two-thirds of these cases were dispatched by customary courts.[94] In many areas, a district commissioner or magistrate could try a case or simply review evidence from the customary court and deem the case closed.[95] Claimants and defendants enjoyed the right to appeal to the statutory courts, though that right was exercised in fewer than one of every 1000 cases.

"The basic assumption of Indirect Rule was that traditional political systems existed on a scale and in a form reasonably adaptable to their

---

[91] McDowell, 815/8/22.

[92] Robertson (1974), 103.

[93] Ibid., 107.

[94] The annual reports indicate total civil, criminal, personal status, and customary law cases in Sudanese territory to be 106,239 in 1949, and 150,199 in the 18-month period January 1950–June 1951. Native benches of magistrates handled most of the civil and criminal cases and summary convictions.

[95] L. James, "The Sudan Police Force in the Final Years of the Condominium," Durham Sudan Historical Records Conference, Durham University, April 14–16, 1982. Sudan Archive, Durham University.

incorporation into [the] colonial system."[96] Devolution supported both "preservation of culture and consolidation of power."[97] Its purpose was to place existing social institutions (customary courts) under the purview of an otherwise illegitimate government (the colonial administration). And, in the opinion of British sources, it seemed to work as the British intended. According to a report commissioned by the SPS, "In areas where the Local Courts are in close and constant contact with the State Courts and the State Police Force, for example the Gezira and the Northern Province, there is a definite tendency for the [Native] Court to follow the same procedure as that laid down by the Code of Criminal Procedure."[98] Over time, tribal leaders and courts began to mimic the approach of colonial authorities. In this way, customary laws and power structures were indelibly altered by the imposition of colonial dimensions and goals.

Advancing the Rule of Law through Legal Education
British investment in Sudanese education, as a tool of colonial legal politics, began with British attempts to create a formal system of education in Islamic law. In the first several years after the imposition of parallel civil and *shari'a* court systems, the Egyptian-born sheikh Mohamed Shakir, the first grand *qadi* of the Sudanese courts, struggled to dispose of the more than 10,000 cases that flooded his courts each year. Arguing there was a lack of qualified people to serve in the qadirate, he petitioned the SPS to create a training school for sheikhs from prominent Arab families. In 1906, the administration created the Gordon College Sheikhs' School to train future *qadis* of the *shari'a* courts. (The British pointedly named the Islamic law school after Charles George Gordon, the British general killed during the Mahdist Islamic uprising.) The school served the colonial regime's purpose of monitoring and controlling legal education in Sudan. Graduates went on to work for the colonial judiciary, and the grand *qadi* reported to the British government annually on the state of the *shari'a* division and Sudan's qadirate.

In 1936, the colonial administration opened the Kitchener School of Law at Gordon College. Prior to that, the legal profession in Sudan had

[96] T. O. Beidelman, "Intertribal Tensions in Some Local Government Courts in Colonial Tanganyika: I," 10(2) *Journal of African Law* (1966): 118–30, at 119.
[97] Trimingham (1949), 253.
[98] Marshall (1953), 100.

been made up exclusively of foreign-trained lawyers, customarily from Britain or Egypt. The purpose of the Kitchener School was to educate Sudanese to staff the legal department, respond to inquiries, draft letters, and write opinions in English. Every two to four years, a new class of about six to ten Sudanese students would enter the two-year legal training program. The school was named after Lord Herbert Kitchener, the first governor-general of Anglo-Egyptian Sudan, who had said at the beginning of Britain's occupation:

> What is now mainly required is to impart such a knowledge of reading, writing and arithmetic to a certain number of young men [in Khartoum] as will enable them to occupy with advantage the subordinate places in the administration of the country. The need for such a class is severely felt.[99]

Lord Kitchener's sentiment that the Sudanese take "subordinate" roles in the country's administration was representative of the mind-set of the British at the time.[100] And some Sudanese accepted that status in order to gain access to the training it entailed. Babiker Awadalla, a 1940 graduate who would decades later become one of Sudan's chief justices, reflected nostalgically on his legal education under British colonial administrators, saying, "The [Kitchener] Law School was proper – we studied [both] common and *shari'a* law."[101] The Sudanese like Awadalla who worked as clerks and assistants to colonial officials were later able to rise to prominence as the country transitioned to independence. In other words, those who worked for the colonial administration benefited from it most.[102] Out of the Kitchener School of Law's first class of graduates emerged a future prime minister, foreign affairs minister, chief justice, attorney general, and senior judges.[103]

---

[99] *Annual Report on the Finances, Administration, and Condition of the Sudan* (1902), Legal Department Chapter, 78.

[100] See also Sharkey (2003), arguing that local recruits in the Khartoum administration, who worked as typists, clerks, and tax collectors, made colonialism function and later would become national elites after independence. Sharkey calls them the "imprisoned challengers of colonialism." For a similar example in French colonial West Africa, see Emily Lynn Osborn "'Circle of Iron': African Colonial Employees and the Interpretation of Colonial Rule in French West Africa," 44 *Journal of African History* (2003): 29–50.

[101] Interview with Babiker Awadalla, former speaker of Parliament, chief justice, and prime minister, in Khartoum, Sudan (February 2007).

[102] See Sharkey (2003).

[103] Hawley (1982), 6.

After independence, the Kitchener School of Law was renamed the University of Khartoum Faculty of Law and became one of the most highly regarded Anglophone law faculties on the continent. One of the University of Khartoum's first law students, who began in 1958, said,

> We were taught proper [British] common law. And we were very happy and pleased with it. Everything was clear to us. And the law was settled – everywhere was English law. It was stable, clear, and really independent.[104]

Education was not universally accessible in Sudan, however. While the SPS supported minimal access to education in the North, establishing Gordon College and some secondary schools, the SPS left education in the South to the discretion of Christian missionaries. One former chief justice of the Sudan judiciary said, "In this country we had the misfortune of being colonized by the British. They isolated the southern part of the country."[105] By the time this man was of university age in 1954, two years before Sudan's independence, the colonial administration had constructed only three secondary schools for a population of nearly nine million – and none of them was in the South.[106] In this way, colonial policies maintained and "institutionalized ethnic and racial entitlements."[107]

While they trained future judges and a handful of common-law lawyers, the colonial administration did not regard mass literacy and education as key priorities. And central control of legal authority and the tight grip on legal education stunted the growth of any organized bar or legal profession during the colonial administration. Many Sudanese, even those who later rose to high posts, concluded that the British "did not want [us] to be educated. They wanted servants and very junior officials to receive orders and carry them out.... They wanted a very small portion [of us] to be educated to a very limited extent, and the rest of the people to be in a complete black out."[108]

[104] Interview with Gasim, former government minister, in Khartoum, Sudan (November 2006).

[105] Interview with senior judicial official 3, in Khartoum, Sudan (January 2007).

[106] These three secondary schools were located in Jezeera, Kordofan, and Omdurman, neighboring Khartoum.

[107] Amir H. Idris, *Conflict and Politics of Identity in Sudan* (New York: Palgrave Macmillan, 2005), 10.

[108] Interview with senior judicial official 3, in Khartoum, Sudan (January 2007).

DOES RULE-OF-LAW PROMOTION HELP CONSOLIDATE STATE POWER?

A 1953 report to the British Foreign Office congratulated the British on their legal project in Sudan: Despite extremely low population density (8.8 million people spread across 1 million square miles), the report argued, Sudan "is covered with such an extensive network of courts that justice is brought within easy reach of all."[109] While these British sources do not reveal the precise location of each court across Sudan's broad landscape, at least some Sudanese did have regular access to the colonial administration through its court system. The British colonial government developed this sophisticated legal system and advanced a model of the rule of law in order to enhance stability, create a veneer of legitimacy and accessibility, and earn a reputation among the Sudanese who encountered it as a benevolent and trustworthy authority. One clear sign that British rule achieved its goals in the areas in which courts were set up was the enormous annual caseload carried by its legal institutions. Presumably, if the Sudanese had no access to or confidence in the British legal system, they would not have turned so readily to regime-run *shari'a*, civil, and native courts to air grievances and resolve disputes. Certainly, the administration argued, the Sudanese trusted the colonial authority to be a neutral arbiter.

Following the early success of the land registry program, between 1908 and 1925 the number of civil suits filed by Sudanese increased 116 percent. From 1910 to 1952 the legal department acted on an average of 45,000 cases a year, reaching a peak of 59,569 in 1927 (Figure 2.4).[110] When the consistently high caseload exhausted the resources of the small judiciary staff, the colonial administration adopted two important strategies: it tied the cost of bringing suits in civil courts to the level of demand, and it devolved judicial powers to local tribal leaders and sheikhs. In 1925, confident enough in the vitality of its court system, the SPS increased the cost of bringing a civil suit from 10 to 25 piastres (equivalent to about half a day's pay), an increase that made the courts considerably less accessible to average Sudanese who were turning to courts to resolve a variety of their problems. The legal secretary wrote

[109] Marshall (1953), 100–1.

[110] Consistent with data from the other years of the colonial administration, crimes were an important part of the caseload. In 1927 half of all cases (33,046) were summary criminal trials resulting in convictions (Figure 2.4).

that the cost increase "has been beneficial in eliminating a large number of cases which ought never to have been brought at all."[111]

Civil and nonsummary criminal cases also fell by 61 percent, from a peak of 20,928 in 1923 to 8,261 in 1929 (Figure 2.4). The SPS used the policy of native administration to help reduce demand on the colonial judiciary; devolution contributed to the steep decline in caseload and number of summary convictions in the late 1920s (Figure 2.4).

The steady growth in the number of cases handled by the *shari'a* division of the legal department (an increase of 75 percent from 1932 to 1952) suggests that the Sudanese also began to trust the qadirate selected and employed by the colonial administration. Even with the annexation of Darfur (a majority-Muslim region) into Anglo-Egyptian Sudan in 1917 and the consequent increase in Muslim population, the colonial administration was able to police the approximately 70 percent of the Sudanese population who practiced Islam by streamlining the *shari'a* court system. While total caseload increased by three-quarters, the number of *shari'a* courts shrank from forty-five in 1915 to thirty-eight by 1952. The reduction in *shari'a* courts is one indication that provision of the Islamic rule of law was limited in colonial Sudan, where millions of Muslims lived. But the British efforts to create and fund *shari'a* courts reflect a broader law-based strategy to support nondemocratic rule.

Aiming to establish a relatively orderly court system and respect for the rule of law did hold unintended consequences for the colonial administration. During the colonial regime, many Sudanese began to expect and then demand an independent judiciary that could serve the public, resolve disputes, and address grievances against the government. Exposure to a legal culture that nominally supported independence inadvertently led the Sudanese to develop a keener sense of Sudanese national identity and desire for statehood.

Law plays an important role in the construction of identity.[112] On one level, law uses a language of abstraction in which the objects of inquiry are rules rather than individuals, leaving persons to become subjects of a governing authority.[113] On another level, having a legal identity (such

---

[111] Annual Report [Legal Department] on the Finances, Administration, and Condition of the Sudan (1925).

[112] Carol J. Greenhouse, "Constructive Approaches to Law, Culture, and Identity," 28(5) *Law & Society Review* (1994): 1231–42.

[113] Noonan, John T., *Persons and Masks of the Law: Cardozo, Holmes, Jefferson, and Wythe as Makers of the Masks* (Berkeley: University of California Press[1976] 2002).

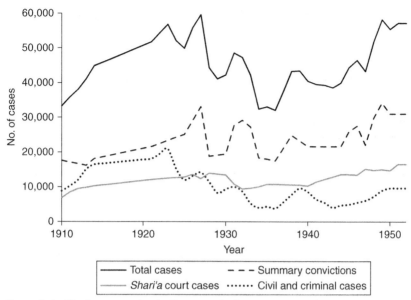

Figure 2.4. Total cases in Anglo-Egyptian Sudan, 1910–1952.
(Noncustomary court cases, including summary convictions, by year)
Note: Data are interpolated for missing years when the Sudan Political Service did not record case events, mainly during World War I.
Source: Compiled by the author using government data from each *Annual Report of the Finances, Administration and Condition of the Sudan,* 1910–52.

as citizenship) forms the basis for claiming rights and privileges. As colonial subjects, the Sudanese were subject to nondemocratic foreign rule imposed upon them. But as subjects of norms promoting equality and the rule of law, the Sudanese saw that the same legal principles that worked to limit their rights could be used to justify independence.

The colonial administration began using legal means to combat opposition as early as 1899 during the adoption of the criminal code. Efforts were consolidated by 1927, when the British adopted a range of new civil and criminal codes. It was no coincidence that revised criminal codes and procedures were imposed after a nationalist rebellion in Sudan in 1924 following Egypt's declaration of independence in 1922. The SPS sought to reinforce British control by increasing surveillance, policing the colonized population, and more closely regulating the behavior of the Sudanese.

Nationalist tendencies successfully silenced by the British during the 1920s powerfully reemerged in the late 1940s. Despite efforts by colonial officials to downplay a growing movement,[114] the strength of the nationalist sentiments could not be denied. According to a senior colonial official writing at the time,

> There is a queer emotional quality amongst these chaps and incipient nationalism, which is usually well subordinated to common-sense but which from time to time comes out.... We must play our hand very cautiously and patiently in these difficult days, and put up with a great deal of unpleasantness.[115]

While SPS officials wanted to seize control of the discussion and impose a definition of what it meant to be a Sudanese person, confidential memoranda reveal SPS struggles over how to create a formal legal identity without inflaming nationalist fervor.

> The position of the Sudanese is indeed anomalous. There is a certain well-defined territory known as the Anglo-Egyptian Sudan, the inhabitants of which are almost entirely Sudanese and known to the world as Sudanese.... Yet ... there is no law defining who are included in the term "Sudanese." Such [a law] would assist in removing certain anomalies and difficulties.... It seems to me that the [government] would do well to *approach this as a purely practical and administrative matter and not as a political question* [emphasis added].[116]

Nearly fifty years after the British took power, the SPS finally adopted the Definition of "Sudanese" Ordinance in 1948 during a time of incipient nationalist fervor. The law's purpose was to "define what the term Sudanese means in laws promulgated,"[117] but it had the effect of confirming Sudanese legal personhood and encouraging claims against British colonial rule.

---

[114] J. W. Robertson, "Speech on Recent Constitutional Developments in Sudan," March 4, 1952. Robertson Collection, Sudan Archive, Durham University, 529/13/17–43.

[115] J. W. Robertson, "Letters to Sudan Agent from 1948." Robertson Collection, Sudan Archive, Durham University, 521/11/65.

[116] Confidential Memorandum of the Office of the Legal Secretary, "Is It Desirable That the Sudan Government Should Introduce Legislation to Define the Persons to Whom the Term Sudanese Should Be Applied?" Robertson Collection, Sudan Archive, Durham University, 517/12/7.

[117] Sudan Government 1948 Ordinance No. 17. Under this ordinance, a person could claim to be Sudanese by domicile and intent to remain, and by grant or birth. The ordinance also includes a section on those "ceasing to be Sudanese," for instance, by taking another nationality.

Sudanese nationalism had been sparked, in part, by Sudan's participation in World War II. Men sent abroad to fight as members of the Sudan Defense Force learned about independence movements emerging elsewhere in Africa and in South Asia. "One of the effects of the war was a greater awareness among educated classes of events abroad. . . . Sudan no longer felt itself remote from other countries," wrote one British official.[118] In addition, Sudanese veterans returned not only possessing new technical skills but also having heard about the founding of the United Nations, which Sudan's neighbors, Egypt and Ethiopia, joined in 1945 as independent states, and about the independence movement in India. Anticolonial sentiment quickly began to ferment among the Sudanese.

The nationalist movement was also spurred by the growth of trade unions in Sudan in the postwar era. Before 1948, trade associations and unions were outlawed by the SPS. But the British Labour Party, elected to lead the House of Commons after World War II, wanted to strengthen trade unions in Britain's colonies, including Sudan. "One of the things the postwar Labour government did was to say [to the SPS] that you must have trade unions."[119] This legal change launched a local labor movement. In 1949, there were 5 unions in Sudan; by 1954, this number had increased to 123, and at the moment of independence in 1956, 135 unions represented 87,355 Sudanese workers.[120] Sudan's largest union, for employees of Sudan Railways, led a number of strikes in the railway town of Atbara during the height of the Sudanese fight for independence (1950–3), shutting down district commissioners' main routes to their provinces and, more importantly, SPS officers' primary routes to England via Egypt. Legal strategies featured prominently in the functions of unions: They "look[ed] after their interests and rights by legitimate action, within the boundaries of the law [and] defend[ed] the rights of [their] members . . . by resorting to legal and other action."[121] Trade union activists and veterans of World War II helped to raise Sudanese consciousness

---

[118] *Annual Report on the Finances, Administration, and Condition of the Sudan* (1944).

[119] Interview with Sir Donald Hawley, former Chief Registrar of Sudan Judiciary (1953–5), in Wiltshire, England (January 2007).

[120] Safwat S. Fanous, "UK Role in Influencing the Rise and Development of Sudanese Political Parties and Civil Society." *Conference on Sudanese-British Relations* (2001). University of Khartoum Dept. of Political Science in collaboration with the British Council.

[121] Niblock (1987), 115.

of the human right to self-determination, which in turn catalyzed demand for independence.

To defuse some of the nationalist fervor, dampen growing enthusiasm among some Sudanese Muslim sects for Egypt to annex Sudan, and prevent outright rebellion against the colonial administration, the British allowed the Sudanese to associate and form political parties. The SPS even appointed a Sudanese-staffed "Advisory Council for Northern Sudan" and allowed the Sudanese to elect representatives to a legislative assembly. (That assembly would eventually become a transitional government in 1953 during the move toward independence.) British officials felt, according to Civil Secretary J. W. Robertson,

> The [Advisory] Council and the Assembly have worked well so far ... questions and motions may not appear to have a great deal of international, or even national importance, but at the same time they deal with the fundamentals of administration and good government, and I think the Sudanese public has a far better idea now of what Government does than they used to have.[122]

The institutions of colonial legal politics ultimately would help to catalyze strategies of legal politics among local elites. After World War II some Sudanese – particularly members of the administrative middle class and graduates of the Kitchener School of Law trained by the SPS – began to use colonial legal institutions against the regime. Colonial courts became tools in the Sudanese campaign for self-determination as political leaders filed successful suits against the government. These often included tort suits claiming government wrongdoing.[123] "It was not uncommon for the government to be sued [directly]. And if the court decided that the [colonial] government had to pay, then the government had to pay."[124] Activists also spoke out against the British authority, in violation of criminal laws, and used their high-profile criminal prosecutions to build sympathy for their cause among the masses. One defendant (who later became a cabinet minister in independent

---

[122] J. W. Robertson, "Letter to Mohammed Eff. Osman Yasin" (semiofficial correspondence), Robertson Collection, Sudan Archive, Durham University, 528/3/18–28.

[123] A case commonly taught at the University of Khartoum law faculty is that of a man who fell during a government function, losing the ability to dance with his wife. The colonial court ruled against the government for failing to make the area safe, the point that the court deemed the proximate cause of the man's injury.

[124] Interview with Donald Hawley, former chief registrar of the Sudan Political Service, in Wiltshire, England, January 2007.

Sudan) requested his trial be conducted by a judge, and not by a district commissioner. He wanted the most respected colonial authority to be seen handing down a criminal penalty for free speech hoping to spark greater social outrage.[125] Such a criminal conviction was sought to (and often did) confer prestige, helping one attain the prominence needed to become a national leader. In these ways, the Sudanese sought their freedom in part by using courts and promoting the very institutions of the rule of law that had been designed to keep them subjects of the Crown.

The first national Sudanese parliament – emerging in 1953 and still working under British tutelage before independence – attempted their first series of law reforms in 1954. Calls for reform – to the press ordinance and penal code – were "motivated by ... their subjection to criminal prosecutions and other forms of restriction to their liberties."[126] Colonial law, they said, was "aimed at killing the national feeling of the people."[127] While the demand for reform continued after independence, little was accomplished because of sectarian fighting, and Parliament was eventually dissolved in the wake of a 1958 coup. The colonial law they sought to repeal persisted.

TOWARD A COLONIAL THEORY OF LAW

British colonial officials in Sudan engaged in top-down legal politics by using legal strategies – drafting ordinances, hiring personnel, and providing limited access to legal education and training – as the means through which they sought to maintain control of the vast Sudanese territory and the diverse and divided Sudanese people. Promoting the development of legal institutions and the rule of law helped to facilitate British control and maintain political order. Encouraging people to believe that legal recourse to the state would make a difference in their lives also enabled the British to claim to themselves, to the Sudanese, and to interested observers that the imperial enterprise was designed not only to preserve the security of the Sudanese territory from foreign encroachment but also to guide Sudanese people to a new kind of political and economic maturity. The statistics recorded by the

[125] Ibid.
[126] Ali Suleiman Fadlalla, "Law Reform in the Sudan: A Brief History," unpublished paper presented at United Nations Development Programme/Ahfad University for Women workshop on law reform, September 2006, 3 (Copy on file with author).
[127] Ibid.

British of the increasing numbers of court cases in colonial Sudan do not reveal qualitatively the extent of people's trust in these courts. But encouraging and even training Sudanese to approach colonial officials within a system governed by laws and not by men helped to generate respect for those institutions, particularly among Sudanese elites. It also stimulated a political battle against the men who controlled those institutions of government.

While the British certainly did not succeed in instituting a robust rule of law in Sudan, promoting a rule-of-law ideology was the cornerstone of the colonial administration. As colonialism reached its twilight in Sudan, the rule of law – however weak it was – became the gift that legally trained colonial officials would leave to what they saw as a politically infant Sudan, to help it achieve status among civilized nations. Their gift would, however, largely benefit the few elites who fought successfully against the machinery of colonialism just enough to gain control of its core institutions. For most Sudanese, the transition to an independent state meant little, and in some cases life became worse after the onset of civil war in the months before Sudan's independence.

Rather than react violently against colonialism, the Sudanese in Khartoum, whose rise to power the British facilitated, unsurprisingly accepted a more civilized battle. Cultivating those institutions and ideas that played a role in catalyzing their political activism, they breathed a postcolonial afterlife into colonial institutions. With few exceptions, the elite guardians of the infant Sudan nursed their state with the same laws and legal institutions that the British had used to control and subjugate the Sudanese across two generations.

Like all foreign diplomats, members of the Sudan Political Service were appointed to serve the interests of the metropole. But unlike many of their colleagues stationed in other British colonies, many SPS officials saw themselves as obligated to serve the Sudanese as well. They sought to promote an authority in Sudan greater than their own: the authority of law. As an abstraction whose power had an exogenous source and served as a constraint on the exercise of raw power by the regime, the rule of law in Sudan was not just lipstick on the face of an authoritarian pig. On some level, however limited it was, norms of fairness did guide Britain's representatives in Sudan.

But by cultivating an image of fairness and justice, the colonial regime was also able to maintain its essentially unjust and authoritarian rule. Promotion of essential tenets of the rule of law, such as an independent judiciary, allowed the British to perpetuate the paternalistic fiction that they were helping civilize the Sudanese and that creating formal spaces for legal education was part of a necessary transfer of knowledge. By providing state legal services to those Sudanese people able to access them, colonial administrators masked what rule-of-law promotion simultaneously provided the regime: an ability to repress domestic political threats, maintain order, and defend British involvement in Sudan.

When studying the use of law as a tool of politics by nondemocratic regimes like the Condominium administration and those subjected to its rule, it is important to recognize that facets and institutions of the rule of law were established and designed in order to serve the interests of the colonial enterprise. Colonial law was deployed to pacify a population, manufacture a veneer of legitimacy, and help maintain the regime's authority over the long term, particularly in the face of encroaching Egyptian involvement in Sudanese affairs. To the extent that promoting the rule of law also helps foster stability and further a concept of justice in the occupied nation, colonial authorities do so by advancing an imperialist agenda.[128]

During the Condominium era in Sudan, British administrators engaged in basic state-building projects such as creating clearly marked territorial boundaries and uniting the inhabitants under a central authority based in Khartoum and supported by district commissioners throughout Sudan. There is no doubt that the British administration imparted its vision of the rule of law to those Sudanese willing to accept it, particularly through courts that worked to resolve civil disputes and claims between Sudanese persons. In 1953, in the twilight of colonial rule, a British Foreign Office report (unsurprisingly assessing British activities in Sudan in a positive light) concluded by quoting the late legal secretary, Sir Charles Cummings: "The Sudanese are a litigious people. I am sure that they value justice most highly; I am not sure about the speed in litigation for sometimes I think that even the winner of a law suit would prefer his triumph to be long draw [sic] out."[129] The report added that a "dissatisfied litigant may resort to further petitioning, to the Governor, Chief Justice or even to the High Court."

[128] See also Martin Chanock, *Law, Custom, and Social Order: The Colonial Experience in Malawi and Zambia* (Cambridge: Cambridge University Press, 1985).
[129] Marshall (1953), 101.

Although the colonial administration called itself the "Sudan Government," the Sudanese people faced multiple layers of legal authority. The vastness and impassibility of much of Sudan's territory meant that for many Sudanese, local familial, tribal, and religious authorities still governed daily life in the most meaningful sense. By the 1950s, the strength of these historic identities and awareness of independence movements abroad sparked efforts among elite Sudanese to wage a battle for self-determination, which was facilitated by the British-installed court system. The SPS accepted short-term political losses, allowing a rapid "Sudanization" of important administrative and judicial posts, in an attempt to assuage the agitators and thwart growing calls by Egyptian supporters to annex Sudan. But law became a tool of resistance and a basis for framing the Sudanese national identity. Colonial rulers used legal resources and tools to achieve their desired ends, and the Sudanese in turn used the logic of the British legal system to help them expel their colonial overlords and achieve self-determination.

The legal leaders of independent Sudan justified and initiated their country's transition to independence by maintaining the essential features of British common law and the legal system it created. Its most striking feature was a fiercely independent judiciary. "Throughout the era of the British administration ... the concept of judicial independence was there."[130] With British pressure, the Sudanese preserved the concept, codifying it in the 1953 Self-Government Statute that guided the country to its independence. Judicial circulars were also preserved, continuing for at least a generation after independence.[131] And as late as 2011, Sudan's corporate and bankruptcy codes, though translated and revised in the 1970s, remained effectively copies of colonial codes drafted by the British. Those Sudanese educated in law by the British would become independent Sudan's government ministers, chief justices, and members of Parliament, who – like the colonial officials who taught them – would use the rhetoric of law and legal certainty to respond to economic or political uncertainty, maintain a veneer of legitimacy, or entrench their authority. While colonial rule formally ended in 1956, actions taken and policies adopted in independent Sudan reveal that colonial legal politics left the nation an enduring legacy.

---

[130] Interview with Donald Hawley, former chief registrar of the Sudan Political Service, in Wiltshire, England, January 2007.
[131] See Fluehr-Lobban and Hillawi (1983).

CHAPTER 3

LAW IN A STATE OF CRISIS, 1956–1989

INTRODUCTION

From the end of the Anglo-Egyptian Condominium in 1956 to the start of President Omar Hassan al-Bashir's military regime in 1989, Sudanese state authorities grappled with the persistent threat of political and economic collapse. Leaders in postcolonial Sudan relied on a variety of methods to manage these threats and ensure the survival of the state. Some used violence and militarism to deal with civil and economic unrest. But all political leaders during this period – whether elected democrats or authoritarian dictators – sought to control law and the legal order. They passed ordinances, built legal institutions, trained legal personnel, and used precious political capital to promote legal theories. In short, they adopted an array of strategies of legal politics to support their own authority and convey a sense of state stability.

In nations governed by a robust rule of law, constitutional law is independent of and transcends current politics, and it functions with some degree of continuity and predictability. In Sudan, which has been governed alternatingly by incompetent democrats and intransigent authoritarians, constitutional law has been used and altered by each regime in pursuit of its own political ends. The tension between theory and reality is neatly illustrated in a conversation I had with one of Sudan's first government ministers, directly involved in the country's first postindependence political stalemate in 1964. The military regime of General Ibrahim Abboud was toppled that year by a popular uprising, and two major democratic parties began to compete for power. The Democratic

Unionists claimed that although they had fewer seats in parliament, their leader, Ismael al-Azhari, ought to be reinstated as prime minister. (He had been ousted in a coup in 1958.) Facing legislative deadlock, the majority party, Umma, offered a compromise – al-Azhari would head the *majlis al-siyada* (Supreme Council) and Umma would select the prime minister. Al-Azhari's party agreed, but the arrangement required a change to the Sudan Constitution, which had originally stated that leadership of the *majlis* would rotate among five named political parties. Umma and the Democratic Unionists argued that this constitutional change was necessary in order to prevent political chaos and demonstrate their respect for the rule of law. A key government minister of the time told me in 2007, "Azhari wanted assurances [from me] that this [arrangement] would be possible legally."[1] Still, political foes accused both Azhari and his competitors of "playing with" Sudan's "sacred" constitution to suit their political purposes.[2] More than forty years after this episode, sitting behind a mahogany desk in his private law office in Khartoum, the former minister reflected, "Of course that's nonsensical. What's wrong with [altering] the constitution to serve a [political] purpose? ... If the stability of the country requires that the constitution be changed, why not [change it]?"[3]

Many Sudanese politicians before and since have asked the same question: in the face of violence, conspiracy, and chaos, what purpose does fealty to legal principles serve? Equally confounding for these politicians has been the question: to which legal principles should one be loyal? As previously described, the legal order in Sudan is best characterized as radically plural. Since the founding of the Condominium, multiple systems – including British common law, Egyptian civil law, Islamic law, and different Sudanese customary legal systems – have been combined in various ways, creating a complex and uneven legal landscape. Law is a particularly messy business in Sudan, where there is no agreed-upon national set of fundamental legal principles, even among democratically minded politicians.

During the three decades following independence, Sudan's legal pluralism was one of the critical features that allowed successive state authorities to reinterpret and redesign the rule of law to fit their

---

[1] Interview with Mansour, lawyer and former government minister, in Khartoum, Sudan (February 2007).

[2] Ibid.

[3] Ibid.

expression of

law = politics

objectives and the political, economic, and social conditions of the day. Rather than reflecting a set of abstract and unchanging legal principles, the rule of law reflected the political priorities and interests of each new administration. To analyze law promotion during the first generation of postcolonial Sudan, I have identified three distinct periods of legal politics in which political elites promoted the rule of law for different ends. During the first period (1956–64), promoting the rule of law was used to foster stability, continuity from the colonial period, and predictability. During the second period (1965–76), it was used to intimidate opponents and establish a grand legacy for a military dictator seeking to crystallize his authority. During the third period (1977–89), it was a tool of regime preservation, a life vest for a drowning autocrat – followed by a momentary revival of an independent judiciary prior to Bashir's dramatic coup in 1989.

In the 1950s and 1960s, Sudan faced a potentially crippling power vacuum in its national parliament. It was the judiciary, instead, that had the trained staff and capability to impose basic social order. British-trained judges continued the work they had previously done in partnership with the Sudan Political Service and maintained a British-imposed legal system in accordance with British common law. To the rest of the world, the fact that the legal system prospered despite political turmoil in Sudan was powerful proof of Sudan's legitimacy as an independent state. And, for a time, it was a safeguard against infringement on the judiciary's own independence. This was a high point for the emergence of a Sudanese common law, as Sudanese judges were able to adapt aspects of British common law to suit their own country. After the first decade, however, when governmental deadlock was replaced with dictatorship, the judiciary was overtaken and a new form of law emerged.

From the late 1960s to the early 1980s, political actors seeking to augment their own power and create a legacy of legal innovation made dramatic changes in the law. First, the legislature tried to reassert its authority, not by bold leadership but by undercutting the power of the judiciary when ostensibly democratic political parties disagreed with judicial rulings. Then, in the early 1970s, President Jafaar Nimeiri sought the wholesale revision of the legal system from one rooted in British common law to one rooted in Egyptian civil law. (Common law is in part based on precedents set by judges in the course of issuing legal decisions. Civil law is based largely on laws written and codified by legislators or administrators.) Nimeiri hoped that this change would pave the way for Sudan and Egypt to unite and form an Arab powerhouse in Africa. That goal, of course, did not come to pass. But Nimeiri successfully, albeit temporarily, strengthened his power by trying to remake Sudan's entire legal structure.

By the early 1980s, economic collapse was imminent and Nimeiri's power was waning. In an effort to stay in office, he attempted once again to remake the legal system. This time, he promoted revisions based on Islamic law, hoping this would win him friends among the devout and distract the nation from its economic woes. But his heavy-handed use of Islamic law, particularly with regard to corporal punishment, awakened the dormant judicial branch. Another even more repressive military regime (under Bashir) would soon rise to power, but this momentary resurgence of judicial autonomy between 1986 and 1989 demonstrated once again how the law can be a tool simultaneously of political oppression and redemption.

LAW AS BALLAST 1956–1964

Before Sudan became officially independent, the British colonial administration put a great deal of energy into shoring up the judicial branch. Colonial representatives closely supervised the work of judges and judiciary officials during the three-year transitional period 1953–5 to ensure the rule of law would be respected. The British were also particularly anxious about Egypt's long-standing attempts to sway influential Muslim sects in Sudan (primarily the Khatmiyya Sufi order); they feared a recolonization of Sudan by its nineteenth-century colonial masters. (Egyptians had colonized Sudan with Ottoman assistance from 1821 to 1884, and the British blamed violent anticolonial insurrections in Sudan in 1924 on the Egyptians.) The British felt that any Sudanese alliance with Egypt after 1956 would subordinate Sudanese interests to Egyptian ones. British colonial officials sought to block Egypt's influence by assigning Egyptians to "menial" positions in the shared colonial administration.[4]

The British saw the common-law system they were carefully assembling for independent Sudan as a bulwark against rising Egyptian influence, and a legacy that the British would leave for Sudan in what they felt was a rapid push to oust them. A stable legal system based

[4] Abdullahi Ali Ibrahim, *Manichaean Delirium: Decolonizing the Judiciary and Islamic Renewal in Sudan, 1898–1985* (Leiden: Brill, 2008), 115.

on British common law enforced and interpreted by Sudanese elites (primarily educated in that system at Gordon College) would make the Sudanese less likely to adopt Egyptian law in the long term. Sudan's first self-governing constitution in 1953 provided for the independence of the judiciary in an attempt to ensure that this common-law system would survive any political turmoil, and the British sent a chief registrar to Sudan with direct responsibility for working with the Sudanese to ensure that the judiciary was a separate unit prior to the 1956 independence.

British-trained Sudanese took over the administrative posts that had been held by the British themselves, and the legal structure put in place by the British administration remained largely intact after independence. This is noteworthy because the rest of the governmental system floundered in turmoil. As much as the incoming national elites wanted the transition to appear orderly and Sudanese-led, the reality was that the "Sudanization" of government was a quick and dirty process that left little room for thoughtful decision making.[5] For example, prior to independence a Sudanization Committee was created to oversee the removal of British officers from administrative posts and the installation of competent Sudanese replacements. Ten months before Britain was scheduled to hand over power, the committee "completed its review of the Sudan Government and sent 260 letters of termination to British officials."[6] But the committee's action had been preempted. Having seen the writing on the wall, many British officials in Sudan had already resigned and given their notice to Whitehall and Khartoum.

Why the rush? Britain and Egypt had been locked in an unhappy rivalry since Egypt had gained independence in 1922. By the early 1950s, the two colonial powers were deadlocked over the future status of Sudan. Egypt had begun to exert heavy pressure on the Sudanese to unite and form a single Arab-African nation with control over the economically vital Nile Valley. The river was Egypt's lifeblood. But to maintain a close relationship with Sudan after their departure, the British wanted the Sudanese to remain independent and free of Egyptian influence. The British ultimately determined that pushing

[5] See, e.g., Peter Woodward, *Sudan, 1898–1989: The Unstable State* (Boulder, CO: L. Rienner Publishers, 1990).

[6] Sir William Luce, Undated manuscript, Luce Collection, Sudan Archive, Durham University, 830/1/82.

the Sudanese toward a rushed independence was the best way to counter Egyptian pressure on Sudan and for the former colony to maintain
friendly relations with the empire.[7] Despite knowing that there were
not nearly enough trained Sudanese to fill key governmental posts and
that anger about being excluded from the political process was rising
among southern Sudanese, the British proceeded to pull out with haste.
It seems that Britain preferred an independent Sudan at war with itself
to a Sudan annexed to Egypt. Predictably, Sudan fell quickly into the
same pattern of pendulum politics that has plagued many postcolonial
African nations, a pattern characterized by wild swings between parliamentary democracy and military dictatorship.[8]

In practical terms, the result of moving so quickly to independence
was twofold: a truly Sudanese system of government did not emerge,
and the weakened form of colonial governance was left essentially in
the hands of amateurs tasked to run an intricate bureaucracy. (These
consequences were consistent across Africa during the decoloniza-
tion process.) While the Sudanese eliminated the colonial post of
governor-general and abandoned the formal divisions between the
financial, civil, and legal departments, they retained personnel in those
departments as the core of the new postcolonial bureaucracy. Shifting
low-level Sudanese clerks into the positions once held by colonial
officials maintained and reified the colonial order. Sudanization was
not a wholesale rethinking of the governmental system; it simply
meant that Sudanese workers now occupied the desks of their former
bosses.

Possibly more problematic was that fact that few Sudanese had
the technical or administrative experience to undertake these positions effectively.[9] The Sudanese had not been trained by the British

---

[7] James Robertson, *Transitions in Africa: From Direct Rule to Independence* (London:
C. Hurst, 1974), p. 94. See also Marjory Perham, "Delicate Transfer of Rule in the
Sudan: Dangers Facing the New Regime," *Times*, June 16, 1954.

[8] Later during the same year as its independence, Sudan joined the United Nations
as a member-state, giving the young nation international legitimacy as a sovereign
entity with recognized territorial boundaries. These boundaries, though, had been
drawn by British colonial administrators between 1898 and 1917, demarcated not
because of local ethnic, religious, or geographic divisions but because of European
imperial interests in Africa. Sudan's new sovereignty fixed these ethnic, religious,
and geographic divisions as internal issues to the newly independent Sudan – making
them now a "Sudanese" problem and no longer an issue of colonial governance.

[9] Perham (1954).

to fill the director-level positions available in the new government. Acknowledging that they were leaving the country in uncertain hands, the former colonial civil secretary James Robertson wrote,

> As far as we British in the Sudan were concerned, we did not object to Sudanisation; we had pushed ahead with it as fast as seemed possible, and had certainly promoted to senior posts some Sudanese who were hardly up to the responsibilities which they had to assume.[10]

British commentators back home criticized the government's actions. Marjory Perham, a prominent columnist for London's *Times* newspaper who wrote frequently on Sudan and other British imperial outposts, argued that Britain's Foreign Office had "little experience in administering African territories and leading them on the way to self-government."[11] Perham's articles angered colonial administrators in Sudan, but she was right to worry about the lack of technical assistance to, and expertise within, Sudan's first democratic government.

To the extent that the newly Sudanized civil service was inadequate to its task, the newly created democratic legislature was equally incapable of providing political leadership. The parliament, essentially controlled by two major parties, divided along sectarian lines and fell victim almost immediately to petty rivalries, religious intolerance, and tribalism. The Umma Party was led by the Mahdi family, descendants of the Islamic Mahdi regime that defeated the Turco-Egyptian colonial occupiers in 1884 (see Table 3.1). Umma was aligned with the Ansar religious sect (made up of the followers of the Mahdist program), and Umma supporters wanted Sudan to remain independent from Egypt. The National Unionist Party, controlled by the Mirghani family, leaders of the Khatmiyya Sufi order, strove for unity with Egypt. These two families also controlled the major daily newspapers in colonial Sudan, *al-Nil* (The Nile) and *Sowt al-Sudan* (Voice of Sudan), and, thus, the primary information sources for many literate Sudanese.[12] The two families were also major players in postcolonial Sudanese politics, often falling into and out of power. (A number of smaller parties, including the Communist Party and

---

[10] Robertson (1974), 151.

[11] James Robertson, "Note to Marjory Perham, Times Newspaper," Sudan Archive, Durham University, 528/3/41.

[12] See J. Spencer Trimingham, *Islam in the Sudan* (Oxford: Oxford University Press, 1949), 268.

Table 3.1. Major democratic political parties in northern Sudan

Political Party	Islamic Sect	Relationship to Egypt
Hizb al-Qawmiyya/Hizb al-Umma [Nationalist/ Umma Party]	Ansar (descendants and followers of the Mahdi)	Advocated separation
Al-Hizb al-Itihadi al-Qawmi [National Unionist Party, later renamed National Democratic Party]	Khatmiyya (descendants and followers of the Mirghani family)	Advocated unity of the Nile Valley

Source: Compiled by the author. *See also* Zaki Al-Bahiri, *Al-Haraka al-Demokratiyya Fi al-Sudan 1943–1985 [The Democratic Movement in Sudan 1943–1985]* (Dar Nahdat al-Sharq, Cairo University, 1990).

various incarnations of the Muslim Brotherhood, also held important political influence.)[13]

The parliament, incredibly, reached its first impasse before Sudan formally declared independence – a remarkable contrast to what would be seen as a steadfast judiciary. Divisions between the two main parties were so sharp that agreement could not be reached on whom to appoint as speaker. Ismael al-Azhari (a leading proponent of annexation by Egypt and head of the National Unionist Party) wanted to appoint his cousin to the post. The opposition Umma Party vehemently opposed the idea of being annexed to Egypt. The outgoing British governor-general ultimately had to intervene to end the standoff. It is not known who first made the suggestion, but Babiker Awadalla, a member of the second graduating class of the law school at Gordon College, was put forward as a candidate for the post. He was one of Sudan's first college-trained judges under the colonial administration and eventually became the only person in Sudanese history to lead all three branches of government – as speaker of parliament from 1953 to 1956, chief justice from 1964 to 1967, and prime minister (earlier he had taken the title of

---

[13] See Zaki al-Bahiri, *Al-Haraka al-Demokratiyya Fi al-Sudan 1943–1985* [*The Democratic Movement in Sudan 1943–1985*] (Cairo University: Dar Nahdat al-Sharq, 1990). While Al-Bahiri's book also speaks to democratic movements during the Nimeiri-led military regime in Sudan 1969–85, it features extensive historical background to the various political parties active in Sudan during the run-up to independence. These included at least three different nationalist parties, eight unionist parties, three southern Sudanese parties, the Communist Party, and three "intellectual" parties (including the Muslim Brotherhood).

vice president under President Nimeiri) from 1970 to 1971. I interviewed the ninety-year-old Awadalla several times in 2007 at his home in Khartoum.

Awadalla had been serving as a judge in a lower court in El Obeid, a trading town about four hundred kilometers southwest of Khartoum, when the call came in 1953 that he should return to the capital. Awadalla was deemed an acceptable choice by the British governor-general, the Umma Party, and the pro-Egyptian Unionists because of his status as a judge in the colonial administration and the expectation that his legal training made him impartial. "I was known to people to be non-aligned," Awadalla said. As a judge under colonial rule, he claimed he had great respect for the law and "didn't apply what was asked by the British [administrators]."[14] This independence made Awadalla a more attractive candidate to the political factions that had been fighting for unity with Egypt, and a suitable middle ground between rival elites.

The Awadalla compromise put out one political fire, but by the time the British formally relinquished control in 1956, the legislature was already caught in a fresh conflagration over Sudan's relationship with Egypt. Because no party held a parliamentary majority and the challenges of building a coalition were too great to overcome, virtually no substantive legislation was passed between 1956 and 1958.[15] No attention was given to creating "fundamental change" in the social or economic structures built up under colonialism.[16] The bureaucracy bulged, however, as party bosses created jobs for supporters and family members. The number of classified government posts rose from 15,868 in 1956 to 39,769 in 1968.[17]

A former Sudanese government official wrote in the 1970s that "the one major lesson [Sudanese leaders] learned was that the parliamentary system created on the model of Westminster was not suited to the conditions of the Sudan."[18] Divided attitudes toward Egypt, in combination with "petty personal squabbles, deep mutual distrust, and

---

[14] Interview with Babiker Awadalla, former speaker of Parliament, chief justice, and prime minister, in Khartoum, Sudan (February 2007).

[15] Zaki Mustafa, *The Common Law in the Sudan: An Account of the 'Justice, Equity, and Good Conscience' Provision* (Oxford: Oxford University Press, 1971), 235.

[16] Tim Niblock, *Class and Power in Sudan: The Dynamics of Sudanese Politics 1898–1985* (London: MacMillan Press, 1987), 160.

[17] Woodward (1990), 117.

[18] Mohamed Omer Beshir, *Revolution and Nationalism in the Sudan* (London: Rex Collins, 1974), viii.

the intransigence of sectarian rivalry" between the two major political parties with the greatest support bases, disabled government officials from crafting and passing useful legislation after independence.[19] British efforts to promote secular democracy following a Westminster model resulted immediately after independence in a political scene dominated by religious discord. Each of Sudan's three attempts at parliamentary government (1956–8, 1964–9, 1985–9) collapsed to authoritarian rule within five years.

In 1958, just two years after Sudan declared independence, General Ibrahim Abboud, a relatively unknown military man, led a successful coup and took over modern Sudan's first independent government. Although Sudan was once again being led by an imposed regime, many Sudanese welcomed the coup because the democratic legislature had been so ineffectual. Abboud's popularity was short-lived; his regime would last for six years – the first and shortest-lasting of Sudan's military rulers. He imposed a repressive military rule and tried to end political rivalries by harassing and forcing political parties underground.[20] In addition, civil war in the South was now in full swing. Sudan's future as a viable state was uncertain.

Despite all of this political and social turmoil, the first years after Sudan's independence were the high-water mark for Sudanese common-law jurisprudence. It may seem odd that a legal system could thrive in the face of such unrest, but fragmented political authority can create space for judicial power to emerge. When a legislative or executive authority is incapable of governance, courts can sometimes fill the void. The first years of Sudan's independence are a prime example of this phenomenon. Political incompetence enabled the judiciary to function independently and contributed to the preservation of judicial autonomy during this period – in many ways just as the British had intended.

The legal structure built by the colonial administration survived the difficult transition to independence. The judiciary functioned

---

[19] J. Millard Burr and Robert O. Collins, *Revolutionary Sudan: Hassan Al-Turabi and the Islamist State, 1989–2000* (Leiden: Brill, 2003), p. 69.

[20] Abboud also tried to promote Islam in southern Sudan, in part by changing the holiday there from Sunday (a Christian holy day, designated by the British in 1918 as the day of rest in southern Sudan) to Friday (the Muslim holy day). He furthered his attempts to Islamize the entirety of Sudan by instituting forced removal of Christian missionaries in 1964. See Giovanni Vantini, *Christianity in the Sudan* (Bologna, Italy: EMI, 1981), 251–3.

much as it had during the colonial administration, interpreting the same laws, resolving disputes, and making determinations guided by a fifty-year-old common-law vision shared by elite legal professionals in Sudan. Members of the Sudanese bar advanced the legal order by sharpening their techniques and procedures related to English common law and integrating some Sudanese legal traditions to allow more effective functioning in the local context. Most importantly, the courts were not agents of the political regime; the political regime was not stable enough to control the courts. Even after General Abboud's coup in 1958, the judiciary retained its independence because of the close relationship between Chief Justice Abu Ranat and General Abboud and the influence wielded by an elite group of British-trained professional jurists.[21]

Why was the judiciary able to go through the transition so much more smoothly than the legislature or civil service? After all, the senior British staff in the legal department and judiciary had either resigned or been forced to leave by the Sudanization Committee, just as in the other departments.[22] The key difference between the judiciary and other administrative or legislative departments was that the British had invested in teaching and training of Sudanese legal professionals and had begun the process of Sudanizing the judiciary long before the move to independence. As early as 1936, Egypt and Britain signed a treaty that stated the *shari'a* division of the judiciary would be staffed exclusively by Sudanese candidates. Non-Sudanese personnel were employed only if no qualified Sudanese candidate was available. This hiring practice allowed Sudanese access to leadership positions in the *shari'a* division of the judiciary considerably earlier than in other departments. The first Sudanese grand qadi, Sheikh Ahmed El Tahir, was appointed in 1947, nine years before independence.[23]

---

[21] See Mohammed Khalifa Hamid, *Al-Nizham al-Qada'i al-Sudani: Tarekhahu, Nizhumuhu, Tatowruhu, Istiqlaluhu, wa Atharahu fi al-Mujtama* [*The Sudanese Judicial System: Its History, Organization, Development, Independence, and Influence on Society*] (Khartoum: Khartoum Press, 2006), 364.

[22] Interview with Sir Donald Hawley, former chief registrar of Sudan Judiciary (1953–55), in Wiltshire, England (January 2007). According to Sudan's self-government statute, the judiciary was to be an independent entity, not answerable to government authority. For this reason, judges argued that the Sudanization Committee had no jurisdiction over the judges and could not remove them, even British judges. Nevertheless, the British judges resigned when it became clear the Sudanization Committee would not acquiesce.

[23] El Tahir replaced Egyptian Sheikh Hassan Mamoun. See Robertson (1974), 100.

british training

Judicial training focused on building a cadre of qualified people to take important leadership roles. In the other branches of government, there was no training to speak of; Sudanese junior staff simply replaced outgoing British officials. But the law clerks who later became judges had been among Sudan's brightest students. The SPS had long encouraged Sudanese who earned top scores on the civil service exam to enter the legal department rather than other government agencies.[24] The courts were imbued with a sense of honor, prestige, and professionalism that the bureaucracy and legislature did not have. According to one of the first Sudanese lawyers, "The ... dignity of law was apparent. The judges had robes and wigs at the time, in the English tradition."[25] The judiciary, with this talented and trained pool of young Sudanese professionals who understood British common law, Sudanese customs, and *shari'a*, was uniquely positioned to keep functioning after the British left. According to the Sudanese lawyer:

> Our judges ... were well trained in English common law. And [their judgments] revealed a good grasp of the fundamentals of common law. [Chief Justices] Abu Ranat and Babiker Awadalla, all of them [wrote and thought] in a very impressive way. And we established a corpus of precedents based on English common and statutory law.[26]

The Transitional Constitution of 1953 formally codified the judiciary as an independent governmental institution. Administration of the new judiciary moved from a colonial legal secretary to a chief justice.[27] The colonial practice of allowing provincial governors under the authority of the governor-general to supervise judges was ended,[28] and management of judges was given over to an independent judicial authority (*al-sulta al-qada'iyya*) led by a chief justice. *Al-sulta al-qada'iyya* was held separate from the new Ministry of Justice, which housed the offices of the prosecutor general (who litigated criminal cases on behalf of the government) and the advocate general (who litigated civil cases on behalf of the government).

[24] Interview with Babiker Awadalla, former speaker of Parliament, chief justice, and prime minister, in Khartoum, Sudan (February 2007). See also Hussein Sir Ahmed al-Mufti, *Tatowar Nizham al-Qadha Fi al-Sudan* [*The Development of the Judicial System in Sudan*] (Khartoum: Sudan Renaissance Library, 1959).
[25] Interview with Abdul Gadir, lawyer and civil society activist, in Khartoum, Sudan (January 2007).
[26] Interview with Sadiq, lawyer, in Khartoum, Sudan (February 2007).
[27] Hamid (2006), 356.
[28] Mustafa (1971), 232.

After independence, the Sudanese decided to maintain the division between civil law and *shari'a* in the judicial branch. *Shari'a* continued to be confined to the narrow fields of personal and family law, although a vocal minority advocated expanding its scope to encompass contracts, property, and crimes.[29] During the 1950s, some important Sudanese intellectuals argued that Sudan's entire system of government should be rooted in Islam. The minister of justice at the time, Sheikh Mudathir Elbushi, publicly stated that common law in Sudan "was not intended for the betterment of the Sudan ... or its progress but rather [was] aimed at killing the national feelings of the people."[30] A former grand qadi, Hassan Mauddathiri, appealed to the Sudanese to reconsider the acceptance of common law promoted by the British, saying it would "encourage people to sip wines and commit adultery, both of which are prohibited by Islam whose principles have been adopted by our people."[31] Lawyers in the Muslim Brotherhood also worried that the laws given to Sudan by the British would facilitate moral conduct antithetical to the tenets of Islam.[32] While many Sudanese Muslims lived according to traditional religious and social norms of conduct, there was not widespread support for wholesale legal reform. At least through the 1960s, outside the Muslim Brotherhood and its supporters, Western norms and dress codes (such as alcohol consumption, Western-style suits for men, short sleeves on dresses for women) were still common, particularly in Khartoum, and the public generally disregarded calls for a more prominent role for Islamic law. One Sudanese lawyer who graduated from law school in 1964 told me:

> [During] this period, there were no problems [in the legal system].
> It was a clear, defined law, [with] clear, defined procedures. It was

[29] For an account of the evolution of Muslim family law in Sudan, see Carolyn Fluehr-Lobban, *Islamic Law and Society in The Sudan* (London: Frank Cass, 1987). See also Shamil Jeppie, "The Making and Unmaking of Colonial Shari'a in Sudan," in *Muslim Family Law in Sub-Saharan Africa: Colonial Legacies and Post-Colonial Challenges*, ed. Jeppie, Moosa, and Roberts (Amsterdam: Amsterdam University Press, 2010).

[30] Ali Suleiman Fadlalla, "Law Reform in the Sudan: A Brief History," unpublished paper presented at United Nations Development Programme/Ahfad University for Women workshop on law reform, September 2006, 3 (on file with author).

[31] See H. Mauddathiri, "A Memorandum for the Enactment of a Sudan Law Derived from the Principles of Islam" (November 1956) Khartoum: Sudan Library (available, Sudan Library 8H Hassan), 2.

[32] Interview with Gasim, former government minister, in Khartoum, Sudan (November 2006).

smooth. And, of course, the judges were really qualified. The studies at University of Khartoum were in English, so it was no problem [for us] to apply [English] laws.[33]

Despite a general desire expressed by the government during this period to drive out colonial influences, Mustafa (1971) convincingly proved that the Sudanese courts continued to rely on British common law. In his analysis, Mustafa surmised that judges simply had a "tendency to apply principles of common law without describing them as such."[34] Thus, they operated as colonial subjects in doctrine if not rhetoric. Mustafa found that judges used English common-law precedent with even greater fervor than they had before independence. Showcasing stability and predictability in the legal system, the average number of cases cited in decisions each year for the ten years after independence was more than four times the yearly average for the preceding twenty years.[35] Mustafa's research also revealed an "excessive resort to, and reliance upon, English books and treatises."[36] In almost half of the cases decided during the first decade of independence, there is direct evidence that the rulings were "influenced by the views expressed in an English book on the subject."[37]

As important as English common law remained, there is evidence that many Sudanese jurists felt grounded in but not chained to its tenets. Jurists trained at Gordon College or by British and American professors at the University of Khartoum aspired to lay the foundations for a Sudanese common law. An American lawyer teaching in Sudan wrote, "The goal seemed that Sudan would be ... guided by English common law but not bound by it, ultimately developing its own common law based on the social customs and ethics of the Sudan as a whole."[38] Cases brought to the High Court were seen as vehicles for developing precedent and an indigenous form of the legal principle of *stare decisis*.[39]

Courts, including the High Court, tended to apply English common law to criminal and tort cases but used the "justice, equity, and good

---

[33] Interview with Shadi, lawyer, in Khartoum, Sudan (April 2007).
[34] Mustafa (1971), 189.
[35] Ibid.
[36] Ibid.
[37] Ibid., at 190.
[38] Egon Guttman, "A Survey of the Sudan Legal System." *SLJR* (1957) at 7.
[39] Mustafa (1971).

conscience" provision in the 1929 Civil Justice Ordinance to build a Sudanese common law in the area of real property.[40] This provision – giving judges sweeping authority to consider principles of good conscience beyond the written text of the law or precedent – had been used during the colonial administration to a create a legal justification for British judges to base decisions on British common law. After independence, Sudanese judges started using the same provision as justification for "depart[ing] from the rules of English law which were considered harsh or unsuitable," such as in resolving land disputes.[41] Because determining property ownership – politically important for maintaining social order and encouraging economic development – is inextricably linked to Islamic inheritance rules and family law, civil property law had to be more cognizant of local tradition than tort or contract law to operate effectively. So, for example, in the 1958 case of *Alam Maximos v. Khadiga Mohammed El Brigdar*, the High Court ruled that while the legal precedent governing this sale of real property may be "true in England ... the hardship of such a rule ... in [Sudan]" should prevent its application.[42]

Judges also increasingly began to cite cases by Sudanese rather than British jurists in their rulings: the number of citations of Sudanese decisions rose from fifteen per year between 1946 and 1956 to more than fifty per year between 1956 and 1966, with the number of total cases holding steady.[43] "Although English law still remained the hard core of Sudanese law and still reigned supreme in most respects, the attitude of the courts [could] no longer be described as one of strict adherence [to English law]."[44] In forging a Sudanese common law, the courts looked to a diverse array of sources, including Indian law,[45] American law,[46]

---

[40] The formula reads, "In cases not provided for by this or any other enactment for the time being in force, the Court shall act according to justice, equity and good conscience." Sudan Government, Section 9, Civil Justice Ordinance, 1929.

[41] Mustafa (1971), 210–11.

[42] *Alam Maximos v. Khadiga Mohammed El Brigdar*, SLJR (1958) at 92.

[43] Mustafa (1971), 220–21. Many of these citations were in land law and in procedure, the areas where Sudan had been developing its own robust jurisprudence.

[44] Mustafa (1971), 210–11.

[45] Ibid., at 194 and 214. See, e.g., *Dairat El Mahdi v. Abdel Gadir Abu Regeila*, SLJR (1960) at 49; *Ali Abu Sam v. Kambal Osman*, SLJR (1962) at 207; and *Maeema Hassan v. Mursi Hassan*, SLJR (1962) at 86.

[46] See Mustafa (1971), 210–11; see also *Fatma Ibrahim v. The Attorney General*, SLJR (1958) at 3; *Khartoum Municipal Council v. Michel Cotran*, SLJR (1958) at 85; *Furmeister and Co. v. Abdel Ghani Ali Mousa*, SLJR (1959) at 38.

LAW'S FRAGILE STATE

Islamic law,[47] universal principles of justice,[48] Canadian legal practices, and simple rules of common sense.[49] In 1956, Sudan's first law review, the *Sudan Law Journal and Reports*, was founded. Edited by European and American faculty at the University of Khartoum, it reported on all major decisions by the High Court and tracked the evolution of Sudanese common law in multiple areas, including property and tort.

Meanwhile, the number of lawyers was doubling every two and a half years, from 30 registered members in the Roll of Advocates in 1956 to 200 in 1964. Two leading law schools existed in Sudan: the University of Khartoum School of Law, which opened in 1936 as Kitchener School of Law in Gordon College, and Cairo University's Khartoum branch campus, which opened in 1955. While the University of Khartoum focused on English common law and taught all subjects except *shari'a* in English, Cairo University focused on Egyptian civil law and taught primarily in Arabic. Divisions between Sudan's two law schools would eventually lead to fragmentation of the legal elite.[50] But during this early period, the institution of a bar exam for all non–University of Khartoum graduates kept legal eyes trained on developing a common-law system for Sudan.

An important 1956 case established the right of the courts to judicial review of government action. The facts of the case were simple: The plaintiff, Mohammed Adlan, had leased land from the Sudanese government since 1949. He held a one-year lease, which was renewed each year. In 1954, the government informed Adlan that it would not renew his lease beyond 1955. Adlan brought suit in Sudan's civil court, asking the judge to issue an order of mandamus to compel the new Sudanese government to renew his lease. His petition failed. He appealed to the High Court, where he failed again. Chief Justice Abu Ranat took the

---

[47] See, e.g., *Heirs of Naeema Ahmed Wagealla v. El Hag Ahmed Mohammed*, SLJR (1961).

[48] *John Fairweather v. Gabriel Gabrielides*, SLJR (1963) at 212. See Mustafa (1971), 212 for a discussion of this case.

[49] Mustafa indicates that the many references to these diverse sources, including Indian and American jurisprudence, came about after visits from senior judges of those countries, who presented law books and treatises to the chief justice for use in the Sudan High Court's library (Mustafa 1971 at 215–17).

[50] The tensions between lawyers of different legal educations were exploited by the Bashir military regime after 1989 to consolidate control using Islamic law and to quell any opposition from lawyers, particularly graduates of the University of Khartoum (see Chapter 4).

opportunity to point out that, while the Court chose not to force the government to renew the lease, it was nevertheless within the Court's ability to do so. The Court, he wrote, "has the power to enforce governmental performance of a legal duty [and thus] to control executive acts, but the plaintiff has not shown he is entitled to this remedy."[51]

After this landmark case, the High Court began to draw explicit comparisons between the scope of judicial review of government action in Sudan and the United States. In the 1958 case *Building Authority of Khartoum v. Evangellos Evangelledes*, Justice Soni for the High Court wrote:

> In the English Constitution, Parliament is supreme. The Legislature there is not bound by any written law of the Constitution. But in the Sudan, as in the United States, the Constitution is supreme. Textbooks are full of cases where the Supreme Court of the United States had declared Legislative Acts of the United States Congress *ultra vires* the Constitution and unenforceable.[52]

The High Court firmly established the power of judicial review, allowing judges to rule against the government where they deemed it appropriate.

Lawyers and former judges also began taking an increasingly public role in politics during the first decade of independence. Among them was Babiker Awadalla, who had served as Sudan's first speaker of parliament in 1953. In 1964, after years of prominent public service, Awadalla publicly renounced General Abboud's military regime. Awadalla encouraged ongoing strikes by civil servants and helped unite the students, women, and trade unionists who each were calling for better representation in national leadership in Sudan. The union movement had blossomed in independent Sudan. Best estimates suggest that there were 150,000 to 200,000 union members by the mid-1960s, up from 87,000 in 1956. With the support of Awadalla and other prominent members of the legal profession, the union-led movement to overthrow Abboud gained much-needed legitimacy.

On October 21, 1964, Abboud's regime fell. It was succeeded by what would become Sudan's longest period of democracy, lasting for

---

[51] *Mohammed Adlan v. Sudan Government, Awad El Sid Abdullah and others*, SLJR (1956) at 64.

[52] *Building Authority of Khartoum v. Evangellos Evangelledes*, S LJ R (1958) at 44. Here, the High Court used Fifth Amendment due process jurisprudence from the United States to interpret Sudan's own constitutional due process clause.

five years from 1964 to 1969. Ironically, this reversion to democratic rule would mark the end of the golden era in Sudanese common-law jurisprudence. Instead of being cultivated by judges interested in legal stability and social order, law became a tool of politicians more directly interested in self-promotion and power.

LAW AS A LEGACY 1965–1976

Between 1965 and 1976, the colonial-based common-law legal structure that had been protected and advanced by the Sudanese judiciary came under assault. First, in a misguided attempt to reclaim its own authority, in 1967 the legislature refused to execute a major decision by the High Court. This led to a showdown between parliament and the Court, which left the judiciary looking marginal and ineffectual. Second, in an effort to jump-start a new movement to unite Sudan and Egypt in the early 1970s, President Jafaar Nimeiri tried to overhaul Sudan's legal system, basing it on Egyptian civil law rather than English common law. He was unable to execute a complete transformation, but did manage to wreak havoc on the legal order.

The new democratic coalition government that came into power after Abboud's 1964 defeat was still dominated by the Umma Party (backed by the Ansar sect) and the newly renamed Democratic Unionist Party (backed by the Khatmiyya Sufi order). And the problems that had plagued Sudan's first democratic government (1956–8) returned in full force. Internecine legislative battles led to deadlock and sapped institutional strength. Britain's *Sunday Times* described Sudan during this period (1964–9) as operating in a "state of democratic chaos."[53] The two political parties were unable to form a working coalition and most ministers continued to fear another coup. Once again, the democratic legislature seemed "unable to spend time actually putting forward policies."[54]

With the major parties sidelined, several minority parties in parliament saw a big upswing in support. The Communist Party in particular came into favor, benefiting from its close association with the popular labor unions that had facilitated the 1964 uprising against Abboud's military regime. Fearing a loss of power, the two major parties passed

---

[53] Geoffrey Sumner, "Tomb Is Key to Sudan," *Sunday Times*, June 1, 1969. K. D. D. Henderson Collection, Sudan Archive, Durham University 539/7/26.

[54] Woodward (1990), 117.

a law in 1965 to dissolve the Communist Party in Sudan. Its members were no longer permitted to serve in parliament, organize, or campaign. The banished Communist members of parliament (MPs) immediately lodged a complaint in the judiciary, requesting that the courts review the constitutionality of the law. (At this point, Sudan was governed by a modified version of the 1956 Transitional Constitution.)

The case reached the High Court in December 1966. Chief Justice Babiker Awadalla wrote the decision, which stated that banning the Communist Party violated Sudan's Constitution and demanded that parliament revoke the law and reinstate the Communist MPs. While some politicians in the coalition government had suggested mediation, the High Court decided to exercise its power of judicial review, as it had been doing for a decade since the *Adlan* case established the principle of judicial review. Awadalla said publicly that judges should not abdicate their legal responsibilities for the sake of political face-saving.[55]

Leaders of the two major parties, convinced that the Communist Party posed a significant threat to democracy and frustrated by their tenuous grip on power, dismissed the High Court's decision as a declaratory judgment and argued that parliament was not required to take any further action.[56] This approach pitted elected representatives desperate for some hold on power against a judicial branch accustomed to decades of deference, even under colonialism. That the parliament evoked the legalist phrase "declaratory judgment" rather than simply ignoring the court's decision is evidence that it still recognized the authority of the judiciary to some degree. But the effect was the same: the legislature refused to follow the High Court's order. Parliamentarians worried that any validation of the Communist Party would facilitate a Communist-led coup against them.

Within a week, certain that parliament would not cede authority to the judiciary, Chief Justice Babiker Awadalla submitted his resignation. His resignation letter was made widely available.[57] He wrote it in Arabic, the language of the people. (The language of law was, at this time, still English.) In his letter, Awadalla took a firm stand against the government's decision not to respect the independence of the judiciary,

[55] Hamid (2006), 387.

[56] Follow-up interview with Hassan, retired senior judicial official, in Khartoum, Sudan (April 2007).

[57] Mansour Khalid, *The Government They Deserve: The Role of the Elite in Sudan's Political Evolution* (London: Kegan Paul International, 1990), 222.

condemned its attempts to interfere in the judicial process, and criticized its refusal to execute the decision of the Court.[58] Almost immediately, Awadalla was hailed as a hero and a martyr for the rule of law.[59] The government's intransigence cost it a great deal of public support but succeeded in significantly weakening the judiciary. With access to neither sword nor purse, any political authority the judiciary possesses is based largely on respect and consent. When rulings against the government are not implemented, a court's potential to disrupt politics and create social or political change wanes.

The Communist Party case actually set in motion a series of events that resulted in the Sudan's takeover by a military dictator willing to use the law to pursue a political and economic agenda. The leader of the coup was Colonel Jafaar Nimeiri, a 1952 graduate of the Sudan Military College and 1966 graduate of the United States Army Command College in Kansas.[60] Nimeiri, who espoused a mix of socialist and pan-Arab ideologies, declared, "The revolution will not allow the application of multi-party liberal democracy again. We have tried liberal democracy in the Sudan. It failed, and we will never go back to it."[61]

Nimeiri was joined by eleven coconspirators: ten other young military officers and the former chief justice, Babiker Awadalla, who at fifty-three years old was the oldest member of the coup leadership. The Communist Party that had been expelled from parliament in 1965 had changed its name to the Socialist Party in 1967. This organization, along with Sudan's trade unions, welcomed the new Socialist government and Awadalla's involvement in it. According to news reports, Awadalla warned "that the regime would execute anyone who opposed it. Public meetings were banned, banks and newspapers closed until further notice, and Khartum [sic] and other civil airports barred to incoming flights."[62]

---

[58] The full Arabic text of Awadalla's resignation can be found in Hamid (2006).

[59] George Gretton, "The Law and Constitution in the Sudan." *The World Today: The Royal Institute of International Affairs*, August 1968, 319.

[60] See "Gaafar Mohamed el-Nimeiri," *Encyclopedia Britannica*. Available: http://www.britannica.com/EBchecked/topic/415488/Gaafar-Mohamed-el-Nimeiri (accessed January 9, 2013).

[61] Untitled manuscript. K. D. D. Henderson Collection, Sudan Archive, Durham University 539/7/29.

[62] Paul Martin, "Army Overthrows Sudan Cabinet" (British newspaper, unknown), May 25, 1969, K. D. D. Henderson Collection, Sudan Archive, Durham University 539/7/18.

Awadalla was quickly installed as vice president and later became prime minister and minister of justice under President Nimeiri. One of Awadalla's first acts was to deal with his former colleagues on the bench. Although Awadalla had received broad public support during the Communist Party case, his fellow jurists had been silent. As chief justice, he had been left to resign alone. After Nimeiri seized power, Awadalla removed all seven members of the High Court. He appointed a former Gordon College law school classmate, Osman At-Tayyib, to be the new chief justice and selected replacement judges more sympathetic to socialist and pan-Arab causes.[63] One former law professor I met speculated that Awadalla fired the judges to exact retribution for the fact that the old regime had accepted his resignation so quickly. This transformation was a dramatic one for a man who had so recently been seen as a great defender of the British-inspired rule of law framework in Sudan. Even General Abboud himself had not dared to dismiss judges in such a heavy-handed and openly political manner. One lawyer recalled how Awadalla's "nature changed radically. He was a liberal. [Then he became] a totalitarian. He ... overthrew a government democratically elected by the will of the Sudanese people."[64]

During one of our interviews at his home, I asked Awadalla over tea and biscuits why he had participated in the 1969 coup that so tarnished his reputation as a common-law jurist and icon of legal integrity. He replied curtly, "I had no intention of delving into politics. I was asked by others to come and assist them in their coup."[65] Awadalla gave few details about how, as a civilian, he decided to join those eleven military officers in the uprising. He simply said that after he submitted his resignation from the judiciary, he began to work in private business. Then a military officer named Farooq Osman Fadlalla, who had been suspended by the Ministry of Defense for suspected insubordination, asked Awadalla to join the group of conspirators.[66]

Awadalla had become quite popular in Sudan in the aftermath of the Communist MPs' legal case, and Nimeiri likely hoped that Awadalla's participation would lend the military-dominated coup an air of respectability and legitimacy. For Awadalla's part, he was "known

[63] Osman at-Tayyib and Babiker Awadalla were classmates in the second class of law students to graduate from the Gordon College Higher Schools, in 1943.

[64] Interview with Abu Musa, lawyer, in Khartoum, Sudan (March 2007).

[65] Interview with Babiker Awadalla, former speaker of Parliament, chief justice, and prime minister, in Khartoum, Sudan (February 2007).

[66] Ibid.

to be non-aligned" with any sect or party in Sudan.[67] But he was intimately connected to Egypt's president, Gamal Abdel Nasser. The two men shared a vision of uniting Sudan and Egypt. They believed that unifying the Nile Valley under one leader would be the first step in creating on the African continent a powerful Arab state that would include Sudan, Egypt, and Libya. Awadalla showed me numerous photos of him and Nasser together during this period. One shows the two of them sitting close on a couch, smiling like old friends. It is likely that the combination of anger at the previous government and hope that Nimeiri's rule would promote Arab unity drove Awadalla to join the cause.

After seizing power, Nimeiri quickly managed to win some popular support. He overhauled the labor codes twice, making them by 1971 among the most progressive in the Arab world. And, in 1972, Nimeiri was able to broker an end to the civil war in the South that had begun seventeen years earlier in the months before Sudan's independence.[68] Because dictators hold legislative and executive power and can remove "squabbling politicians" who stand in the way of reform, it is sometimes easier for military regimes not facing meaningful competition to enact bold changes on behalf of the people than for democratic governments to do the same.[69] In Sudan, the Nimeiri regime was aided by the fact that the opposition parties remained disorganized and were able to do little except fight among themselves.[70]

---

[67] Awadalla reflected on his experience as a junior Sudanese judge working during the Anglo-Egyptian Condominium. A British judge of the High Court once inquired whether he was a communist: "He asked if I was a 'fellow traveler.' I said no ... this is politics, and [as a judge] I haven't trodden on the field.... From there, I went to my court and wrote a complaint to the chief justice relating this incident. I said that I realized that to accuse someone of communism was an offense in England, but I hope something would be done in my case.... [Ultimately] after statements published in the *Daily Telegraph* in which this British judge in Sudan said he did not feel Sudan deserved its independence, he tendered his resignation." Interview with Babiker Awadalla, former speaker of Parliament, chief justice, and prime minister, in Khartoum, Sudan (February 2007).

[68] As part of the peace deal, President Nimeiri took on a vice president from southern Sudan, Abel Alier, who had negotiated the peace agreement on behalf of the South, ending Sudan's first civil war. Similarly, in 2005, President Bashir accepted a vice president from southern Sudan, John Garang, who negotiated the peace agreement on behalf of the South, ending Sudan's second civil war.

[69] Woodward (1990), 135.

[70] See Mohamed Ahmed Mahgoub, *Democracy on Trial: Reflections on Arab and African Politics* (London: Andre Deutsch, 1974). See also Khalid (1990).

But there was one legal obstacle to Awadalla and Nasser's pan-Arab vision that included uniting the Nile Valley: Sudan was the only large, predominantly Arab state without an entrenched civil-law legal system. Given the procedural differences between common-law and civil-law systems, Sudan's legal code needed to be rewritten to make it more consistent with Egypt's. Awadalla and Nasser perceived that reconfiguring the legal system was a crucial step toward promoting unification and ensuring the smooth operation of economic and legal systems after unification.

To get the president's buy-in, Awadalla played on Nimeiri's desire to leave a grand legal legacy. Even though he was new to power, Nimeiri knew that his political authority would not last forever and he aimed to leave his mark on Sudan's legal system, which he saw as the foundation of any great state or civilization. "A lawyer told Nimeiri, to flatter him, that Napoleon had made a name for himself, not for his conquests, but because of the law – the Code Napoleon," Awadalla said.[71] This brand of flattery enticed Nimeiri to approve Awadalla's monumental change in Sudan's legal system from common law to civil law, or *qanoon Nimeiri* (Nimeiri's law), as he hoped it would be known.[72]

With Nimeiri's blessing, Awadalla enlisted twelve Egyptian civil law jurists to Sudan in 1971 to lead a law reform commission. Within a year, the commission transformed Sudan's legal system from one based on more than seventy years of common-law precedent to one based on Egyptian civil law, itself originally drawn from the Napoleonic Code. They drafted a civil code governing "contract, tort, sale of goods, agency, and private international law"[73] in 1971 and a code of civil procedures in 1972. The committee also pushed forward the Judiciary Act of 1972, merging the civil and *shari'a* divisions that the British had created at the turn of the century.

At the same time, however, the alliance between Awadalla and Nimeiri was crumbling. They split as enthusiasm toward the proposed unification of Sudan, Egypt, and Libya began to fade among regime elites and across Sudan. Many Sudanese wanted to put the notion of

---

[71] Interview with Babiker Awadalla, former speaker of Parliament, chief justice, and prime minister, in Khartoum, Sudan (February 2007).

[72] Ibid.

[73] Salman Salman, "Legal Profession in Sudan: A Study of Legal and Professional Pluralism," in *Lawyers in the Third World: Comparative and Developmental Perspectives*, ed. C. J. Dias et al. (New York: International Center for Law and Development, 1981), 240–1.

unity with Egypt to rest, especially as Sudan was finally reaching an agreement to end the civil war.[74] In 1972, just as Nimeiri was signing peace accords in Addis Ababa with southern Sudanese leaders and gaining great fame across Africa for ending a protracted civil war, Awadalla quietly moved with his family to Egypt to retire permanently from Sudanese politics.

The changes to the legal system proved ephemeral as well. Many lawyers and judges had simply refused to follow the shift in legal systems, and, by 1973, the year after Awadalla's departure, common law was restored as the basis of Sudanese government. A lawyer who worked as a judge under Nimeiri during the 1970s said, "For me, coming back from London [with a master's degree in law], I found that ... the law had changed to the continental system. But I'm not trained in that system. So I found it difficult to make a judicial pronouncement on any dispute."[75] Another lawyer in Sudan at the time said simply, "Lawyers could not accept it."[76]

In 1973, Nimeiri ushered Sudan's first permanent constitution into existence. For the previous twenty years since the signing of the 1953 self-governing agreement (itself meant to be replaced by a permanent constitution by the time of independence in 1956), political parties embroiled in sectarian battles moved from one transitional agreement to another, in between military coups. Politically divided, they had been unable to agree to any permanent governing document for the country. Nimeiri, on the other hand, gained a great deal of political capital from ending the civil war. With political authority squarely in his hands, Nimeiri oversaw the constitutional change and rapid economic growth in the mid-1970s, supported by private foreign investors from the Gulf and the International Monetary Fund. The historian Robert O. Collins has labeled this brief period as Nimeiri's "heroic" years.[77]

While the legal system reverted to its colonial British roots, the shift from common law to civil law and back again within just three years created lasting confusion in the application of law in Sudan. Egyptian civil law remains a strong influence and source of law in Sudan, in part because many judges who had trained at Cairo University's Khartoum

---

[74] Salman (1981), 242.

[75] Interview with Sadiq, lawyer, in Khartoum, Sudan (February 2007).

[76] Interview with Rafiq, lawyer and opposition leader, in Khartoum, Sudan (April 2007).

[77] Robert O. Collins, A History of Modern Sudan (Cambridge: Cambridge University Press, 2008), 119–121.

Branch were appointed during that period and then applied civil-law jurisprudence to cases they heard in Sudan.[78] Lawyers also continue to cite prominent Egyptian jurists in their petitions and briefs before courts, including Abd al-Razzak al-Sanhuri, the primary author of Egypt's civil code. The repeated changing of the source of law in Sudan – from British common law to Egyptian civil law to Islamic law, while maintaining Sudanese influences in each – has generated increased political space for elite maneuvering, and a more selective or strategic application of the law by political elites.

As we sat together in his living room, Awadalla sought to vindicate himself and justify actions he had taken during the 1970s:

> I tried very hard. I asked Abdel Nasser to bring me twelve of his best legislative drafters. I didn't want English law to be applied in Sudan forever. We are Arabs. You can't expect Egypt and Sudan and Arab countries to be governed by English law. [I thought], "We can have a code like the Egyptians [have]." Unfortunately the procedural code couldn't be digested by the existing [common-law] lawyers. Their objection was to the [new] procedures. Instead, they canceled it all. If I were English, I'd be proud of the common law. If I were French, I'd be proud of the Code Napoleon.[79]

Shrugging his shoulders and opening his palms to the sky above us, and echoing the comments of many lawyers and civil society activists I met in Sudan, Awadalla sighed, "But now, what do we have here in Sudan? We have no law. No law."[80]

Despite their agreement with Awadalla on the current state of Sudanese law, many members of the Sudanese bar still view him as having done more damage to the nation's judiciary than all of the military despots combined. His firing of the High Court judges opened the door for future purges of the judiciary. His politically motivated conversion from common law to civil law dismantled the legal system, revealing

---

[78] Founded in 1955, Cairo University-Khartoum Branch taught Egyptian civil law to its students. It was from its inception not seen to be as prestigious a law faculty as the University of Khartoum's, which had been widely recognized as the top law school in Anglophone Africa. Nevertheless, Cairo University-Khartoum Branch graduated more lawyers in Sudan annually than University of Khartoum did, meaning that its graduates (soon outnumbering the common-law-trained graduates of University of Khartoum) were more receptive to civil law influences in Sudan.

[79] Interview with Babiker Awadalla, former speaker of Parliament, chief justice, and prime minister, in Khartoum, Sudan (February 2007).

[80] Ibid.

its vulnerability to manipulation in the decades following the end of the colonial enterprise. Awadalla, one of the most prominent defenders of judicial autonomy, was the first (so openly) to remake the postindependence legal order into a tool of the political elite. According to one lawyer, Awadalla "virtually destroyed the judiciary [he] so carefully [helped to] build up."

One of the most noteworthy aspects of this episode of authoritarian legal politics is the fact that, just as Nimeiri believed that resolving the civil war would give him the widespread support he needed, he also believed unequivocally that dominating the legal order – through his overhaul of the legal system – would be his ticket to political greatness, territorial expansion, and lasting relevance. While his regime was antidemocratic and motivated by political self-interest, Nimeiri and his military leaders were not antilaw. On the contrary, the changes they imposed were based on an understanding of the formality and malleability of law. He wanted to use law and the legal order to shape the political trajectory of the nation. In a political environment as unstable as Sudan's, Nimeiri saw the legal system as one of the few areas where he could exert lasting influence.

LAW AS SAVIOR 1977–1989

President Nimeiri's attempts to remake the legal order did not end with the importation of Egyptian civil law in the early 1970s. In 1983, in response to a deepening economic crisis, Nimeiri once again undertook an ambitious program of legal reform. This time he attempted to redraft all Sudanese laws in accordance with Islamic law. Because of an economic crisis, precipitated by his administration's socialist policies adopted in the late 1970s, Nimeiri needed the support of the politically strong Muslim Brotherhood. He sought desperately to exercise control over the legal order, not to foster stability or build a grand legacy, but to stave off forced retirement.[81]

The economic decline started in the late 1970s when Nimeiri, self-confident in his sense of unrestrained authority, revoked legal

---

[81] For a similar argument about Nimeiri's political use of Islamic law in the context of the development of Sudan's Islamic jurisprudence, see Olaf Köndgen, "Shari'a and National Law in the Sudan," in *Sharia Incorporated: A Comparative Overview of the Legal Systems of Twelve Muslim Countries in Past and Present*, ed. Jan Michiel Otto (Leiden: Leiden University Press, 2010), pp. 181–230.

protections for private businesses and foreign investors unaffiliated with his government. Despite cases brought by private lawyers on behalf of investors, the judiciary mostly acquiesced to Nimeiri. His security forces confiscated many private businesses, including trading companies, oil companies, cinemas, and raw materials exporters in the fertile Blue Nile River basin east of Khartoum. Most of these large enterprises failed shortly after they were confiscated; untrained government bureaucrats often hired through nepotism proved unable to run the complex organizations. Driving through the two working-class cities of Omdurman and Khartoum North in the 2000s, one could still see along the roadways the remains of factories shuttered as a result of these confiscations more than thirty years earlier.

Wealthy investors left Sudan in droves (along with the International Monetary Fund), and business owners who stayed were harassed by the government. Operations at the Gezira Scheme, once the world's largest agricultural program, came to an almost complete standstill. The confiscations and ensuing economic decline led the Sudanese currency to be devalued: one Sudanese pound had been worth three U.S. dollars in the 1960s. By the late 1970s, one dollar bought three Sudanese pounds.[82] Workers were left to suffer through devastating inflation. By 1982, annual inflation had reached a record 40 to 50 percent. According to one account:

> The cost of nearly every basic commodity, including meat, fruit and vegetables, flour and petrol has more than … quadrupled in the last decade. In one of the worst cases, the cost of a kilo of meat had risen by 1980 to ten times what it was in 1970. Transportation has become a daily source of stress [and] woefully inadequate, the result being long queues and occasional outbursts of fighting. Meanwhile, wages have been held down and the inability of workers to keep pace financially with the rate of inflation has meant an unprecedented number of strikes…. [And] an increase in the government regulated cost of petrol and bread … brought about widespread demonstrations.[83]

The country was headed toward economic and social collapse, and a new civil war was starting in the South after a rebellion by southern

[82] By 2005, 1 USD bought 2,500 Sudanese pounds. In 2007, Sudan tied its currency to the dollar and then reconfigured it so that 1 USD would be equal to approximately 2.5 (rather than 2,500) pounds. The official rate was modified again in mid-2012, making 1 USD worth 4.4 pounds.

[83] Fluehr-Lobban (1987), 176–7.

members of the military in early 1983. Nimeiri had all but lost the popular support he had earned a decade earlier through his labor reforms
and negotiated end to the first civil war. Nimeiri was still receiving
considerable military aid from Russia and China,[84] but as before he
needed domestic backing to survive. In an effort to build a new base
of support, in 1977 Nimeiri instituted a policy of "national reconciliation," an attempt to form a coalition with the dominant opposition
parties. The three major parties Nimeiri tried to draw together were
the Umma (affiliated with the Mahdi sect and led by Sadiq al-Mahdi,
a great-grandson of the original Mahdi), the Democratic Unionist
Party (affiliated with the Khatmiyya Sufi order and led by Mohammed
Osman al-Mirghani), and the Muslim Brotherhood (an Islamic party
led by Sorbonne-educated lawyer and professor, Hassan al-Turabi).

Nimeiri was not always an ally of the Muslim Brotherhood. But it
was gaining support in Sudan through the charismatic leadership of
Hassan al-Turabi and the general inability of other political parties to
move beyond their impasses. In 1975, the Muslim Brotherhood had
successfully convinced Nimeiri's government to translate the laws of
Sudan from English (the language of the colonizer) into Arabic (the
lingua franca of the people in the capital city and surrounding areas).
When the reconciliation between the Umma and Democratic Unionist
Party fell apart by 1979, the Muslim Brotherhood saw an opportunity
to push Nimeiri for much more.

To reinforce his tenuous grip on power, Nimeiri led the national reconciliation in 1977. Within a year, though, Nimeiri was losing favor
with what were relatively impotent opposition parties, whose leadership
began to realize he had little intention of keeping his promises to them.[85]
Seeing an opportunity to advance *shari'a*, the Muslim Brotherhood
openly committed itself to the regime, and Nimeiri rewarded them by
appointing its leader, Hassan al-Turabi, as attorney general.[86] To placate
his new partners, he also appointed a law reform commission to begin
"Islamizing" Sudan's laws to ensure consistency with Islamic jurisprudence, and, to buy himself more time, he announced new decentral-
ization measures: dividing northern Sudan into five semiautonomous
regions. The changes would not last, as Nimeiri failed to keep his
promises to devolve power out of Khartoum.

---

[84] K. D. D. Henderson Collection, Sudan Archive, Durham University 539/7/47.
[85] Collins (2008), 130.
[86] Ibid.

In a final effort to stay afloat, in 1983 Nimeiri – a military man who in the past had aligned at different times with the International Monetary Fund and with socialists abroad – astonishingly declared himself a sheikh. He passed what is now referred to as the notorious *qanoon september* (September law) after authorizing lawyers for the Muslim Brotherhood to redraft the legal code according to their interpretation of Islamic law. Nimeiri agreed that Islamic laws relating to crime, tort, and property could be implemented across Sudan in Muslim and non-Muslim regions alike. He "change[d] the [1925] Civil Procedure Act to outlaw interest rates [according to Islamic law], and he introduced four or five sections in the penal code to introduce *shari'a* punishments of amputations and flogging."[87] Some lawyers I met told me that they felt the most important legal changes were limited to the penal code. But the effect of Nimeiri's manipulation of the legal system was lasting. For example, the 1984 Civil Transactions Act has remained for at least a generation the basis for all noncriminal civil law in Sudan.

Why would a leader make dramatic legal change in the face of economic crisis and ailing social support? Why not push to reform the economy and reduce inflation as he had in the past? Why not invest in education, social services, or subsidies to win back popular support? In the case of Sudan, Nimeiri calculated that installing a repressive legal order was the quickest and surest way to impose order, compel obedience to his authority, and quash dissent. Calling this new legal order "Islamic" was more than useful window dressing. It allowed Nimeiri to govern as an autocrat while claiming that he was adhering to religious proscriptions and respecting the rule of Islamic law. He was able to use religiosity and law as covers for a harsh governmental crackdown.

According to changes in the *qanoon september*, judges were required to follow Islamic law as derived from the Quran and Sunna, absent other relevant legislation.[88] This obligation led to the heavy use of *huduud* punishments in Sudan.[89] *Huduud* (literally, "borders") refers to a class of fixed punishments, such as amputations and stoning, that are

---

[87] Interview with Sadiq, lawyer, in Khartoum, Sudan (February 2007).

[88] Government of the Republic of the Sudan, Judgments (Basic Rules) Act of 1983.

[89] *Huduud* punishments are stipulated for seven crimes in Islam. Sudan recognized five of them in 1983: simple theft, aggravated theft, defamation or other libelous activities, consumption of alcohol, and adultery. Apostasy was later codified formally in Sudan's 1991 criminal code. The seventh *huduud* punishment is for rebellion against government.

issued for certain crimes that are "claims of God" such as theft, forni-cation, and consumption of alcohol.[90] Sudanese courts became known for the widespread imposition of such punishments, often before the opportunity to appeal. But rather than targeting those who commit-ted the most egregious sins, corporal punishment under Nimeiri largely targeted poor residents of outlying areas who went to Khartoum to find work and were deemed likely to organize against Nimeiri's failing dicta-torship. His courts often delivered immediate punishments, including *huduud* punishments for non-*huduud* crimes, demonstrating the power of the state over society.[91]

Judges and lawyers who worked within the Nimeiri administra-tion told me separately of a "new hostility" in Sudanese society after the passage of the September laws.[92] Growing antagonism in partic-ular between lawyers and judges facilitated a sense of uncertainty in the application of the law and of corporal punishment, particularly as common-law judges were replaced with ideological supporters.[93] Corporal punishment is the most visible and lasting artifact of the last few years of Nimeiri's repressive rule. (Corporal punishment did not end with Nimeiri's demise. I witnessed several floggings at courthouses while researching this book between 2005 and 2010.) It is a ritual that reinforces state authority, as well as the state's claim to derive its authority from religious scripture. In Sudan it is "the climactic emo-tional point of the criminal law – the moment of terror around which the system revolve[s]."[94]

While some judges did what they were told, the new legal order did not sit well with many of them. Accustomed to the separation between civil and *shari'a* divisions, many judges had difficulty applying religious laws in which they had little training or experience.[95] A small number

---

[90] Interview with retired senior judicial official 1, in Khartoum, Sudan (February 2007). This official had been a member of the law reform commission that would later implement the *huduud*.

[91] Rudolph Peters, "The Islamization of Criminal Law: A Comparative Analysis," 32(2) *Die Welt Des Islams: International Journal for the Study of Modern Islam* (1994): 264.

[92] Interview with Talal, lawyer, in Khartoum, Sudan (April 2007).

[93] Interview with Shadi, lawyer, in Khartoum, Sudan (April 2007).

[94] Douglas Hay, "Property, Authority, and the Criminal Law," in *Albion's Fatal Tree: Crime and Society in Eighteenth Century England*, ed. Douglas Hay, Peter Linebaugh, John G. Rule, E. P. Thompson, and Cal Winslow (New York: Pantheon Press, 1975), 28.

[95] Fluehr-Lobban (1987), 51.

went on a short-lived strike to protest the implementation of *huduud* punishments. When I asked a southern Sudanese non-Muslim judge why he was not dismissed under Nimeiri, he said that the Sudanese president "wanted non-Muslims to be seen to be applying the Islamic laws."[96] He was not the only one who saw through Nimeiri's ploy to use an Islamic rule of law to maintain a grip on political power. Indeed, a culture of respect for the rule of law still existed among judges and lawyers of a certain generation. Moreover, facing economic collapse and rising prices, most Sudanese people would not accept the claim that Nimeiri's authority was suddenly given by God, and they denounced his actions in what would become a people's revolution to overthrow him in 1985.

Nimeiri's heavy-handed and dramatic use of the law ultimately led to his undoing. In early January 1985, the government arrested seventy-year-old Mahmoud Mohammed Taha, accusing him of *ridda* (apostasy). While apostasy is a crime punishable by death under the *huduud* system, it was not incorporated into Sudanese law until six years later, in 1991. Taha was a leader of the Republican Brotherhood, an Islamic movement in Sudan that openly opposed the type of *shari'a* codified by the Nimeiri government. Taha and his followers had been distributing anti-Nimeiri circulars. Nimeiri's specially constituted court found Taha guilty of the Islamic crime of apostasy, though it was not yet a crime under Sudanese law. Taha was hanged in public on January 18, 1985.

The Taha execution was supposed to demonstrate how far the government would go to stamp out dissent. But instead of acting as a deterrent to activism, the special court case and ensuing execution enraged the Sudanese people and sparked a wave of anti-Nimeiri mobilization. Trade unions held major strikes across Khartoum and received public assistance from opposition leaders and leading lawyers who had been dismissed as judges by Nimeiri.[97] Most important, Nimeiri lost the support of the military. In April 1985, just months after the Taha execution, a nonviolent *intifada* (uprising) led by Sudanese military officers overthrew Nimeiri's sixteen-year dictatorship. The military officials formed a one-year interim government to oversee a peaceful transition to democracy. Elections were held in April 1986, and the military

---

[96] Interview with Nasim, member of Parliament, in Omdurman, Sudan (May 2007).

[97] Interview with Gasim, former government minister, in Khartoum, Sudan (November 2006).

council turned over power to a civilian government led by Prime Minister Sadiq al-Mahdi of the Umma Party.

In an attempt to reclaim the rule of law after what they felt were years of manipulation and abuse, a group of independent lawyers demanded that the new democratic government of Sudan formally invalidate the execution of Mahmoud Mohammed Taha on the grounds that he was punished for an act that was not a crime at the time of the alleged offense, in violation of Sudan's constitution. The case went before a panel of High Court justices.[98] Enjoying a renewed sense of independence, and with the support of the public and political elites, the constitutional panel invalidated the earlier court ruling that had led to Taha's execution:

> The trial and appellate courts had acted against express provisions of the law, assumed legislative powers and created the criminal offense of apostasy, which was not part of the indictment and was not defined as a criminal offense by the laws in effect at the time the acts in question were committed.[99]

In 2007, I met with one of the justices who had served on this panel. "Everything was too late," he sighed. Taha had already been executed. But, he added, invalidating the execution was the proudest moment of his career.[100] The new administration accepted the High Court's decision and reversed the ruling against Taha.

The 1986 judgment seemed to hold the promise of a return to the kind of judicial independence not seen in Sudan since Awadalla's resignation nearly twenty years earlier in 1967. But the judiciary, so badly weakened, was not able to resurrect itself as an autonomous force before the window of opportunity shut. The new democratic administration suffered from the same ills that had plagued Sudan's previous attempts at representative democracy from 1956 to 1958 and from 1965 to 1969. A lawyer who served as a minister of government in both the 1960s and 1980s reflected:

> There was a striking resemblance between the 1960s and 1980s in [terms of] instability. That instability led to the collapse of both

---

[98] There was no separate Constitutional Court in Sudan until 1998, when it was formed under President Bashir.

[99] *Asma Mahmoud Mohamed Taha and Abdel Latif Amr Hisballah vs. the Sudan Government*, SLJR (1986) at 163.

[100] Interview with Hassan, retired senior judicial official, in Khartoum, Sudan (February 2007).

democracies. There were [the same] differences between the ruling parties, Umma and DUP, the same differences within [each] party, with the opposition trying to exploit all these differences. So that led to the collapse of the first [1964–9] and second [1985–9] democracy.[101]

In both eras, political disagreements between the major parties led to a standstill that opposition parties were able to exploit. In the 1980s, that opposition was led by the National Islamic Front (NIF), an incarnation of the Muslim Brotherhood led by Hassan al-Turabi.

> Just as the communists had done, the NIF in the 1980s tried to utilize to the best of their ability the differences between the Umma and DUP. They were infiltrating the government, and succeeded in [leading] this *coup d'etat* that brought them to power until today.[102]

In June 1989, the NIF and a group of young military leaders executed a takeover of Prime Minister Sadiq al-Mahdi's nascent democratic government. The elected government was replaced by the self-proclaimed leader of the "National Salvation Revolution," General Omar Hassan al-Bashir.

A PERMANENT STATE OF TRANSITION 1956–1989

For nearly three and a half decades after independence, Sudan existed in a state of political and legal transition as its myriad leaders struggled to maintain authority. In the course of these struggles, law became detached from its colonial origins and became a tool of successive regimes. Taken together, the three periods of legal politics analyzed in this chapter show how law and the legal order can play many different roles in a chaotic political environment and how easily they can be challenged and manipulated. In Sudan, the desire to reinforce authority by engaging in legal reform was too compelling for leaders like Babiker Awadalla and Jafaar Nimeiri to ignore. They turned to legal strategies to control the populace, and they used their ability to dictate the law itself to create an image of omnipotence. And like the British before them, their political goals influenced their views of the rule of law and how its constituent elements could be marshaled to support their authority and the stability of the state.

---

[101] Interview with Mansour, lawyer and former government minister, in Khartoum, Sudan (February 2007).

[102] Ibid.

The initial period after Sudan's independence was a golden age for the rule of common law: judges and lawyers maintained a reputation for professionalism and the legal system functioned autonomously from politics. At a time of political uncertainty and sectarian conflict, Sudan's judges, including the nation's second chief justice, Babiker Awadalla, worked to build a system of Sudanese law based on domestic precedent, British common law, and other international influences. By the 1970s, however, law had become an instrument of sectarian rivalries and authoritarian politics. Awadalla and then-President Nimeiri, for instance, manipulated the legal system in order to push a pan-Arab political agenda, create a Napoleonic legal legacy, and distract the nation from its social and economic crises.[103] There was a brief moment in the late 1980s when the judiciary tried once again to operate as an independent branch of government. But this revival effort was thwarted by the rise of the Bashir military government in 1989. These changes in the legal order create a complex layering of laws and systems in which lawyers and judges must work. Describing the state of the nation when Bashir assumed power, the historian Peter Woodward wrote, "Sudan seems endlessly trapped in a cycle of ineffective civilian and military regimes, with neither form of rule apparently capable of breaking out of the vicious circle of decay."[104] In many ways, Sudan's legal order was as abused and traumatized by these postcolonial political machinations as its people were.

[103] See also Massell (1968).
[104] Woodward (1990), 239.

CHAPTER 4

AUTHORITARIAN LEGAL POLITICS AND ISLAMIC LAW, 1989–2011

INTRODUCTION

In colonial Sudan, the British administration adopted strategies of legal politics to buttress its authority and foster an image of benevolent despotism. The British set up legal institutions that resolved grievances in a manner that benefited the regime but also accommodated Sudanese religious structures and existing modes of dispute resolution. After independence, successive Sudanese administrations also turned to legal politics to create stability, as Sudan swayed dangerously between political stalemate and collapse, and to enhance their own stature. In 1989, the decades of political instability came to an end. For a quarter-century Sudan has been dominated by the authoritarian government of President Omar Hassan al-Bashir. Like his predecessors, Bashir made decisive use of the law and legal institutions to support his regime's authority. But, having learned from his predecessors' mistakes, Bashir also turned the law into a servant of his political agenda to an extent unmatched by any of Sudan's previous governors.

In June 1989 General Bashir, a shrewd observer of Sudanese politics who quickly rose through the ranks of the Sudanese Army, led a group of fellow officers in a bloodless military coup against the ineffectual democratic government of Prime Minister Sadiq al-Mahdi. Bashir and his narrow circle of deputies (including Hassan al-Turabi, one of Sudan's most outspoken political figures and legal professionals) understood that an independent judiciary and uncontrolled legal order would pose a threat to their authority. Immediately they set out to put the sweeping power of the legal profession under executive control.[1] In deciding on a course of action, Bashir took inspiration from his predecessors. Like former president Nimeiri, Bashir addressed the problem posed by successive changes to the Sudanese legal system by imposing a single legal framework based on a unified version of Islamic law. Unlike Nimeiri's efforts on this score, the Bashir regime's approach was decisive, sweeping, and lasting. Like the British, Bashir put substantial resources into building new courts and law schools. Also like the British, Bashir attempted to create a veneer of legitimacy, to secure law and order, and to inculcate his own legal ideology in the Sudanese by investing in legal services, legal education, and the creation of efficient courts. Unlike that of the British, Bashir's military-dominated regime was able to expand its legal empire into areas that the colonial administration did not have the resources or cultural credibility to access. Bashir and his first chief justice, Jalal Ali Lutfi, went out of their way to create and oversee an extensive legal apparatus, including the establishment of special courts, public order courts, and popular defense courts.[2] Building a wide-ranging network of courts operating under Islamic law, the regime aimed to maintain an image of legal integrity despite its ruthless conduct during the civil wars and humanitarian crises in southern Sudan and Darfur.

Having studied what previous regimes did and why they fell, Bashir and those who advised him sought to control the work and lives of lawyers, judges, and legal academics to an unprecedented degree. Sudanese legal professionals played critical roles in the toppling of his predecessors, so the Bashir administration rather ingeniously devised ways to undermine their ability to organize. In particular, the regime built a system of law schools that teach Islamic law, in a form approved by the regime, and graduate a steady stream of like-minded attorneys. The number of lawyers trained in Bashir's academies grew at a rate quadruple that of the Sudanese population. As older lawyers well versed in common law retired and died, they were replaced by a generation of lawyers who have known little more than the Islamist political practices sanctioned as law by the regime.

---

[1] See Burr and Collins, *Revolutionary Sudan: Hassan al-Turabi and the Islamist State, 1989–2000* (Leiden: Brill, 2003). Burr and Collins argue, inter alia, that the Bashir regime quickly purged the legal profession as part of a broader strategy of securing control shortly after seizing power. This chapter provides primary evidence for these actions, gathered from the government and from important judges and lawyers working within and at times opposing it.

[2] Burr and Collins (2003), 19.

Governors of fragile states use legal strategies, including developing a judicial administration to resolve citizen disputes, to build up a functioning state apparatus. They expand the law to build the state in an effort to promote their legitimacy, while they curtail the law elsewhere, such as by designing a national-security apparatus to monitor citizen behavior and by prolonging a devastating civil war. Bashir's brand of authoritarian order was rooted in manufacturing legal systems, institutions, and ideologies to maintain longevity. But the insidious nature of authoritarian legal politics is that citizens are encouraged to and do rely upon the laws and courts created by the regime, shaping their daily experiences and contact with each other and government personnel.

In this chapter, I investigate how the authoritarian government of Omar Hassan al-Bashir, a regime that had little social support when it took power, helped to secure its longevity through legal politics, specifically its uses of the law and legal institutions as political resources. In essence, Bashir's regime studied the lessons of history in Sudan and retooled the strategies used by previous governments to manipulate both the legal profession and the legal order to advance Bashir's own political ends. Strengthened legal institutions would provide a public resource for citizens seeking to resolve private disputes through litigation and would also create a space for grievances against the regime to be managed, processed, and defused, helping to promote stable authoritarian governance. This chapter details the regime's actions with respect to three main groups of legal professionals – members of the bar association, the bench, and the legal academy – and the impact of these actions on the legal order as a whole.

CONTROLLING THE BAR ASSOCIATION

Within days of commandeering the government in 1989, Bashir's military regime took dramatic action against the legal community. In contrast to the previous military regimes of Abboud (1958–64) and Nimeiri (1969–85), who were backed into efforts to control the private bar, Bashir and his compatriots moved quickly to launch a full frontal assault against the legal profession. They captured and imprisoned key leaders of the bar association (some for longer than a year). They shut down the bar association's main office in Khartoum and quickly reopened it for business with loyalists in command. Why would the bar association be a prime target? What threat did these unarmed lawyers pose to Bashir's military takeover? The bar association had been a driving force behind the dismantling of both the Abboud and Nimeiri regimes, and Bashir realized that it would eventually come after him, too – unless he found a way to keep it in check. Rather than shut it down entirely, Bashir invested precious capital to create an appearance of support among the bar.

The source of the bar's strength lay in its history as the favored off-spring of Sudan's former British masters. More than in any other realm of social or civic life, the British had made serious efforts to develop Sudanese competence in the practice of common law. Commenting on the extent to which British-trained Sudanese lawyers felt loyal to their British sponsors, a retired high-ranking Bashir judicial appointee recalled to me the "great responsibility" he felt not to embarrass his British teachers back home when he went to Britain to pursue a master's degree in law. "I worked more than anybody there, believe me, just to free myself [of this potential embarrassment]."[3] The Sudanese bar developed a culture of professionalism and entitlement because of its privileged position under British rule.

As detailed in Chapter 2, the British had set up a small law school at Gordon College in 1936 that graduated six to ten Sudanese every two or three years. The primary purpose of training a select group of Sudanese was to create an elite cadre of civil servants to serve as judges and deputies within the colonial administration.[4] Law students were encouraged to think of themselves as the future leaders of Sudanese government. The secular system at the University of Khartoum – widely considered to be among the best law schools in Anglophone Africa – effectively inculcated British legal norms and mores in students. With the exception of *shari'a*, all classes were taught in English, and instructors expected their Sudanese students to be completely fluent. Professors marked exams as if they had been taken at the University of London, which until the early 1960s awarded external degrees to students graduating from the University of Khartoum.

For several decades after independence, entry into the legal profession was reserved for an elite group of students and geared toward public service. It was a small and tight-knit community – professional bonds trumped political, regional, and religious differences. Even around the time of independence when disagreements over the

---

[3] Interview with senior judicial official 3, in Khartoum, Sudan (January 2007).

[4] Interview with Sir Donald Hawley, former chief registrar of Sudan Judiciary (1953–5), in Wiltshire, England (January 2007).

compartmentalization of Islamic law started to emerge, the powerful ties formed at the small, elite law school helped lawyers transcend political disagreements. (Bashir would later exploit these differences of opinion over the role of Islamic law in his Islamization campaign.) According to one lawyer:

> You know, [though] we are ... colleagues from the University [of Khartoum] ... politically, yes, we are *very* different. But if I have any occasion, he comes to my home. If he has any occasion, I go to his home.... Sometimes we talk politics, but we don't take knives, you know [laughs].[5]

The bar association first became active in Sudan in the 1930s. At that time, because the colonial administration limited Sudanese access to legal education to fewer than a dozen men each year, the bar's membership was originally made up of mostly foreign lawyers. After Sudanese independence, *niqabat al-muhamiyyin* (the lawyers' union) became the primary representative of Sudanese lawyers' interests in the country. Its role was conceived primarily as protecting the independence of the legal profession and securing its interests. "Private [legal] practitioners are free thinkers," said one Sudanese lawyer. "We are not controlled by any government office. Historically, [we] acted through [our] association, the bar."[6] While the bar licensed an average of only thirty new lawyers a year between 1956 and 1981, it had real influence in politics. And as the population of lawyers grew, so did the bar's institutional importance. "It's the association of all the thousands of lawyers in Sudan.... If any statement of all these lawyers [declared] that laws go against the Constitution, the statement would make all the difference."[7]

Prestigious education, collective strength, and facility with both English (the language of professionals) and Arabic (the language of the people) meant that, in the first decades after independence, bar association members were uniquely positioned to command the public's trust and lead efforts to mobilize citizens. Many older Sudanese lawyers still speak with pride about the guidance legal professionals provided to the nonviolent people's movements that toppled both the Abboud

---

[5] Interview with Talal, lawyer, in Khartoum, Sudan (April 2007).

[6] Follow-up interview with Hassan, retired senior judicial official, in Khartoum, Sudan (April 2007).

[7] Ibid.

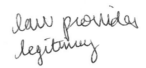 *law provides legitimacy*

military regime in 1964 and the Nimeiri military regime in 1985. A well-respected judge, Babiker Awadalla, gave vociferous speeches in support of trade union strikes, which lent much-needed legitimacy to the 1964 revolution against Abboud.[8] (Chapter 3 details Awadalla's role as the country's first speaker of parliament in the 1950s, its second chief justice in the 1960s, and its prime minister and minister of justice in the early 1970s.) The participation of legal professionals added intellectual firepower that made the masses of angry students and working-class Sudanese much harder for the regime to ignore. Sympathetic judges were also able to protect organizers' freedom of movement during government-imposed curfews, enabling protesters to keep up the pressure at critical moments.

An understanding of the bar association's historical relationship with the Sudanese government is necessary to explain why Bashir felt threatened enough by it to take action against it so swiftly after rising to national power. During the Nimeiri regime, the bar association actively sought out political cases to publicize governmental abuse and protect the right of revolutionaries to free association. "In the early 1980s, I defended many workers and students," said a former senior official of the bar. "Anyone who had a political case, we were there. The bar association was there."[9] Well-known lawyers delivered major speeches at street rallies, demanding that Nimeiri step down from power and be replaced by a democratically elected administration. After helping to topple Nimeiri in 1985, the bar association in Khartoum nurtured the development of the Sudan Human Rights Organization, which brought cases against the ousted security forces for kidnapping and torture of civilians.[10] In the words of one Sudanese advocate, "[independent] lawyers were very powerful in Sudan, before this [Bashir-led] government."[11]

When Bashir seized power, Sudan was reeling from several years of deadly droughts, floods, famine, and civil war. As an unelected leader, Bashir enjoyed very little public support. He knew that his reign would

[8] George Gretton, "The Law and Constitution in the Sudan." *The World Today: The Royal Institute of International Affairs*, August 1968, 319.

[9] Interview with Gasim, former government minister, in Khartoum, Sudan (November 2006).

[10] Follow-up interview with Abdul Gadir, lawyer and civil society activist, in Khartoum, Sudan (January 2007).

[11] Interview with Zacharia, lawyer and legal awareness workshop facilitator, in Khartoum, Sudan (May 2007).

be short-lived unless he found a way to unify the country and neutralize the bar's ability to mount an effective opposition. Bashir took fast action against the legal community by immediately shuttering the bar association's headquarters. In response, the leadership of the bar signed a desperate letter of protest and requested a meeting with Bashir or his deputies. According to human rights reports, some did manage to meet with Bashir's political deputy, Brigadier Hamadien, several days after the coup. Hamadien promised that he would follow up with them soon. "Security agents then moved the same night to arrest all those who signed the memorandum, and sent them directly to ... prison."[12]

According to lawyers I met who were targeted in the raid, national-security forces arrived at their homes and took them either to Sudan's notorious prisons at Kober and Port Sudan or to "ghost houses" or other unofficial prisons to be tortured. Ironically, one of these unofficial prisons was set up in the "confiscated offices of the ... Sudan Bar Association."[13] While details given to me did not enable me to verify how many lawyers were targeted in the raid, it was clear that the most prominent leaders of the bar association were imprisoned for a period lasting twelve to fourteen months. Undoubtedly traumatized by his experience of imprisonment, one lawyer and opposition political leader told me in a hauntingly distant voice, "I have spent ten years and three months of my life in prison and was [once] sentenced to death."[14] The imprisonments had a devastating effect, not only on those targeted, but also on the legal profession as a whole, effectively chilling prodemocracy activism and quieting legal opposition to Bashir's rule.

In addition to his heavy-handed militarism, Bashir took more subtle steps to undermine the cohesiveness of the legal community. Since the departure of the British, tensions within the elite ranks of the bar had been growing over the proper role of Islam in Sudanese law. Lawyers were split on the issue in part depending on where they had received their legal training: the University of Khartoum emphasized common

---

[12] Jemera Rone, *Behind the Red Line: Political Repression in Sudan* (New York: Human Rights Watch, 1996). See also Africa Watch, *Sudan – inside Al Bashir's Prisons: Torture, Denial of Medical Attention and Poor Conditions* (Washington, DC, 1991), 174.

[13] Africa Watch (1991).

[14] Interview with Rafiq, lawyer and opposition leader, in Khartoum, Sudan (April 2007).

law, Cairo University's branch campus in Khartoum emphasized
civil law, and Jama'at Omdurman al-Islamiyya (Islamic University of
Omdurman) emphasized *shari'a*. These tensions grew more significant
over time, particularly since Cairo University graduated more lawyers
(trained in Arabic) each year than Khartoum. According to a senior
government lawyer, "Based on the university where they studied,
[we] had [attorneys and judges] applying three different types of laws
[common, civil, and Islamic]."[15] With few exceptions, lawyers trained
primarily in English common law in the years following Sudan's 1956
independence gravitated toward a style of government modeled on the
secular British system while confining Islam to personal and familial
law for Muslims. They argued that allowing Islam to form the basis of
commercial, banking, and criminal law (especially for non-Muslims)
would further fracture an already deeply divided country. Lawyers
trained primarily in *shari'a* tended to promote a government run
according to the tenets of Islamic law. They argued that secularism
was a remnant of colonial rule and that Islam should be freed from
the compartmentalization that Britain had imposed. Lawyers I met
who had been trained primarily in Egyptian law at Cairo University's
Khartoum campus tended to be split in favor of promoting Islamic
law as the basis of governance or confining it to govern legal matters
related to marital or family property.

While these ideological differences over Islam had emerged well
before Bashir's coup, his policies exacerbated tensions and caused deep
and lasting fragmentation and discord. Most importantly, the Bashir
government launched a program of Islamization with the goal of uniting Sudan under its particular vision of Islamic law. (Bashir borrowed
from the Hanafi school, itself transplanted into Sudan during the nineteenth century by Turco-Egyptian colonial administrators who sought
to consolidate control over Sudan's diverse ethnic groups.) As part of
this program, in 1991, the Bashir government adopted a new criminal
code claiming to be rooted in Islamic law. This criminal code, in force
throughout the Bashir administration, was largely similar to the one
put forward by the Nimeiri administration during its Islamization program in 1983. The major difference was the addition of a penalty for
the crime of *ridda* (apostasy). This addition was crucial; it cemented
the notion that disagreements with the government's rule would be

[15] Interview with senior government official in Khartoum, Sudan (March 2007).

akin to disrespect of Islam, a crime punishable by death. Other legal changes under Bashir included adoption of Arabic-only policies in education and government, enforcement of conservative dress for women, and movement of the nation toward a conservative vision of an Islamic state.[16]

The routine administration of the law under Bashir is laden with religious symbolism. The faithful are called to prayer five times per day via loudspeakers installed in courthouses, halting legal proceedings midsentence. Corporal punishment, echoing the words of the legal historian Douglas Hay, is routinely used as a "splendid occasion for lessons in justice and power."[17] Many Sudanese courthouses are designed like Western-style motels, with two floors of courtrooms opening onto exterior corridors. Floggings (many, if not most, for alcohol-related offenses) are administered in these open walkways or terraces alongside courthouse buildings, visible and audible to those on the premises and passersby on the street.[18]

The changes to the law made by the Bashir regime intensified tensions between Islamists and secularists in the bar, leading to the fragmentation of the legal profession over the role of religion in the legal system.[19] The few remaining older lawyers trained during the 1950s and 1960s at the University of Khartoum continued to tout the virtues of secular common law and Western political liberalism, while many in the younger generation of lawyers and law students were being similarly seduced by the appeal of a formal legal system seen to be rooted in an immutable and infallible (religious) law that would rise above the political chaos or authoritarianism familiar to the Sudanese.[20] Evidence of fragmentation appears largely in court proceedings – while

---

[16] See Burr and Collins (2003), 21.

[17] Douglas Hay, "Property, Authority, and the Criminal Law," in *Albion's Fatal Tree: Crime and Society in Eighteenth Century England*, ed. Douglas Hay, Peter Linebaugh, John G. Rule, E. P. Thompson, and Cal Winslow (New York: Pantheon Press, 1975), 57.

[18] Administering corporal punishment under Sudanese law for the possession or production of alcohol may "exceed traditional Islamic jurisprudence." Olaf Köndgen, "Shari'a and National Law in the Sudan," in *Sharia Incorporated: A Comparative Overview of the Legal Systems of Twelve Muslim Countries in Past and Present*, ed. Jan Michiel Otto (Leiden: Leiden University Press, 2010), 210.

[19] Interview with Watani, lawyer, in Khartoum, Sudan (March 2007).

[20] Interview with Talal, lawyer, in Khartoum, Sudan (April 2007).

younger lawyers generally cite Islamic *hadith* (accounts of what the Prophet Muhammad said, did, or permitted by omission) and Egyptian jurists like al-Sanhuri, older lawyers trained in the common law prior to the 1970s continue to cite to Sudan's (now outdated) common law. Evidence of fragmentation is also seen in the new legal culture Bashir has sought to create, in which early graduates of the University of Khartoum have been expelled from government jobs, because of the university's "colonial heritage," which, according to lawyers, inculcated in its graduates "some kind of liberal, sort of, mind" seen to be threatening to the regime.[21]

In addition to sowing discord and exploiting the fragmentation within the bar, Bashir imposed legal controls over the bar to limit its independence. He knew he needed to create "legal" legitimacy for his rule, so he went to great lengths to change laws and work within the scope of those changes – an appearance of respect for the rule of law. His government formally took steps to amend Sudan's Advocacy Act, passed under the Nimeiri government in 1983, so that the bar association would be categorized as a trade union. While it had imposed restrictions on some of the bar association's activities, the act nevertheless maintained the bar's independence from government. But Bashir also seized control of the Registrar of Trade Unions, the agency that monitors the actions of trade unions. Doing so effectively brought the bar under the authority of the executive branch. Since then, Bashir has been able to exercise total control over its operations.

While the Islamist wing of the bar had no more than a limited role in the association prior to 1989, it has led the association since the coup. Nonaligned lawyers have decried elections for the Sudan Bar Association leadership as fraudulent. After the 2006 election, they claimed that lawyers unsympathetic to the government were unable to vote when poll workers told them their bar license numbers did not match the official roll. They also claimed that regime supporters were given falsified bar licenses to present to poll workers, and that the bar elections were unfair and undemocratic because only one polling site was created and placed in the capital city, making it impossible for lawyers outside Khartoum to vote. Prior to these elections, the bar leadership declared the association the "independent [and] representative

---

[21] Interview with Hassan, retired senior judicial official, in Khartoum, Sudan (February 2007).

body of the Sudanese lawyers."[22] But that claim is belied by allegations of the bar's acquiescence to Bashir's dictatorship:

> The government is trying to create a new legal culture in the bar, on their side. Liberal lawyers are left to being individuals. The [government] knows the bar is their institution: They rely on it to defend them. For example, protesters against the [government's construction of the Merowe] dam [in 2007] were killed ... [and] the bar said nothing.[23]

When bar association leaders did speak out in the 2000s, it was typically to support government policies. According to a Sudanese lawyer, bar leaders "say that human rights in certain respects are against Islamic ... concepts [and] stand against [Western aid agencies] from the perspective of Islam and this regime."[24] In 2009, the African Union called for hybrid courts to be set up in Sudan to try war crimes suspects related to the atrocities committed in Darfur. The bar association leadership responded quickly to support the regime by appealing to Sudanese law: "The Sudanese constitution and laws reject the participation of foreign judges in Sudanese courts."[25]

A small group of progressive lawyers still tries to operate outside the government-sanctioned bar to defend human rights. One lawyer successfully argued before the High Court that his client – a pregnant displaced woman whose husband had disappeared nearly a decade earlier, presumably a casualty of war – should be legally considered unmarried. Had she been found guilty of adultery, her punishment would have been death by stoning.[26] Another lawyer convinced a majority of the judges of the Constitutional Court of Sudan, set up by President Bashir's government after the 1998 Permanent Constitution, that civilians should not be tried before military courts.[27] Speaking of the legal aid organization he founded in Darfur, a local lawyer told

---

[22] Interview with senior official, Sudan Bar Association, in Khartoum, Sudan (June 2005).

[23] Follow-up interview with Hassan, retired senior judicial official, in Khartoum, Sudan (April 2007).

[24] Interview with Sadiq, lawyer, in Khartoum, Sudan (February 2007).

[25] "Sudan Says No to Hybrid Courts for Darfur Crimes," *Sudan Tribune*, September 21, 2009. Available: http://www.sudantribune.com/Sudan-says-no-to-hybrid-courts-for,32543 (accessed January 9, 2013).

[26] Interview with Maher, legal aid attorney from Darfur, in Khartoum, Sudan (June 2005).

[27] Interview with Abdul Moneim, lawyer, in Khartoum, Sudan (February 2007).

me, "We had cases of people who were tortured. Relatives and friends could not raise their voices to say anything [about the torture]. It was only the lawyers who could stand up for that, against the atrocities and violations."[28]

But these are isolated cases. It is very difficult for lawyers outside the Bashir regime to organize collectively, particularly when seeking constitutional judicial review of regime actions. While Bashir created institutional avenues for public-interest lawyering and the construction of the rule of law, he controlled them to prevent real engagement with the regime. Institutional constraints on the Constitutional Court, for instance, prevent it from wielding authority as Sudan's Supreme Court (*mahkama al-'uliyya*; also earlier called the High Court) had in years past. To start, President Bashir created a Constitutional Court separate from Sudan's Supreme Court and appointed its nine justices, who serve eight-year terms. The Court has original and sole jurisdiction over all constitutional matters. Its decisions may not be appealed. (The Supreme Court is the court of last resort for all nonconstitutional cases.) Lengthy delays – largely from an accumulation of hundreds of unresolved cases in which justices must apply the defunct 1998 constitution – and court fees of more than USD 1,000 prevent public-interest cases from emerging. High cost in time and finance makes court access unaffordable except to the wealthiest investors. While Bashir appointed some of the justices on the advice of minority parties, including the Sudan People's Liberation Movement (SPLM), these jurists form the outvoted minority of the bench. The purse strings of the Court are also closely monitored and controlled. The Constitutional Court occupies a dilapidated one-story building at a busy intersection in downtown Khartoum, a far cry from the modern air-conditioned office tower housing the Supreme Court down the road. According to one senior attorney familiar with the inner workings of the Constitutional Court, "no one is holding any hope" that it will help the Sudanese people achieve the justice embedded in their constitution and bill of rights. After reading recent opinions of the Court, he concluded that "from the perspective of the writing and academic standards, it was poor. From the perspective of justice, it was worse."[29]

[28] Interview with Hani, lawyer and member of Parliament, in Khartoum, Sudan (April 2007).

[29] Follow-up interview with Mansour, lawyer and former government minister, in Khartoum, Sudan (June 2010).

In addition to controlling and obstructing institutional access to the rule of law, as described in detail later in this chapter, Bashir has altered the system of legal education in Sudan in order to undermine the prestige of the legal profession and its tight-knit culture. Stable government jobs have become more difficult to obtain, driving many lawyers into private practice, where many remain impoverished – long-term clients are few, and monthly salaries are not guaranteed. Lawyers strapped for money to buy food or pay rent are less likely to engage in pro bono or reform work. One young lawyer told me about her failed efforts to promote constitutional judicial review and reform-oriented activities among fifteen of her reform-minded colleagues. They were too preoccupied with earning a decent living to concern themselves with activism, she told me. "The bar association now is [not] concerned with legal aid," agreed another attorney.[30]

CONTROLLING THE JUDICIARY

In addition to targeting members of the bar association, Bashir sought to limit the ability of judges to pose a threat to his regime. Like lawyers, judges had long been on the front lines of antiauthoritarian activism in Sudan. According to one judge, in 1964 during the Abboud military regime, "I used to issue permissions for people ... to move after the curfew. [Lawyers] like Dr. [Hassan al-] Turabi and others who were interested in getting rid of the military regime – they were the ones ... allowed to move at night."[31] Bashir moved quickly to constrain judicial independence under his program of Islamization. Along with purging the bar association, he fired unsympathetic judges and kept remaining judges under his thumb by issuing employment contracts that had to be renewed annually. And he made massive investments in court infrastructure to advance his regime's legal priorities and extend his reach well beyond Khartoum.

Long before Bashir's rise to power, during the 1950s and 1960s, Sudan's judiciary almost entirely comprised of graduates of British-built law schools, who were trained in English common law. Many of them had graduate degrees from prestigious institutions in Great Britain, including Cambridge, Oxford, and Edinburgh. As part of his efforts

---

[30] Interview with Talal, lawyer, in Khartoum, Sudan (April 2007).

[31] Interview with Gasim, former government minister, in Khartoum, Sudan (November 2006).

to centralize control of Sudan under a unified Islamic law, between 1989 and 1994, Bashir fired more than three hundred judges,[32] many of whom had received their law degrees from the University of Khartoum, and replaced them "with *shari'a*-trained personnel."[33] One lawyer who observed this weeding-out process explained:

> The system of education [at the University of Khartoum] formed your mind to approach legal problems comparatively. So the addition of *shari'a* as a major source of law in the late 1970s wouldn't have resulted in much harm. But what [the Bashir government] did was to dismiss those judges properly trained in all legal systems applicable to Sudanese law and [replace them] with those trained only in *shari'a*.[34]

Some judges having backgrounds in common law were allowed to keep their jobs thanks to nepotism or other social connections. One former judge described to me how his job was saved by his close friendship with the chief justice at the time.[35] This judge believes that the administration purposely assigned him to certain cases to boost its legitimacy: he would cast a minority vote in Supreme Court panels (of three judges) and the regime could claim that judges were free to dissent. He ultimately resigned because he did not want to be fodder for regime propaganda.

Among the judges who retained their positions on the bench, the removals bred fear and prevented them from expressing opinions counter to the Bashir government. One senior judiciary official under Bashir recalled the "butchery" of the judiciary during Bashir's early years and the "very harsh" atmosphere in which judges operated.[36] The administration started requiring judges to wear uniforms, for example. A small inconvenience, perhaps, but a powerful symbol of the loss of judicial independence. The renewable one-year contracts provided no job security. "There were no rights for judges," said a retired Supreme Court justice:

> Anyone with a voice would just be dismissed, without any rights or procedures. The only guarantee for judges had been the High Judicial

[32] Rone (1996); Africa Watch (1991).

[33] Interview with Shadi, lawyer, in Khartoum, Sudan (April 2007).

[34] Interview with Mansour, lawyer and former government minister, in Khartoum, Sudan (February 2007).

[35] Interview with Hassan, retired senior judicial official, in Khartoum, Sudan (February 2007).

[36] Interview with senior judicial official 3, in Khartoum, Sudan (January 2007).

Commission. But at first even the Commission's powers were given to the Chief Justice. So he was everything. And so he could advise the President to dismiss a judge, and he'd be dismissed.[37]

Judges who left the bench in order to become law professors found themselves similarly squeezed. It was no coincidence that when some of Sudan's most liberal-minded professors returned after the end of the civil war, the government in 2007 announced a plan to combine the professors' union with the staff workers' union, thereby reducing faculty bargaining power over their wages. Professors united in opposition behind their most senior colleagues, most of whom were older than sixty-five and trained by the British at the University of Khartoum. As their criticism of the government grew louder, Bashir announced a new mandatory retirement age of sixty-five in order to make room for younger faculty. By refusing to pay the salaries of unruly faculty, the administration effectively quieted an uprising by adopting an outwardly unconnected legal change. The professors filed a case in the Constitutional Court arguing that the order violates the 2005 Interim National Constitution and demanding to be reinstated. But the lawsuit stalled as a result of the backlog of cases on the court's docket.

Judges have also had to swallow the party line. Jalal Ali Lutfi, Bashir's first chief justice, is perhaps the most infamous example of judicial accommodation to political authority. In 1967, Lutfi published an article in the *Sudan Law Journal and Reports* in which he rejected the widespread application of non-common-law sources in Sudan. "There is nothing wrong with the way followed in receiving and applying English law in the Sudan," he wrote. "For the building of a sound Sudanese legal system we must never sever our relation with the past and demolish what has taken more than half a century to build."[38] A little more than two decades later, Lutfi became a crucial ally of Bashir and the key legal component of the Bashir regime's Islamization policies, shoveling the last pile of earth over the grave Bashir had dug for the common law. Lutfi oversaw the gutting of the Khartoum-educated judiciary and, in a much-discussed case, approved the execution of two men for an act not considered criminal under common law. The case occurred in the early 1990s after Bashir seized power. Two Sudanese

---

[37] Follow-up interview with Hassan, retired senior judicial official, in Khartoum, Sudan (April 2007).

[38] G. A. Lutfi, "The Future of the English Law in the Sudan." *SLJR* 219 (1967) at 236.

men (named as A. Georges and Magdi Mahgoub) were convicted of possessing foreign currency and sentenced to death by a special court. Because the use of Western currencies in Sudan was common practice, particularly among wealthy investors, one of Lutfi's subordinates recalled, "I went to see [Chief Justice Lutfi], and I told him that [the court's decision] was wrong, that no person should be executed for possession of [foreign] currency, that it was a political decision in which he should not have involved himself. But he refused to listen to my advice."[39] The two accused men were executed.

A small subset of judicial personnel vocally supported the Bashir regime, believing it was their duty to help reconceptualize the legal order according to Islamic law. A senior judiciary official, initially trained in the common law by the British, said that he did not hesitate to join Bashir's government because, as he put it, "I knew that if I refused, God would punish me: 'Who are you to refuse? I made you what you are [and] facilitated everything for you.'"[40] In 1998 Bashir appointed the first chief justice of the Sudan judiciary who was trained in a law faculty that emphasized *shari'a*. This appointment led many of the old-guard Khartoum-trained judges and lawyers to question the chief justice's credentials because he lacked a robust education in common law and what they saw as politicization of *shari'a* under the Bashir regime. With limited exceptions, this old guard sees legal training that emphasizes *shari'a* as an indicator of Islamist political leanings, often dismissing the substance of *shari'a*-based education if it is not integrated with comprehensive study of Sudan's common-law heritage. In general, a perception exists among legal professionals that the judiciary's reputation has eroded significantly, particularly since 1990. Some even lament the loss of the colonial judiciary. One lawyer insisted, "Judges and lawyers [prior to Sudan's independence] were [more] prestigious and well-informed compared to now."[41]

CONTROLLING ENTRY INTO THE LEGAL PROFESSION

The Bashir regime made its most lasting impact on the legal order through its reshaping of Sudan's legal education system. Bold academic

[39] Interview with Hassan, retired senior judicial official, in Khartoum, Sudan (February 2007).
[40] Interview with senior judicial official 3, in Khartoum, Sudan (January 2007).
[41] Interview with Abdul-Haq, lawyer, in Khartoum, Sudan (July 2010).

reforms enabled the government to indoctrinate huge numbers of law students with regime-approved Islamic ideologies, to expand its influence outside Khartoum and to develop a more compliant population of future legal practitioners.

The Turco-Egyptian colonial administration in Sudan in the nineteenth century, the British in the first half of the twentieth century, and the Sudanese military dictators before Bashir had also viewed the legal academy as a useful tool of legal politics to promote regime stability. But when Bashir took power, Sudan's system of legal education was in a sorry condition. It had been badly damaged in the 1970s and 1980s as a result of Nimeiri's failed socialist policies, drastic budget cuts, devaluation of the Sudanese currency, and skyrocketing inflation. Professors taught heavy course loads and had little or no release time for research. Limited access to technology, daily power cuts, and the intense Sudanese heat restricted the amount of work that faculty and students could do each day. Libraries had restricted their purchases of new books, particularly works in English.[42]

Legal education was also as fragmented and layered as Sudan's system of laws, with curricula varying widely. At the University of Khartoum, even students who had wanted to specialize in *shari'a* had to demonstrate proficiency in common law before specializing in religious law. But during the early 1990s, the Bashir government undertook a so-called educational revolution aimed at expanding access to higher education, particularly in law, and unifying all law school curricula around the teaching of *shari'a*.[43] The regime had several reasons for focusing its attention on law school reform. First, increasing the number of lawyers was one key strategy for lessening the cohesiveness of the historically tight-knit legal community. Second, state-sponsored schools would provide a space in which students would learn about and internalize state-approved ideologies and expectations. More universities meant

[42] The dearth of English-language scholarly materials is due in part to economic sanctions imposed on Sudan since the 1980s. Texts found at major bookstores in central Khartoum, including al-Dar al-Sudaniyya lil Kutub (Sudan Bookstore), are for sale at prices inaccessible to most Sudanese. Academic journals are similarly outdated or costly, and proprietary online databases are unavailable. Some materials, though, may be found at cultural centers affiliated with foreign embassies.

[43] For an analysis of the self-proclaimed "educational revolution" by the Sudan government during the early 1990s, see Ali Abdalla Abbas (September–October 1991). "The National Islamic Front and the Politics of Education," *Middle East Report*, No. 172, pp. 22–5.

more students educated to support the regime. (And law schools are easier and cheaper to launch than medical or scientific schools, which require new technology and costly labs.)[44] Third, expanding access to legal education was a way to build support outside Khartoum.

In the five years from 1990 through 1994, the government increased the number of institutions granting law degrees in Sudan from four to sixteen (Map 4.1).[45] The Bashir administration opened more law schools than had all previous governments combined. It was determined to extend its legal authority beyond the capital city, where its power was most concentrated: with the exception of a new Police College in Khartoum that taught law, all of the new law faculties were founded outside the capital (Map 4.1). In total, every Sudanese law school was launched by a nondemocratic government.

Educational reform was an extension of Bashir's larger Islamization efforts. Today, almost all educational programs are conducted in Arabic, and *shari'a* is the basis of all legal education.[46] "They Arabized everything," said one lawyer, a 1960s graduate of the University of Khartoum, "even the University of Khartoum law faculty. We used to have all courses except *shari'a* law in English."[47] Around the time of the signing of the peace accords in 2005, first-year law students began to be required to enroll in the "Introduction to Law" course taught in English. Most, however, take their exams for this and their other courses in Arabic, the language they understand well. The combination of Arabization and the growth in the number of law schools "was very bad on the performance of the legal profession," this lawyer continued, and it coincided with reductions in office staff and research funding

---

[44] Education specialists in Sudan have documented the eroding quality of higher education, and the challenges faced by understaffed departments and undertrained teachers. See, e.g., Mohamed El Amin Ahmed El Tom, *Higher Education in Sudan: Towards a New Vision for a New Era* (Friedrich Ebert Stiftung and Sudan Center for Educational Research, 2006).

[45] The total number of universities granting law degrees is twelve. One of these universities, Al-Qur'an al-Karim, opened campuses in five cities. Note that Juba University relocated to Khartoum during the civil war (1983–2005), and Islamic University Omdurman began in the mid-19th century as an institute for the study of Islam (see Map 4.1).

[46] Some schools received exemptions to teach in English, including the University of Khartoum Faculty of Medicine (where Sudanese professors claimed they only knew complex medical terminology in English) and elite private schools in the Khartoum region.

[47] Interview with Abu Musa, lawyer, in Khartoum, Sudan (March 2007).

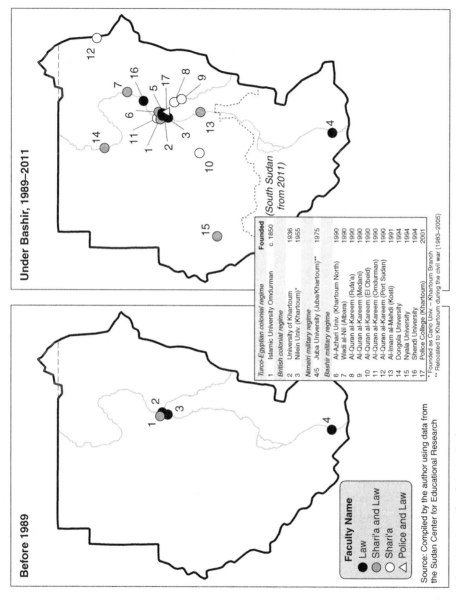

Before 1989

Under Bashir, 1989–2011

Faculty Name

● Law
● Shari'a and Law
○ Shari'a
△ Police and Law

	Founded
Turco-Egyptian colonial regime	
1 Islamic University Omdurman	c. 1850
British colonial regime	
2 University of Khartoum	1936
3 Nilein Univ. (Khartoum)*	1955
Nimeiri military regime	
4/5 Juba University (Juba/Khartoum)**	1975
Bashir military regime	
6 Al-Azhari Univ. (Khartoum North)	1990
7 Wadi al-Nil (Atbara)	1990
8 Al-Quran al-Kareem (Rufa'a)	1990
9 Al-Quran al-Kareem (Medani)	1990
10 Al-Quran al-Kareem (El Obeid)	1990
11 Al-Quran al-Kareem (Omdurman)	1990
12 Al-Quran al-Kareem (Port Sudan)	1990
13 Al-Imam al-Mahdi (Kosti)	1991
14 Dongola University	1994
15 Nyala University	1994
16 Shendi University	1994
17 Police College (Khartoum)	2001

(South Sudan from 2011)

* Founded as Cairo Univ. – Khartoum Branch
** Relocated to Khartoum during the civil war (1983–2005)

Source: Compiled by the author using data from the Sudan Center for Educational Research

Map 4.1. Law faculties in Sudan.

137

for faculty.[48] A partner in one of Sudan's major law firms concurred: "I need [associate attorneys] who can speak and write in English. I cannot find these qualities [in recent law graduates]."[49] The English language was branded an enemy to the Arabization programs built under Bashir during the 1990s, but its relevance could not be overstated for conducting international business and securing foreign investment in Sudan. A senior administrator at one of the few English-language educational institutions in Sudan recalled that complaints had been filed in the 1990s with the Ministry of Education about that school's use of English. The minister publicly stated that he would shut down the school if it did not start abiding by the Arabization program. But, according to school administrators, the complaints quieted, and the following year, in an about-face, the government official sent his child to study at the elite school, despite the policy's enforcement elsewhere.[50]

To the extent that English common law is still part of the legal curriculum, it has been effectively marginalized. After the 2005 peace agreement that ended more than two decades of fighting in Sudan's north-south civil war, some of the old British-trained lawyers returned to Sudan and to their faculty positions at the University of Khartoum. They founded one-year certificate programs for international human rights professionals and taught introductory courses in general jurisprudence using British sources. But these courses are kept separate from the regular curriculum and may mutate or disappear as these professors retire. Lawyers I met in Sudan would refer to a common-law-trained lawyer from the old guard of the legal profession as "one of the remnants of the [old] University of Khartoum" as it was before Bashir seized control.[51]

While the government's educational initiatives have been successful in terms of centralizing control and spreading a state ideology rooted in Islamic law, they have not improved the quality of education nor built widespread support for the regime. "Legal education itself deteriorated," said one lawyer, echoing the views of dozens of lawyers, law students, and professors I met.[52] By 2011, there were no small tutorials

---

[48] Ibid.
[49] Interview with Talal, lawyer, in Khartoum, Sudan (April 2007).
[50] Interview with Leila, school administrator, in Omdurman, Sudan (June 2005).
[51] Interview with Hassan, retired senior judicial official, in Khartoum, Sudan (February 2007).
[52] Interview with Sadiq, lawyer, in Khartoum, Sudan (February 2007).

138

Table 4.1. Lawyers per capita in Sudan

Year	1956	1960	1970	1980	1990	2000	2005	2010
Citizens per Lawyer	483,871	141,112	67,211	37,386	8,934	3,893	3,638	3,547

Source: Compiled by the author, using data provided by Sudan Judiciary, Bar Admissions; and World Bank Development Indicators through 2010.

anymore, and class sizes had exploded. During the 1950s and 1960s, the University of Khartoum Faculty of Law graduated between fifteen and twenty students each year. By 2011, more than two hundred law students enrolled in each class year; they were taught by the same number of faculty (about fifteen full-time professors). According to a former law faculty dean:

> The government wanted to control everything including education, so they set up lots of law schools. But to have a good school, you need students, professors, and libraries. But especially outside of Khartoum, the professors were not qualified. Many of them are party members. So you have places that look like universities but are not universities.[53]

The program of Islamization has also come under attack. A former top-ranking official in Bashir's government who had been educated at the University of Khartoum argued:

> As far as I'm concerned, Islamization and Arabization does not profit from knowledge. Knowledge has no tribal affiliation or political affiliation whatsoever. And this is our Islam: look for knowledge wherever you find it. Our [Arabic-language] proverb even says go to China if you have to: "*Atlabu al-'ilm wa low fi-seen.*" [Seek knowledge even if it is as far away as China.] Therefore, a book written in English, there's much to learn from that book.... When they abandoned English in our schools, we deprived our ... children from a whole world [of knowledge]. In the West, they have culture and discoveries. We are obliged [to] look at it. If we don't, we are limiting our knowledge to a narrow space. At the same time, we are behaving against our own Islamic teachings.[54]

[53] Interview with Haroob, former law dean, in Khartoum, Sudan (October 2006).

[54] Though this person is a major public figure closely aligned with President Bashir, I have chosen to keep his/her identity anonymous because of the sensitivity of this statement made to me. The interview was conducted in Sudan in 2007.

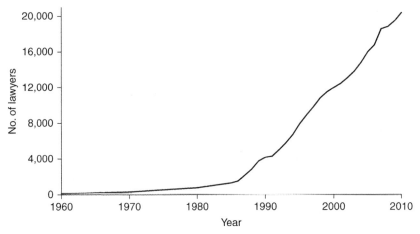

Figure 4.1. Number of lawyers, 1956–2010 (total registered with Sudan Bar Association, by year).
Source: Compiled by the author, using data provided by Sudan Judiciary and Bar Admissions.

One important consequence of the regime's educational reforms has been the enormous increase in the number of lawyers in Sudan. While the population growth rate averaged 2.3 percent annually under Bashir, the growth rate in the number of lawyers was four times that – roughly 9.2 percent per year. Development experts describe such trends in terms of professionals per capita. When Sudan became independent, the ratio of lawyers to citizens was 1:484,000. By 1970, that ratio was approximately 1:67,000, and, by 2010, it was down to 1:3,500 (Table 4.1).

In the thirty-three years before Bashir's takeover (1956–89), successive governments issued 4,000 legal licenses. In the first two decades under President Bashir for which data were made available to me (1989–2010), the government issued 14,500 legal licenses (Figure 4.1).

Another way of viewing the data is the number of new lawyers entering the Sudanese market each year (Figure 4.2). Between 1956 and 1980, forty new lawyers entered the labor market each year. In the 2000s, eight hundred to one thousand new lawyers joined the workforce each year.

These numbers substantiate, in the case of Sudan under Bashir, two hypotheses about the impact of authoritarian legal politics on the legal profession (Figure 4.2). First, military coups and crackdowns on the legal profession in Sudan precipitated a dramatic drop in the number

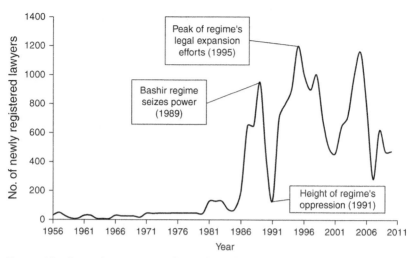

Figure 4.2. Critical junctures in the Bashir administration, measured by newly registered lawyers.
Source: Compiled by the author, using data provided by Sudan Judiciary and Bar Admissions.

of new lawyers emerging. Between 1989 and 1991, the number of lawyers in Sudan fell precipitously because established lawyers were either jailed or exiled and young people were unable or unwilling to join the profession.[55] Second, it is a testament to the efficacy of Bashir's legal and educational reforms that so many new lawyers have been licensed since 1991.

The evidence points to the Bashir administration's high level of confidence in being able to control a large legal community. There is, after all, a long history of legal professionals leading mobilization efforts against despotic regimes in Sudan, and Bashir's own mistrust of the legal profession is well documented. But his administration understood that repression of the old legal guard was not sufficient to ensure its longevity. To stamp out judicial independence and fragment the legal order, the Bashir administration realized it had to flood the legal marketplace within and beyond Khartoum with young loyalists trained in Arabic and the regime-approved *shari'a*. A largely diffuse legal profession also ensured that lawyers would be constrained from

[55] For information on purging in the legal profession in 1989–91 in Sudan, see *Beset by Contradictions: Islamization, Legal Reform and Human Rights in Sudan*, Lawyers Committee for Human Rights, 1996.

intense organizing as they had done in the past against authoritarian governments.

Not only did the Bashir government shift the substantive basis of legal education, but by creating a glut of new lawyers, it triggered labor market conditions that limited political activism. Law school graduates in Sudan have four basic options: to become a judge, government lawyer, private company lawyer, or independent advocate. (An increasingly prominent fifth option for law school graduates is seeking contractual employment with a local or foreign nongovernmental organization operating in Sudan.) Since there are a limited number of government, judicial, corporate, and NGO posts – and an enormous number of law graduates – most new lawyers are forced into private practice. To obtain a private advocate's license, a student must graduate from a registered law school in Sudan, pass the seven-day *mu'adalah* (bar exam),[56] and complete a one-year apprenticeship (often at minimum wage) with a lawyer in practice for at least ten years. Even after all this, many new lawyers find it impossible to get ahead without high-level connections to the ruling party. According to one lawyer:

> Most of the investors, they like things done [quickly]. If [a well-connected lawyer] wants to meet the governor of Bank of Sudan, he will ring [the governor] on his mobile [telephone]. I cannot do that. It would take me five or six weeks to meet the governor of the Bank of Sudan. I'd have to ring his secretary. But any of those people can do it.[57]

In this environment, most lawyers struggle to find work and earn little more than Sudan's minimum wage even in the years after their apprenticeships. Few can afford to specialize in one area of law but instead take any cases they can find in any field, including criminal, tort, contract, and property. With such heavy competition for even the most low-paying cases, many lawyers are unable to consider pro bono or reform-oriented cases. The Bashir regime helped to saturate urban

---

[56] The seven subjects on the bar exam are criminal law, criminal procedure, civil procedure, Islamic jurisprudence, contracts, evidence, and Islamic law of personal relationships (marriage, dissolution, and inheritance), up from four subjects until the mid-1980s (criminal law, civil law, evidence, and contracts). Each subject is given in a single three-hour exam, with seven consecutive days of exams for the seven subjects.

[57] Interview with Gasim, former government minister, in Khartoum, Sudan (November 2006).

markets with a glut of young lawyers inculcated in its strict vision of legal progress.

In the 2000s, contrary to the notion that enthusiasm for international human rights and the rule of law was the purview of younger generations, Sudan became a place where older judges and lawyers trained in English common law were Western-identified and viewed rights in a Western sense. Younger judges and lawyers trained in Islamic law generally did not. Their concept of rights was rooted in part in the immutability of Islamic law and in individual duties and responsibilities. (Chapter 5 looks more closely at diverse Sudanese perceptions of rights as compared to the notions of rights promoted by the international aid community involved in Sudan.) As older lawyers stop practicing, it will be increasingly difficult to inculcate in the young Sudanese Western legal practices, mostly conceived in languages with which they are unfamiliar.

REFORMING THE COURTS: "SHORTENING THE JUDICIAL SHADOW"

Bashir has embraced the British colonialists' strategy of expanding government infrastructure and making the legal system highly accessible to ordinary citizens, which the postcolonial governments before Bashir had been unable to do. "The difficulty," explained a top judicial official appointed by Bashir to lead the effort, "comes when you try to manage a country like Sudan. It is very big in area. To govern such a big country with so many cultures, it is not an easy job."[58] The way to create governable subjects across a vast and divided geography, as Bashir and his deputies determined, was not to decentralize power, but to extend the reach of the centralized authority as far as possible. During the 1990s, the Bashir regime undertook a massive campaign to expand the Sudanese court system, building hundreds of new courthouses. This policy became known within the administration as *taqsir al-zhul al-qada'i* ("shortening the judicial shadow"). The substantial investment in court construction reveals the Bashir government's interest in displaying to Sudanese citizens at least some appearance of accessibility.[59]

---

[58] Interview with senior judicial official 3, in Khartoum, Sudan (January 2007).

[59] I corroborated evidence through interviews with lawyers and senior officials and by using documents I was able to obtain from the Bashir administration. Future

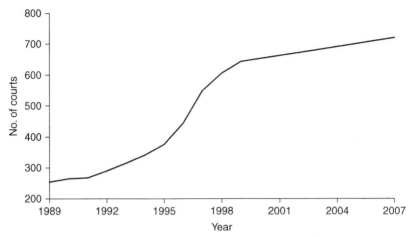

Figure 4.3. Number of courts under President Bashir.
Source: Author, based on data collected at and certified by Sudan Judiciary
Department of Statistics.

Publicly, the government argued that bringing courts and administrative agencies closer to the people enables citizens to interact more directly with their government and enhances governmental responsiveness. Explaining that some citizens had to travel two days or more to take their petitions to the nearest court, a leading judicial official involved with the program said his goal was purely to help the people of Sudan:

> The policy behind this is just to minimize the cost and the trouble people take, because here in Sudan the standard of living is very low. Most people depend on their manual work and time. They have to leave their work and families unattended. Therefore, we thought it was better to move [the courts] to them, rather than making them come to Khartoum.[60]

Between 1989 and 2007, the number of statutory courts in Sudan increased from 254 to 721 (Figure 4.3).[61] Bashir also created a network

research would require full geospatial data of both courts and population density to argue whether these courts were as accessible as the regime had hoped. I attempted on numerous occasions between 2005 and 2010 to access these data from Sudanese government officials, bureaucrats, and archives. But the precise location of each of the hundreds of Sudanese courts remains classified.

[60] Interview with senior judicial official 3, in Khartoum, Sudan (January 2007).

[61] During the second civil war, the Sudan People's Liberation Army (SPLA) controlled many rural areas in southern Sudan. I was unable to access court statistics

of specialized courts, such as those focusing on taxes, customs, electrical and telephone service, and intellectual property.[62] Concomitant with Bashir's expansion of the number of courts was his administration's political carving of Sudan into smaller administrative units, increasing the number of states from nine when he attained power in 1989 to twenty-six by 1998.[63] The judicial official who led the operation from 1994 to 1998 explained that his efforts were supported by others in the administration. Though the judiciary took no money from the Ministry of Finance to construct and fund these hundreds of new courts, it applied existing court fees to the new ventures.[64]

Following the British strategy of co-optation, Bashir's government used local leaders from outside Khartoum who were aligned with and paid by the regime to staff these administrative offices and courts. The regime actively "promoted" loyal staff in Khartoum by returning them to their homelands outside the capital to instill the regime's values beyond the capital. Instead of being seen as government-controlled outsiders, these magistrates are perceived as local (and in many cases they are members of local families) and therefore as legitimate authority figures. Because the Bashir regime is itself *of* Sudan in a way that the foreign colonial administrators never could be, it was much more successful at winning over local leaders, who then executed government policy. Similar to the buildup of law schools in key cities in Sudan, the judiciary's reach extended deeper and broader, to areas where previous foreign governments led by the Egyptians and the British failed to gain entry.

from these areas. Thus, data and policies described in this chapter refer only to the sixteen states of northern Sudan and southern "garrison" towns controlled by the Khartoum-based government during the civil war – Juba, Wau, and Malakal. Informal networks of customary courts continued to exist in sparsely populated areas and villages that the government was unable or unwilling to control, as well as in encampments for displaced persons. Note that the most complete data on courts are for the period between 1989 and 2005, during Sudan's most comprehensive court-building project.

[62] The Sudan government claimed its intellectual property court, located in Khartoum, was the first of its kind in Africa and the Middle East. Lawyers I met separately mentioned that it was not yet hearing substantial cases, if any at all.

[63] See Jennifer Wood and Clifford D. Shearing, *Imagining Security* (Cullompton, UK: Willan, 2007). On these mechanisms of governance that extend the reach of central power into rural areas, see also N. Rose and P. Miller, "Political Power beyond the State: Problematics of Government," 43(2) *British Journal of Sociology* (1992): 173–205.

[64] Interview with senior judicial official 3, in Khartoum, Sudan (January 2007).

Bashir's strategy to increase the number of courts led to wide-ranging uses of the legal system across different areas of law – property, criminal defense, labor, and contract, among others. A young lawyer I met represented a woman who had been fired from her job without receiving the government-mandated severance pay. "I went to the court, and I won the case," she told me. The company was found at fault and would "have to do what the judge said."[65] In another case, this lawyer sought permission from the Ministry of Justice to file suit against the minister of higher education. (According to Article 83 of Sudan's Civil Procedure Act, amended by the Bashir government in 1995, the Ministry of Justice must grant permission to citizens seeking to file suits against a government official.) Her client was a student who had been promised a full scholarship to attend medical school. But the government rescinded its funding two years into his education. Such cases are typically resolved under the threat of litigation once the minister of justice requests an official reply to the complaint from the relevant government department. Lawyers in different areas of Sudan also told me of citizens – usually friends or distant family members – who ask for assistance in business transactions (*shughul al-mu'amalat*) such as drafting contracts to prevent exposure to litigation.[66] And a major church in Sudan – otherwise deeply active in promoting human rights and peace building – was mired in a lengthy appeal against the buyer of what the church had argued was its wrongfully sold property. (A former priest had stolen church documents and sold the property to a buyer, who argued he purchased the church property in good faith from someone – a priest – he thought was authorized to sell it.)[67] These examples represent some of the myriad ways that citizens and organizations experience state law even in what is otherwise one of the world's most fragile states. While some lawyers do allege harm committed by government ministries against their clients, even these cases do not seek to challenge or supplant the regime's authority. Instead, by turning to the judiciary to resolve everyday citizen disputes, these cases and the threat of litigation itself help to solidify that authority and, ultimately, to build the state through law.

In addition to building new court infrastructure and encouraging citizens to use it, Bashir created the Public Grievances and Corrections

[65] Interview with Malika, lawyer, in Khartoum, Sudan (October 2006).
[66] Interview with Jamal, layer, in El Obeid, Sudan (May 2007).
[67] Interview with Ishmael, church leader, in Khartoum, Sudan (June 2010).

Board in 1998. The board, which occupies a medium-sized building in central Khartoum and answers to the president and National Assembly, is described by the administration as a kind of catchall appellate body for complaints against the judiciary or other parts of the government. According to the government, the purpose of the board is

> to remove away patent injustice, clear away grievances, assure effi-ciency and purity in the practice of the State and systems, or the final executive or administrative acts, and also to extend to justice after the final decisions of the institutions of justice [including] a) such patent injustices as may result from ... final judicial decrees [and] b) such injuries, as may arise out of abuse of power, or corruption, by state organs.[68]

In reality, while the board is a tool for channeling and diffusing public grievances, it may not be a true arbiter of justice. During its first seven years of operation, the board received 10,559 complaints and dismissed 10,495 (99.4 percent) on the grounds that they suffered "from either failure to exhaust all legal or administrative remedies, or [failure to] reveal grounds to justify interference [of the Board]."[69] Like local courts during the colonial period, the board serves to enhance control by ensuring that grievances against the state are directed to a single government agency often to be quashed.

As the Bashir regime expanded the number and geographic distribution of courts, it focused particular attention on the development of criminal courts. Investment in criminal law and courts is a means through which governments extend their authority and ensure social order. (The British in colonial Sudan also used this strategy; it is a phenomenon prevalent in and beyond Sudan and across periods.) Prior to 1989, Sudan had roughly equal numbers of criminal, civil, and personal status courts: seventy to eighty of each type. While the numbers of all three types of courts increased under the Bashir regime, the number of criminal courts grew at the fastest rate, nearly quadrupling from 82 to 314 in 2006, the latest year for which data are available (Figure 4.4). By 2006, 44 percent of all courts in Sudan were criminal courts.

Unsurprisingly, the existence of more criminal courts led to more criminal cases. By 2005, there were more than four times as many criminal as civil cases recorded in Sudan and more than twice as many

---

[68] Judge Mohammed Abuzeid, "The Public Grievances and Corrections Board (Ombudsman) of Sudan" (2007) Khartoum.

[69] Ibid.

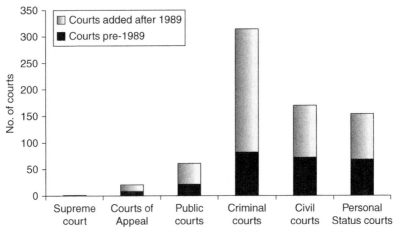

Figure 4.4. Growth in number of courts under Bashir, 1989–2006 (by type).
Source: Author, based on data collected at and certified by Sudan Judiciary
Department of Statistics.

criminal as personal status cases (Figure 4.5). (Despite increasing
divorce rates, four personal status courts were closed between 1999
and 2007, while sixty-one new criminal courts were opened.) The rise
in the number of adjudicated criminal cases results from the fact that
these cases are tried in a summary fashion, an approach first employed
by the British. In 1999, the latest year for which time-series data are
available, the average criminal case reached resolution in just eighty
minutes, compared to two and a half hours for Muslim personal status
cases and more than four hours for civil claims. Summary punishments
are particularly common in cases of alcohol production or possession,
in which the accused can receive forty lashes before a judge without
even a lawyer present.[70]

There are several reasons why the Bashir administration put so much
focus on building up the system of criminal courts under an Islamic legal
code. Nondemocratic states often use criminal law as a tool of political repression. While licensed lawyers maintain immunity from some
forms of prosecution, many whom I met have been harassed, detained,
and arrested by national-security officers for their legal-aid work, particularly for representing the poor. It is no coincidence that the period

[70] *Mahakim al-Jana'iyya al-Sha'abiyya* (People's Criminal Courts) are constituted by
the chief justice of the Judiciary, usually to try petty crimes.

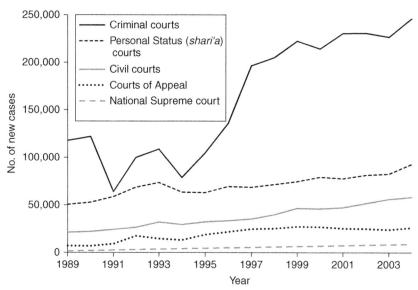

Figure 4.5. Judicial caseload, 1989–2005 (by court and year).
Source: Author; data from *Al-Iqtisad wa al-Mal* [Economics and Finance], Sudan Judiciary, February 13, 2006.

of greatest increase in criminal cases was the mid-1990s, at the height of Sudan's civil war and of the government's simultaneous program to "shorten the judicial shadow." Data, however, on the kinds of criminal cases heard by the courts are inaccessible; the regime has been hostile to inspection by researchers.[71] Evidence from speaking with judges, lawyers, and aid workers, and from visiting courts in urban areas, indicated that the regime's efforts at criminalization focused disproportionately on those most likely to agitate against the regime. These persons included opposition-party officials in Khartoum and residents of desert encampments surrounding the capital city. In 2007 and again in 2012, the government immediately arrested and imprisoned opposition party leaders alleged to have led street protests against the regime and the rising prices of food and fuel.

[71] I made many attempts in 2010 to update previously collected data on courts and to obtain more complete data on criminal jurisprudence in Sudan. But despite early assurances from government staff that these data would be made available to me, I was told in July 2010 that no further data would be open to inspection by researchers.

Relatedly, the Bashir regime focused on building up its criminal capacity in part because it committed itself to a program of strict Islamization as a tool to stabilize Sudan. In order to be seen as a credible religious force, the regime had to establish and enforce Islamic criminal laws (such as the prohibition on alcohol) throughout the country. War-displaced persons from Darfur and southern Sudan commonly reported to me that police arrests for the possession or sale of alcohol were rampant. Those who live in these encampments perhaps have the most to complain about with regard to the regime (and the least to lose, having fled their already-burned villages), but the cycle of displacement, poverty, arrest, and punishment that they endure maintains their subjugation under the regime's law. Finally, by relieving local customary law authorities of their jurisdiction over criminal codes and conflict resolution, the regime was able to consolidate its own authority in Khartoum and elsewhere.[72]

BASHIR'S LEGAL LEGACY

Located just steps from the Nile River, the long two-story building housing the Sudanese judiciary administration is the nation's oldest continuously used public structure. Built by the British in 1907 for the colonial legal secretary and his staff, today it houses the chief justice and his staff. All of Sudan's postindependence chief justices have sat in the same office where the British legal secretaries sat, and in many ways the chief justices have performed the same role. They oversee a judicial system designed primarily to appease and disempower the Sudanese people. More than simply sharing the same space, the judiciary under Bashir has been dedicated to the same repressive goals as Sudan's former colonial masters.

In many ways, however, Bashir's legal revolution has been more successful and more complete. By drastically increasing the number of courts, law schools, lawyers, and judges operating under the same regime-approved version of Islamic law, Bashir's government can claim to have unified the legal order, silenced dissent, and neutralized potential challengers to an extent previously unknown in Sudan. Bashir used both military might and legal mastery to facilitate his control of what has become to date Sudan's longest-running government.

[72] See Martin Shapiro, *Courts: A Comparative and Political Analysis* (Chicago: University of Chicago Press, 1981).

Bashir's longevity is remarkable in the context of postcolonial Sudan, though his regime's efforts to create legal stability rest on shaky ground. Despite the citizenry's increased uses of courts, it remains debatable whether Bashir's turn to legal politics fully remade the military regime to appear more legitimate and moderate. Many lawyers believe that the quality of the legal system has been so horribly eroded that it cannot be sustained in its current form. One private practitioner (and short-term government appointee under Bashir) complained about judgments rendered against his clients in a recent private business dispute, saying his experience with the judiciary was "so bad ... I wrote pages citing laws and Islamic *fiqh* (jurisprudence).... The [Islamic] law says one thing, but [the judges] do something entirely different." He clarified: "It's not corrupt. It's arbitrary – or at least unexplainable."[73]

Another of the most common criticisms regards the lack of training in common law and English language. Young lawyers and law students say they need to be bilingual in English and Arabic in order to do the most lucrative kind of legal work in Sudan – working for clients in the booming oil industry. "We're facing a real problem in the profession," said one lawyer, "because of all the graduates, you can only find a very few who are qualified."[74] Young lawyers I met spoke about the difficulty of completing their one-year apprenticeships in order to obtain an advocate's license, as few lawyers have time or funds to train and pay apprentices. According to one young lawyer, those with sufficient funds will "buy the pupilage certificate without actually doing the training," further debasing the quality of lawyers emerging from Bashir's new law faculties.[75] Lawyers I met agreed that the standards of legal professionalism have dropped. Private lawyers had once looked for work with local or foreign companies, but without the requisite skills they now seek private work that links them to high-ranking government officials, where, in the words of one lawyer, "they will be able to gain more, economically."[76] And a twenty-two-year old recent law graduate lamented that in the profession she was about to enter she found a clear "lack of respect" among lawyers and between lawyers and judges, with "no sense of time management."[77] Like her senior colleagues in the bar, she, too,

---

[73] Follow-up interview with Mansour, lawyer and former government minister (June 2010).

[74] Interview with Talal, lawyer, in Khartoum, Sudan (April 2007).

[75] Interview with Raw'ah lawyer, in Khartoum, Sudan (July 2010).

[76] Ibid.

[77] Interview with Mina, lawyer, in Khartoum, Sudan (July 2010).

expressed frustration that judges seemed to lack knowledge, even of the Islamic legal philosophy in which they purportedly had been trained.

Among the groups of law students particularly ill served by the Bashir government's educational practices are South Sudanese obtaining their legal training in the North. I interviewed several young lawyers in Juba (named the capital city of South Sudan in 2011), who had been schooled exclusively in Arabic in the new law schools established by Bashir during the 1990s. They arrived in Juba between 2005 and 2010 to find that all professional work would be conducted in English, so their opportunities to practice have been limited. Many were hired by the government, which set out to train them to conduct all official business in English. According to an aid worker with the United Nations Development Programme (UNDP) in South Sudan, fourteen of seventeen lawyers and judges the agency sent to Uganda for special legal training in 2006 were sent back immediately "largely due to poor English skills."[78]

There is evidence of a perception among Sudanese lawyers that the Bashir regime's preoccupation with judicial efficiency has led to widespread miscarriages of justice. The administration takes great pride in being able to claim that 95 percent of court cases are resolved before the end of each calendar year, in contrast to the molasseslike judicial systems in many countries. But a number of lawyers separately told me that the regime pays bonuses to judges who are able to clear their dockets at the end of the year. The conclusion is undeniable that some judges rule in haste, while others refuse to hear legitimate cases. There are stories of judges who simply will not take any cases in the month of December.

The operational failings of the judicial system – which in the 1950s was hailed as a model of the diffusion of common-law jurisprudence – combined with the pathologies of civil war and autocratic rule have degraded public confidence in the government. What does this mean for an authoritarian government like Bashir's – that is, under what conditions might there be space for renewal and change in Sudan? Two related possibilities emerge.

First, there are certainly rumblings within the legal profession and some evidence of outside agitation on the part of the legal profession to promote democracy in Sudan. Much of the public remains mistrustful of

[78] Interview with Elizabeth, expatriate lawyer and aid worker, in Juba, South Sudan (April 2007).

the regime and exhausted by its lengthy rule. Cracks within the Bashir regime's wall certainly are expanding, and in 2012 Bashir announced his intention to step down as head of the ruling National Congress Party by 2014. But many lawyers I met suggested privately to me that their fears of what might occur after Bashir were worse than what they knew of Bashir. So they remained operating day to day, working within the great number of new courts Bashir opened by accepting short-term clients and cases as they arrived.

Second, it may be the case that Bashir has dug his own grave. That is, in his efforts to manipulate the legal order to punish enemies (real and perceived), install supporters, and impose a particular ideology, he has unintentionally tipped the first domino in a row that will end with his own downfall. Despite Bashir's 2010 national election victory (boycotted by prominent opposition parties), the lack of confidence in the political system and his regime's purposefully narrow education of several generations of lawyers and judges may lead to a situation in which the regime does not have the human or institutional resources to continue, and it may then collapse from the inside.

But Bashir's command of the law remains firm as of this writing, and – barring a full democratic overhaul of government that could take years to occur – it may continue long after Bashir relinquishes the reins of political power. Like his expansion of the military and national-security apparatus, his administration's legal efforts have been powered by grow-ing profits from oil exports. (These profits, though, certainly began to diminish after the secession of South Sudan in 2011.) No state leader in Sudan has been as capable for as long – economically, militarily, legally. While he was the first Sudanese state leader to agree to the indepen-dence of South Sudan, he also brutalized the region before letting it go. The legal profession under Bashir has not been the calling of the elite that it used to be. The bench has largely been co-opted, and the bar is unlikely to be an agitator unless its independence is restored.

An authoritarian government can impose a top-down interpreta-tion of legal politics – manipulating the legal system to punish ene-mies, installing supporters and judges to handle people's grievances and claims, and foisting a particular legal ideology on the nation – but it cannot in the *longue durée* force the public to trust or legitimize its rule. The lack of public support for the Bashir regime's legal transformations may eventually lead to heightened activism and dissent. Egypt, Sudan's northern neighbor, experienced a monumental power shift in 2011 (among other countries in the region) after a lack of public support for

President Hosni Mubarak's thirty-year reign spilled onto the streets and into the military that had earlier zealously supported his rule. After the signing of Sudan's 2005 Comprehensive Peace Agreement, some local lawyers took advantage of new opportunities to engage in work that promoted principles of the rule of law and democracy, by partnering or working directly with Western aid agencies. Those agencies teach lawyers and judges about the rule of law, and the Sudanese trainees are expected in turn to activate this knowledge in Bashir's courts, ultimately to reform Sudanese law and politics. But legal education by foreigners investing in Sudan (from common-law education by the British in the 1950s and 1960s to human rights education by aid agencies in the 2000s, detailed in Chapters 5 and 6) has worsened tensions within the profession. Promises of lucrative funding from abroad to work in human rights or in rule-of-law promotion have not led to a substantial reorganization of the legal profession. Rather, the attraction to these humanitarian forms of legal politics has created a new playing field on which lawyers compete with one another for international attention and funding, just as they continue to compete for clients to take cases before Bashir's new courts.

CHAPTER 5

LAW AND CIVIL SOCIETY, 1956–2011

INTRODUCTION

Thus far this book has focused on the behavior of state actors regarding the rule of law and legal institutions in Sudan. I have argued that law and legal strategies matter in highly unstable environments precisely because powerful state actors wield them as weapons in a campaign of legal politics. In Sudan, from the start of the colonial period to the present day, state actors have relied on legal resources as primary means to advance political agendas. Sudan's longest-ruling president, Omar al-Bashir, carefully analyzed the experiences of his predecessors and achieved a greater degree of control over the legal order than any previous administration. Legal institutions and the legal profession have served almost entirely to protect his regime's hold on power.

But nonstate actors have their own parallel story to be told about the use of legal tools and resources. Since Sudan became independent, foreign aid workers, international development agencies, and Sudanese civil society activists have also relied on law and legal theory in their efforts to oppose authoritarianism and empower Sudanese citizens. This chapter and the next address how nonstate actors in Sudan have sought to harness the power of the law through humanitarian legal politics, specifically through strategies for empowering the poor to use legal mechanisms to promote democracy, development, human rights, and peace – and the consequences of these actions.

This chapter provides a brief history of Western-originated humanitarian legal initiatives in Sudan during the last sixty years and then

looks deeply at current rights-based development programs. I describe
the growth and change in civil society and contemporary on-the-ground
initiatives operating in Sudan. This descriptive chapter lays the ground-
work for Chapter 6, where I analyze the consequences of humanitarian
legal politics within an authoritarian state. The international aid community has put its full political and financial muscle behind what it
calls a rights-based approach, but surprisingly little empirical study has
been carried out of these programs in authoritarian states like Sudan
struggling with decades of civil war.

HISTORY OF LEGAL DEVELOPMENT INITIATIVES
IN SUDAN

To understand the current approach to humanitarian legal politics
in Sudan, it is necessary to examine the history of foreign assistance
and related interventions by expatriate or transnational interests in
the country. The decades after independence have seen three distinct
phases of Sudan's experience of law reform and legal empowerment.
Each phase highlights the Sudanese experience of a global project
aimed at developing the global South through law. Immediately following Sudan's independence in 1956, foreign intervention focused
on building up and Sudanizing legal education. During the 1970s and
1980s, legal interventions were largely suspended in favor of direct
service and humanitarian relief. From the mid-1990s to 2011, international aid focused on integrating relief and advocacy by promoting
rights-based development programs to counter state repression and
foster a culture of rights recognition among Sudan's most vulnerable
persons, those displaced by atrocities and civil war in Darfur and the
South.

Early postcolonial legal interventions focused almost entirely on
maintaining the legal educational system established by the British.
While Western expatriate educators in Sudan had a stated interest in
Sudanizing the legal academy, they acted with a clear bias for preserv-
ing Western control over the academy and promoting Western-style
education that saw English common law as the foundation of democratic state building. The British permitted Gordon College to be
renamed the University of Khartoum, a gesture meant to symbolize
a break from the colonial past, but the institution itself was still very
much foreign-run through the 1950s. For example, responsibility for
law reporting in Sudan – which began in 1926 under the colonial

administration, with the colonial *Digest of the Decisions of the Court of Appeal of the Sudan* – transferred in 1955 from lawyers in the colonial administration (led by Donald Hawley, the judiciary's chief registrar) to European and American scholars at the University of Khartoum (led by Professor W. E. D. Davies).[1] British and American expatriates continued to fill senior faculty and administrative positions at the university. Curriculum changes had to be approved by the University of London, where University of Khartoum student exams were sent to be marked. Sudanese law graduates received "external" bachelor of laws (LL.B.) degrees from the University of London, making them eligible for coveted positions in elite postgraduate degree programs in Europe and America. Khartoum's most promising law graduates would travel abroad to get their master's or doctoral degrees from some highly prestigious universities and then "return to hold high positions in the Ministry [of Justice]."[2] This mirrored a colonial pattern of training elites abroad to replace colonial judges and educators. Western educators at the University of Khartoum Faculty of Law felt great affection for the place and its young Sudanese faculty but knew their job was "to train ... replacements as quickly as possible."[3]

Several years after independence, debate among Sudanese professors over whether the University of Khartoum should maintain its relationship with the University of London moved to the fore. Some argued that the external degree programs ensured quality and international recognition, while others thought that degrees should be awarded by Sudan's own leading university. Those with more nationalistic sentiments won. The University of Khartoum divorced itself from the University of London and started awarding its own degrees in the early 1960s. Without the University of London's backing, the University of

---

[1] See Egon Guttman "Law Reporting in the Sudan," *International and Comparative Law Quarterly* (1957): 687. See also William Twining. "Law Reporting in the Sudan." *Journal of African Law* 3(3) (1959): 176–8.

[2] Interview with Mansour, lawyer and former government minister, in Khartoum, Sudan (February 2007).

[3] Interview with former law professor 1 of the University of Khartoum, in London, England (October 2006). According to an early dean of the University of Khartoum Faculty of Law, his European predecessor, Elcana Tenenbaum, "wanted a qualified Sudanese to succeed him. But ... he got attached sentimentally to the faculty. He did not want to leave until ... there was someone to take his place." Interview with Mansour, lawyer and former government minister, in Khartoum, Sudan (February 2007).

Khartoum's reputation and prestige quickly waned. By the mid-1970s, many fewer Sudanese students were entering postgraduate programs abroad. British law professors commented that their universities began to grow "cautious about Sudanese degrees" and that "admissions committees were snippy" toward Sudanese applicants in a way they had not been earlier.[4]

During the 1960s lawyers in the United States launched what would become known as a law-and-development movement, which was originally based on a "vague notion that law ... was helpful to development."[5] With primary funding from the Ford Foundation and the U.S. Agency for International Development (USAID), scholars began studying the impact of investing in legal education in developing countries, particularly in Latin America. "Law and modernization" programs were started at Stanford University, Yale University, and the University of Chicago. It was "a wonderful and optimistic time," recalled one participant.[6] The operating principles of the movement were threefold: (1) law is central to economic development,[7] (2) lawyers understand and can encourage institutional reform, and (3) educating local lawyers and judges can close the gap between "the law in the books and the law in action in developing countries."[8] Between 1966 and 1976, the Ford Foundation invested substantial resources to develop a range of new programs related to legal education in non-Western societies. The president of the Ford Foundation at the time justified his new spending

---

[4] Telephone interview with former law professor 1 of the University of Khartoum, London, England (April 2008).

[5] Telephone interview with former law professor 2 of the University of Khartoum, East Lansing, Michigan, April 2008.

[6] See Leah Larson-Rabin, "Introduction to the 25th Anniversary Issue: Happenstance and Memory: A Legacy of Law and Development Scholarship and Policy in Legal Education," 25 *Wisconsin International Law Journal* 209 (2007): 214 (citing University of Wisconsin Law Professor Larry Church).

[7] Legal scholars saw room for lawyers to shape the design of postcolonial economic development because economists' "training and feel for social problems is all too often completely lacking. The general attitude is that such problems are 'someone else's problems,' the result being that the economist is often blind to the implications of his plan." See Robert B. Seidman, "Law and Development: A General Model," 6(3) *Law & Society Review* (1972): 312.

[8] See "Law and Development Movement." World Bank. Available: http://siteresources. worldbank.org/INTLAWJUSTINST/Resources/LawandDevelopmentMovement. pdf (accessed January 9, 2013). See also Elliot M. Burg, "Law and Development: A Review of the Literature and a Critique of 'Scholars in Self-Estrangement,'" 25 *American Journal of Comparative Law* (1977): 492.

in these areas by arguing that the law "must be an active ... force. It is both urgent and right that the law should be affirmatively and imaginatively used against all forms of injustice."[9]

This movement gained followers and practitioners around the world, including in the Horn of Africa.[10] But it largely bypassed Sudan. International law-and-development interventions had completely stalled in Sudan by the 1970s because of a number of competing factors: the autonomy and decline of the University of Khartoum, President Nimeiri's pseudosocialist rule, legal machinations over the switch from a common-law to a civil-law system, and debate in American academic circles over the (lack of) effectiveness of legal development strategies in developing countries.[11] In the early 1960s the Ford Foundation funded one program in Sudan known as the Sudan Law Project. According to its program director, its purpose was to "collect [and compile] the judgments of the Sudan courts."[12] This project helped to develop and finance the publication of the *Sudan Law Journal and Reports* (*SLJR*), an academic journal reserved for the publication of important High Court decisions and law-review articles. The *SLJR* remained as of 2011 the primary court reporter in Sudan. Lasting through the Bashir administration, it has been used to print the legal opinions of High Court judges, along with a limited number of academic articles.

Not only foreign legal assistance, but also other humanitarian forms of aid to Sudan halted in the 1970s as the country headed toward political and economic catastrophe under Nimeiri. (Despite their formal expulsion in 1964 by President Abboud, some missionary societies were able to continue their humanitarian work, particularly through medical clinics and schools in rural areas.) Although President Nimeiri

---

[9] Ford Foundation (2000). *Law: Ford Foundation Grantees and the Pursuit of Justice*, 5.

[10] A memo by James Paul to the Ford Foundation encouraged the foundation to engage in law-and-development interventions in Ethiopia, since it was one of the few areas in the region that the British had not captured. He later became the first dean of the law school at Addis Ababa.

[11] See James A. Gardner, *Legal Imperialism: American Lawyers and Foreign Aid in Latin America* (Madison: University of Wisconsin Press, 1980). See also John Henry Merryman "Comparative Law and Social Change: On the Origins, Style, Decline & Revival of the Law and Development Movement." 25 *American Journal of Comparative Law* (1977): 457–91. See also David M. Trubek and Marc Galanter, "Scholars in Self-Estrangement: Some Reflections on the Crisis and Development Studies in the United States," *Wisconsin Law Review* (1974): 1062–1102.

[12] Telephone interview with former law professor 2 of the University of Khartoum, in East Lansing, Michigan (April 2008).

repeatedly tried to distract the nation from its mounting calamities by advocating adoption of *shari'a*, outside the elite Sudan Bar Association offices in Khartoum, law was not a pressing issue for the new wave of international or Sudanese aid groups.

During the 1980s, Sudan faced repeated economic and humanitarian crises both under Nimeiri and during the short-lived democratic administration that followed. Wild inflation, economic and political instability, and a renewed civil war conspired to make Sudan an inhospitable place for long-term international development for law or human rights, as aid agencies made immediate decisions in response to urgent needs. Between 1984 and 1987, northern Sudan and Darfur experienced devastating droughts, followed by unprecedented rainfall and disastrous flooding in 1988. This series of natural disasters prompted the growth of an indigenous civil society movement focused on providing humanitarian relief. Previously, a diffuse set of civic organizations existed in Sudan, notably trade unions (which had been co-opted under Nimeiri), sports associations, cultural clubs (organized almost exclusively according to national background, including Greek, Syrian, Lebanese, American, and German), religious groups (including a branch of the international Red Crescent Society), and a volunteer-run environmental conservation association that had begun among professors at the University of Khartoum.

Sudan's large-scale humanitarian crises of the 1980s drew the attention of foreign media, aid agencies, and NGOs. Casualties were widely reported, and images of emaciated children in the desert were broadcast throughout the Western world. Aid groups had to rely on Sudanese counterparts with local knowledge to provide them with access to areas where they sought to intervene and to people whom they sought to serve. Sudanese counterparts relied in turn on these aid groups for contractual employment and stable incomes. In the words of one long-time activist, "Most of the local NGOs [in Sudan] started [in order] to respond to some local crisis – food, medical care – since there was no government."[13]

New civic organizations came into existence to accept the influx of capital from abroad, many of them adopting the same crisis-response posture as their funders, addressing immediate needs by setting up health clinics, food delivery centers, water purification systems, and

---

[13] Interview with Lok, civil society network director, in Juba, South Sudan (April 2007).

schools. Aid concentrated on provision of humanitarian relief, particularly in the Darfur famines in 1984–5 and through Operation Lifeline Sudan, an agreement of the Government of Sudan, the Sudan People's Liberation Movement/Army, and the United Nations, to allow humanitarian access to the South during the civil war.[14] In this context of catastrophe civil society in Sudan began to take its contemporary shape by 2011, with direct ties to and funding from abroad in response to humanitarian crises at home.

As soon as President Omar al-Bashir took power in 1989, the Sudanese civil society and international aid community that funded it came under heavy attack. Bashir imprisoned unknown numbers of civil society workers as well as leaders of the bar association. Activists who also held paid governmental positions were fired. Bashir consolidated his power by imposing a unified Islamic law, dismissing judges and government lawyers trained in common law, and limiting the independence of all legal personnel. The Ford Foundation was driven out of Sudan altogether, transferring its operations to Cairo in a move to protect its regional operations shortly after the Bashir government was installed. Without government salaries or funding from international foundations or NGOs, many Sudanese lawyers and civil society activists lucky enough not to be imprisoned either fled the country or went underground.

Largely silenced or exiled by the Bashir regime, many civil society activists who had in the 1980s responded to Sudan's humanitarian crises gradually returned from exile starting around 2004, when it was clear that a peace deal was materializing and the regime would be likely to lift some of its previous restrictions on their activities. These humanitarian activists began to reconstitute themselves as justice activists. They began to integrate their past work in humanitarian relief with new ideals of legal empowerment. The seeds for this later work in law began during their imprisonment or exile in the 1990s. I asked a Sudanese lawyer who facilitates legal-awareness workshops in encampments for internally displaced persons when the idea of promoting the rule of law began to emerge in Sudanese civil society. He said that the earliest work for the rule of law and good governance began around 1992, during the Bashir regime's aggressive posturing against perceived threats

---

[14] For a particularly lucid interpretation of the international community's response to the Darfur famines in the 1980s, see Alex de Waal, *Famine That Kills: Darfur, Sudan*, 2nd ed. (Oxford: Oxford University Press, 2005).

from civil society. "It was … *shari'a*, dictatorial, one rule, one party, one opinion."[15] He said this focus on the rule of law was an organic and local response to escalating government repression, not an idea introduced by the international aid community. But little work could successfully emerge, as Bashir concentrated resources on strengthening the national-security apparatus.

Sudanese activists who fled abroad were exposed to new ideas as they worked in exile to promote the rights of Sudanese. A Sudanese civil society quickly emerged in Cairo, and with it, foreign funding. "I think all the money and organizations that came to Egypt that supported this Sudanese civil society in Cairo were either [focused on Sudanese] culture or [on] legal [issues], human rights, [and] victims of torture."[16] Sudanese civil society activists were not driven by an interest in development, property rights, or investment, but rather by a desire to secure basic human rights to life and freedom of association, movement, and work. Echoing the frustrations of many activists I met, a lawyer complained about the arbitrary nature of authority in Sudan by saying that the regime applies laws as it wishes: "If they want the law to apply to some [people], they apply it" to those people.[17] Returning to Sudan or reemerging from silence after the 2005 peace accords, they believed the rule of law would help strengthen civil society and encourage the government to respect the limits of its power under the law.

While the desire to integrate direct service and legal empowerment originated in part within Sudan's civil society groups, and from the relationships they formed abroad, this change of direction was also necessitated by the sanctions imposed by Western nations against Sudan beginning in the mid-1990s. Bashir's military coup against a democratic administration allied with Western nations, his imprisonment of activists with contacts to Western aid groups, his hospitable policies during the 1990s toward the world's then-most-wanted terrorists including Osama bin Laden, and the brutal civil war against ethnic minorities in southern Sudan led Western governments, particularly the United States, to impose these sanctions on Bashir. Starting in 1997, U.S. sanctions levied against Sudan targeted the government and its burgeoning oil industry. But they also had the effect of leaving Sudanese civil

---

[15] Interview with Zacharia, lawyer and legal awareness workshop facilitator, in Khartoum, Sudan (May 2007).

[16] Interview with Tamir, NGO director, in Khartoum, Sudan (May 2007).

[17] Interview with Shadi, lawyer, in Khartoum, Sudan (April 2007).

society groups in an uncertain position, particularly as more restrictive rounds of sanctions emerged over the following decade. (A later round of U.S. sanctions against Sudan followed in 2008, and sanctions have been extended annually through at least 2013.) While some types of humanitarian relief were still permissible, many activists could no longer ask for funding for development activities such as building schools without running the risk of violating restrictions on economic growth, particularly when the construction of educational institutions or medical clinics could not proceed without local government buy-in (and, typically, payment to local government for permits). Financing human rights awareness and empowerment campaigns began to be a relatively safe alternative, and one the international community ardently encouraged. One longtime women's rights activist in Sudan said:

> All the EU [European Union] countries and the USA [told us] that they can't pay for development activities [anymore] – like building a school, a health center, a women's resource center.... We used to do development [and] income generation activities in rural areas. But now they stopped all developmental activities. We changed our activities in [our] association from a developmental approach to awareness-raising and advocacy activities.[18]

Undertaking these legal development and advocacy activities in Sudan was not without its risks. Organizations involved in promoting human rights and the rule of law not only were forced to cede direct service provision to a host of new organizations affiliated with or tacitly supporting the Bashir regime, giving it fresh advantage in the battle for the hearts and minds of impoverished Sudanese, but were also prime targets of the state's security apparatus throughout the 1990s and 2000s.

The signing of the Comprehensive Peace Agreement (CPA) on January 9, 2005, created a major new opening for foreign and domestic organizations to reengage in legal development and rule-of-law activism, seeking to make direct impacts on the poor and their relationship with government. The agreement ended decades of civil war by creating a six-year transitional government in Khartoum and a semiautonomous government in southern Sudan. Government appointments and national elections, though widely boycotted, helped to position minority parties – including the Sudan People's Liberation Movement,

---

[18] Interview with Nahda, women's rights activist, in Omdurman, Sudan (June 2005).

the political party that would lead South Sudan to its 2011 independence – in Parliament and cabinet positions in Khartoum. The changes set the Bashir regime on its heels for a time, while new aid programs earmarked for Sudan sought to help the nation's poorest to rebuild from the war. As war waned in the South, rapidly increasing hostilities in Darfur as early as 2002 led to an additional influx of aid dollars and programming efforts designed to assist a separate set of war survivors.

Western governments that had signed the 2005 CPA as witnesses were suddenly more likely to be able to obtain permission from the Sudan government to inject new funds into civil society and build the capacity of grassroots groups. Permission was by no means easy to gain (many aid workers complained privately to me of the regime's recalcitrance), but it was typically granted, particularly when foreign groups seemed to focus energy on humanitarian relief and to restrict activities seen as supporting political opposition parties. Representatives from international agencies including the United Nations Development Programme and the newly approved United Nations Mission in Sudan (UNMIS) arrived in the country, hoping to fill what was agreed to be a rule-of-law vacuum by building up the law and people's knowledge of the law. But during this time Bashir remained the country's president and chief decision maker. His tight control of administrative agencies meant that all humanitarian work (by Sudanese or foreign groups) approved by his regime was closely monitored. Aid agencies certainly confronted the Bashir regime and sought to exert pressure on it to respect human rights. But under the auspices of humanitarian relief led by the United Nations and its donors, their efforts focused on financing and building the capacities of civil society agencies that sought to work directly with Sudan's massive population of displaced persons.

SUDANESE CIVIL SOCIETY

The influx of foreign aid and technical support after 2005 greatly altered Sudanese civil society. In 2010, nearly four thousand NGOs were officially registered with the Sudanese government's Humanitarian Aid Commission, up from just a few hundred in 2000.[19] The commission,

---

[19] While precise data from the Humanitarian Aid Commission are not publicly available, these numbers have been separately corroborated by Sudanese sources familiar with the commission's work.

often labeled by Sudanese and expatriates with its English acronym, HAC, is the regime's mechanism for monitoring aid work in the country. According to many sources, this seeming boom in civic activism is actually a construct of the Bashir regime in response to increased foreign aid to civil society groups. The number of organizations that operated independently of government influence hovered somewhere around three hundred, less than 10 percent of the official total. The great majority of newly registered organizations were simply fronts run by loyal members of Bashir's National Congress Party or, in the words of one activist, the "wives of government men."[20] Most were nothing more than a banner and letterhead approved to operate by the regime and existed largely to siphon international donor funds away from independent NGOs that relied on those funds to operate. Said another:

> These government-oriented NGOs take the money. Believe me they do nothing. I'd love to see what they do. Because we never see them around. Only in some meetings they appear. But then when they talk, you feel they are not doing anything. They set up so many NGOs. They knew money was coming, not to government, but to NGOs ... and [the government-oriented NGOs] succeeded [in taking it].[21]

Closer scrutiny reveals that three hundred still probably overestimates the number of independent groups existing in Sudan during the interim between the end of civil war in 2005 and the secession of South Sudan in 2011. Civil society activists tended to operate in small, interconnected circles, and the same names were associated with a number of organizations. With the exception of a few larger groups that have five to ten paid staff, most NGOs were actually just a single person with the vision and determination to write a mission statement. Some individuals single-handedly ran multiple NGOs out of one office or, more commonly, with no office, just a mobile telephone. Many of these organizations formed in direct response to the increase in international funding available for civil society groups, labeled by their funders as their "implementing partners" after the Comprehensive Peace Agreement was signed in 2005. Even the largest organizations were small, with two or three computers, a few dusty filing cabinets, an insubstantial library of English and Arabic texts, and some tables and

---

[20] Interview with Sohir, NGO director, in Khartoum, Sudan (June 2005).
[21] Interview with Najima, NGO founder, in Khartoum, Sudan (February 2007).

Table 5.1. International aid groups in Sudan, 2005–2011, by type

Type of Group	Examples
International/ intergovernmental bodies and financial institutions	United Nations agencies (e.g., FAO, OCHA, UNDP, UNICEF)
	African Union
	European Union
	Arab Bank for Economic Development in Africa
	World Bank
Foreign diplomatic missions and country-sponsored aid programs	U.S. Agency for International Development (USAID)
	German Development Service (Deutscher Entwicklungsdienst, DED; renamed Deutsche Gesellschaft für Internationale Zusammenarbeit, GIZ)
	British Department for International Development (DFID)
	Dutch and Norwegian governments
Foreign or international NGOs	Médecins sans Frontières
	Oxfam
	Save the Children
	Church World Service
	Development Alternatives International (DAI)

Source: Compiled by the author.

chairs. At best, they had intermittent electricity. When I returned in 2010 to organizations I had visited in 2005 and 2006–7, I found that while some had shut down, others had gained additional resources as a result of increased international funding and new staff transferring from international aid organizations expelled by Bashir in 2009. These new hires introduced new ideas for funding and capacities for operations management and proposal writing.

Sudanese NGOs obtain funds from a range of international donors, including intergovernmental bodies, foreign diplomatic missions, country-sponsored aid programs, and large foreign or international nongovernmental organizations (Table 5.1). Under this model, the real work of human rights promotion is outsourced from the foreign aid community to local NGOs. In contrast to older state-centric or economic models of development, this shifts the burden of action from large, bureaucratic institutions to local activists with direct access to target populations.

Precise numbers are difficult to obtain, but informed personnel agree that the vast majority of aid to Sudanese NGOs is dispersed by agencies of the UN, such as the United Nations Population Fund (UNFPA) and

UNDP.[22] Foreign governments or international NGOs fund these UN agencies, which in turn contract with local NGOs to perform projects valued at USD 250,000 or more. The UN agency is responsible for overseeing the work of the local NGOs. Sudanese NGOs are asked to submit reports (almost always in English) outlining their organizations' use of the funds and impact on society. Foreign embassies may also directly fund local NGOs to perform small-scale projects in the range of USD 10,000 to USD 30,000. Because United Nations agencies, the UNDP in particular, tend to operate the most (and most influential) development programs in Sudan, I focus on UN-funded legal-empowerment activities in this analysis.

In addition to NGOs, a handful of self-labeled civil society networks (*shabaqaat*) operate in Sudan.[23] These are umbrella organizations with a small staff of their own who seek to represent a number of separate NGOs working in a specific field such as human rights, civil society development, or the prevention of female genital mutilation. NGOs join such groups in order to be part of the international debates and gain access to calls for funding proposals, which are funneled via the networks from UN agencies to civil society groups. The director of one human rights network explained, "Our network does not implement its activities.... [We] try to get funds from international donors and to fund organizations in our network."[24] Some *shabaqaat* disclose the number of groups they represent – if they have a large number of members, they have more influence when applying for funds or seeking to engage the government on a policy issue. But many keep this information hidden, raising questions about their legitimacy. I asked one leader of a civil society network to see the list of NGOs in his network. The printout he gave me listed nearly seventy Khartoum-based NGOs. But many of these groups had no contact information, and some groups

[22] The UN agencies most active in Sudan by 2011 included the following: Food and Agriculture Organization (FAO), United Nations Office of Crisis and Humanitarian Affairs (OCHA), United Nations Development Programme (UNDP), United Nations Population Fund (UNFPA), United Nations Fund for Women (UNIFEM), and World Food Programme (WFP). This is in addition to two military peacekeeping missions – the United Nations Mission in Sudan (UNMIS) and the United Nations–African Union Mission in Darfur (UNAMID).

[23] Networks are also the names attached by informal groups of civil society activists to their work in the same field, when they meet sporadically to strategize or share experiences – for example, lawyers who work in human rights or environmental preservation.

[24] Interview with Ahmed, lawyer, in Khartoum, Sudan (November 2006).

carried the same contact information. According to several NGO leaders, some of the *shabaqaat* have been co-opted by government-oriented (in some cases, government-run) NGOs, sometimes labeled by the acronym "GONGO."

> These are not organizations [in the network]. They are just names. One of them, we met him in the registration process, he was a staff member in the Humanitarian Aid Commission! He – one of the government members in HAC – has an NGO! [Laughs]. So this was our experience with networks. We are no longer in any of the networks.[25]

It is common for self-proclaimed civil society activists to have multiple, sometimes competing roles as they try to balance their activism with their need to earn a living. I met many civil society activists in Khartoum, Juba, and El Obeid who also work as low-level or midlevel government bureaucrats. Government jobs provide a guaranteed, if meager, monthly income. Most NGOs are unable to provide regular salaries to their workers because these organizations rely on project-specific funding that is often doled out by the United Nations only on the basis of documented expenditures. Independent activist lawyers also accept a wide range of private cases in order to underwrite their legal aid and human rights work.

An elite group of educated English-speaking Sudanese is employed as full-time "national staff" by international NGOs, embassies, or United Nations agencies. While Sudanese national staff sometimes earn as little as one-tenth what expatriate staff earn, the monthly pay is much higher than at local NGOs and is guaranteed for the duration of an employment contract. In some cases, these jobs provide opportunities for Sudanese to travel and work abroad and to participate in periodic conferences and networking events sponsored by international aid organizations.

RIGHTS-BASED DEVELOPMENT PROGRAMS

During the decades when aid work had largely stalled in Sudan, the international aid community had begun to embrace a new approach to legal development in postconflict settings, transitional democracies, and unstable states. Known as a rights-based approach to development, it is founded on a normative concept of universal human rights. The

[25] Interview with Najima, NGO founder, in Khartoum, Sudan (February 2007).

approach was articulated as early as 2001 by Mary Robinson, then the UN high commissioner for human rights, as

> a conceptual framework for the process of human development that is normatively based on international human rights standards and operationally directed to promoting and protecting human rights. The rights-based approach integrates the norms, standards and principles of the international human rights system into the plans, policies and processes of development.[26]

When minimal access to Sudan was finally possible, what foreign governments and aid agencies had to offer were legal interventions designed to educate oppressed individuals about conceptions of human rights and the rule of law circulating in international aid groups and the UN system.[27]

[26] Presidential Fellow's Lecture by Mary Robinson, United Nations high commissioner for human rights, to the World Bank, on December 3, 2001, "Bridging the Gap between Human Rights and Development: from Normative Principles to Operational Relevance," Available: http://www.unhchr.ch/Huricane/Huricane. nsf/60a520ce334aaa77802566100031b4bf/2da59cd3ffc033dcc1256b1a0033f7c 3?OpenDocument (accessed January 9, 2013). In a UN Security Council report (2004), former UN secretary-general Kofi Annan called on all UN agencies to adopt such an approach, one that Ban Ki-moon continues to implement, based on a 2003 interagency statement of common understanding of the rights-based approach. See UNICEF (2004) "The Human Rights-Based Approach: Statement of Common Understanding," in *State of the World's Children (Annex B)*. Available: http://www.unicef.org/sowc04/sowc04_annexes.html (accessed January 9, 2013). See also United Nations Development Programme and United Nations Population Fund (2007) *Regional Program Document 2008–11: Latin America and the Caribbean*, New York: United Nations; and Arbour, Louise (2008) "Foreword," in *Claiming the Millennium Development Goals: A Human Rights Approach*. HR/PUB/08/3. Geneva: United Nations Office of the High Commissioner for Human Rights, http://www. unhcr.org/refworld/docid/49fac1162.html (accessed January 9, 2013). See also UNICEF, "Human Rights Based Approach: Statement of Common Understanding among UN Agencies" (also published as Annex B in State of the World's Children 2004). See also United Nations Development Fund for Women, "CEDAW and the Human Rights Based Approach to Programming: A UNIFEM Guide." The UN is not alone, as foreign aid agencies also deploy similar rights-based approaches using a common language. See Rosalin Eybin, "How to Make a Rights-Based Approach to Development Work: A DFID Perspective" (Lecture to the Overseas Development Initiative, on file with author).

[27] The Ford Foundation published a book of its international funding of law-related interventions, Mary McClymont and Stephen Golub, eds., *Many Roads to Justice: The Law-Related Work of Ford Foundation Grantees around the World* (Ford

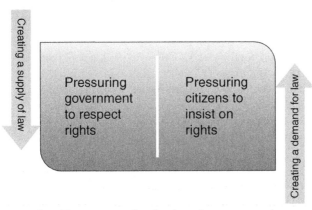

Figure 5.1. Humanitarian legal politics by promoting law to government and to citizens.
Source: Author.

Rights-based development activities in Sudan can be divided into two types: supply-oriented and demand-oriented programs (Figure 5.1). Supply-side initiatives seek to increase the capacity of government personnel to abide by international human rights norms. They provide training for judges, police, and prison administrators regarding broad legal issues. For judges and police, sessions may focus on the rights of the accused, while for newly appointed legislators, sessions may offer technical assistance on drafting laws that are consistent with human rights treaties. Demand-oriented initiatives seek to foster a grassroots sense of entitlement to basic human rights. Such programs are intended to stimulate the political consciousness necessary for a people to demand their own liberation.[28] The programs assume that not only does a vacuum of law exist, but a vacuum of *knowledge about* law exists as well.

Foundation, 2000), citing legal activism, public interest litigation, and the work of nonlawyers acting as legal resources, in such diverse places as China, Chile, Bangladesh, and Eastern Europe. See also *Pathways to Justice: Access to Justice with a Focus on Poor, Women, and Indigenous Peoples* (United Nations Development Programme Cambodia, 2006). In Section 1.2.2, in defining implications of a "human rights-based approach" for access to justice in postconflict settings such as Cambodia, the report labels access to justice as a "right" (30). The report also argues that Cambodian citizens fail to express their social needs because of a "lack of rights awareness" (37). Section 2.2 describes the 477-page report's "human rights–based" methodological approach.

[28] See Mark Fathi Massoud, "Do Victims of War Need International Law? Human Rights Education Programs in Authoritarian Sudan," 45 *Law & Society Review* (2011): 9.

Educating oppressed people to be aware of and fluent in the language of human rights, so the theory goes, will provide them the impetus and tools necessary to make real claims against their governments.

Between 2005 and 2010, the United Nations Development Programme's operations in Sudan directed approximately USD 60 million toward top-down legal development, roughly divided between supply-side institutional activities and demand-side justice and human rights programs. Supply-side efforts comprised giving direct support to the judiciaries of northern Sudan (USD 5 million) and southern Sudan (USD 4.6 million, including the Southern Sudan Ministry of Legal Affairs and Constitutional Development) and developing the police and prison infrastructure of southern Sudan (USD 19 million). Demand-side activities included "access to justice" and "strengthening the rule of law" programs (USD 20.5 million in northern Sudan including Darfur; USD 11 million in southern Sudan).[29]

Considerable supply-side development activities have targeted governmental institutions such as courts. Judges are seen as vessels of the rule of law and protectors of private-property rights and personal freedoms. Academic studies of rule-of-law aid have similarly focused on the aid community's work with judges, legislators, and governmental institutions to achieve their broader development goals.[30] In Sudan, for example, a range of internationally funded judicial-training programs has taken place. I met a variety of private consultants who trained judges from the Supreme Court of Sudan in Khartoum, or the Supreme Court of South Sudan in Juba. The consultants stay in the country for a few days to a few months and offer training on technical legal issues and the content of international human rights treaties. Other judges travel abroad when their schedules permit, often to Europe. Sudan's presidentially appointed Constitutional Court, for instance, was designed with its own technical bureau and training department to provide continuing education courses to justices.[31] Some justices

---

[29] Financial data have been accessed from project scope documents made public by UNDP Sudan. Available: http://www.sd.undp.org/focus_democratic_governance. htm (accessed January 9, 2013).

[30] See, e.g., Amanda Perry Kessaris, *Law in the Pursuit of Development: Principles into Practice?* New York: Routledge (2010). See also Stephen Humphreys, *Theatre of the Rule of Law: Transnational Legal Intervention in Theory and Practice* (Cambridge: Cambridge University Press, 2010).

[31] Under the terms of Sudan's 2005 Interim National Constitution, Sudan's "presidency" that appointed the Court was constituted as a single office of three

have had the opportunity to work with American and European professors at the Max Planck Institute for Comparative Public Law and International Law, in Heidelberg, Germany. As part of a "Global Knowledge Transfer" project funded by the European Commission, the German Ministry of Foreign Affairs, and the Norwegian government, the institute has been working since 2002 to support "constitutional development ... by offering its legal advice and professional training" to judges and state officials in Sudan and other countries.[32] Scholars at the institute helped draft Sudan's 2005 Interim National Constitution and, after the Constitution went into force, held a series of workshops in Germany with high-ranking Sudanese officials, including Sudan's Constitutional Court justices, Supreme Court judges, advocate general, and Ministry of Justice employees. Training sessions focused on alerting Sudanese justices to the types of disputes that may go before the Constitutional Court and helping them think about how these issues relate to Sudanese and international laws.[33] One judge who attended the sessions in Heidelberg told me the course was "very helpful" and "very effective" in honing the legal skills of Sudanese judicial personnel.[34]

But heavy criticism has also been directed at these interventions. A foreign law professor who drafted sections of Sudan's Interim National Constitution and trained judges throughout the region remarked that mock exercises in the training sessions do not respect the decades of judicial experience that participants have in carefully deciding complex cases within a multiplicity of legal systems and in the context of heavy-handed regimes. He said this gap between the trainers and participants results in judges or officials who "don't latch onto these kinds of [trainings]. It's a mixture of 'We don't want to' and 'We can't.'"[35]

persons. These were President Omar Hassan al-Bashir; first vice president Salva Kiir Mayardit, who succeeded John Garang after his death in 2005; and second vice president Ali Osman Mohamed Taha. Bashir held final authority for all decisions within the presidency.

[32] "Sudan Peace Project." Max Planck Institute for Comparative Public Law and International Law. Available: http://www.mpil.de/ww/en/pub/research/details/know_transfer/africa_projects/sudan_peace_project.cfm (accessed January 9, 2013).

[33] Clemens Feinäugle, Tilmann Röder, Verena Wiesner, eds., *Max Planck Compilation of The Papers and Proceedings of the Heidelberg Seminar on Potential Disputes Before the Sudanese Constitutional Court*, Max Planck Institute for Comparative Public Law and International Law (2006, draft on file with author).

[34] Interview with senior judicial official 1, in Khartoum Sudan (December 2006).

[35] Interview with law professor and judicial-training consultant, in England (September 2006).

The long-term effects of judicial-training programs in general remain to be seen. Lawyers in Sudan have decried the inconsistent nature of court rulings. "It's so bad," concluded one lawyer.[36] He went on to say that the training sessions are "not going to lead anywhere" because of the complexity of Sudanese law and suggested that Sudanese persons, not foreigners, conduct them. Even the brightest Sudanese lawyers have difficulty understanding Sudan's confounding pluralistic and politicized legal traditions, making it unclear how European or American professors even less conversant with Sudan's multilayered justice system can presume to be of help.[37]

Significant and less-documented legal development work in Sudan focuses on the demand side by seeking to build awareness and capacity among disadvantaged populations. The three most common demand-side activities are conducting legal awareness workshops, training "paralegals," and building grassroots justice centers. Despite minimal reporting of these efforts, they constituted about half of UNDP's USD 60 million rule-of-law spending in Sudan between 2005 and 2010.

International aid groups have funded Sudanese NGOs to conduct legal awareness workshops for residents in the encampments around Khartoum where survivors of war have been displaced. More than any other legal intervention, these workshops exemplify the logic of demand-side legal development: if people understand their rights, they can mobilize to demand those rights from government officials. According to one Sudanese workshop facilitator, "If you spread knowledge among a lot of people, and the people are aware of their rights, then they begin to practice, it becomes a challenge for our justice system."[38]

I observed fifteen legal awareness workshops in camps for war-displaced persons and remote villages outside Khartoum. Participants gather in thatched-roof community centers, one-room schools, and dilapidated health clinics. Workshops tend to last three to eight days, and sessions are held mostly from 1:00 p.m. to 5:00 p.m., so that those who commute to urban centers for work do not sacrifice a full day's pay to attend. Sandwiches and soft drinks are provided by facilitators at the

---

[36] Follow-up interview with Mansour, lawyer and former government minister, in Khartoum, Sudan (June 2010).

[37] Ibid.

[38] Interview with Sohir, NGO director, in Khartoum, Sudan (June 2005).

start (or, at times, the end) of each session, and there is usually a tea break midway.

The trainers are either staff members of a Sudanese NGO or independent lawyers or activists under contract with an NGO. Many NGOs facilitate dozens of workshops a month for hundreds of participants. NGOs rarely select the participants themselves. Rather, they work with local community leaders who select participants, with the stipulation that at least half be women. Community leaders often nominate themselves and members of well-known families in the community. In order to broaden their reach, some workshops are billed as "training-of-trainers" workshops to encourage attendees to share the knowledge with others.

One major topic is covered on each day of the workshop. The range of topics for each day's workshops is diverse; they include international law (human rights and women's rights under the Universal Declaration of Human Rights and the Convention on the Elimination of All Forms of Discrimination against Women, or CEDAW), constitutional law (the Interim National Constitution and its Bill of Rights), the Comprehensive Peace Agreement, nonviolence, and peace building. Despite the lack of resources, the workshops have the look and feel of an educational setting – a classroom, a teacher, and a curriculum. The NGO provides pens, paper, and an easel. The facilitator stands in front of the room near the easel, and participants sit on iron benches or stiff-backed chairs facing the facilitator. While there is some lecturing, the workshops are meant to be interactive. A facilitator will lead brainstorming sessions by dividing the class into small groups that meet and then report their responses to the entire class. Discussion questions are broad and open-ended: "What does the constitution mean to you?" "What is democracy?" "What are democratic values?" Although discussions can be quite theoretical, some of the information included in the workshops is directly relevant to the lives of displaced survivors of war. For example, the workshops teach them that they have the right to consult a lawyer if they are arrested. The final day of a workshop is customarily dedicated to an informal graduation ceremony in which participants receive certificates of participation, sing and dance, and speak about what they will do with what they have learned.

NGOs often face real challenges in accessing target populations. For example, in order to conduct workshops at Sudan's largest women's prison, Omdurman Prison, NGO activists I met who were seeking to conduct legal-empowerment interventions had to gain entry by providing humanitarian aid. Omdurman is a densely populated city just across the White Nile river from Khartoum. Because many inmates are either nursing or pregnant when they are arrested, the prison population includes many infants. But Omdurman Prison is responsible only for feeding its inmates. To alleviate the crisis, activists offered to provide food for the inmates' children. "We tried to get [the prison guards'] trust by giving meals to children, by doing humanitarian work," said the coordinator of the program. "Then we started legal aid."[39]

A manager with the NGO said, "Sometimes you can go to the Omdurman Prison and ask the women [about their experiences]. Some of the women – a great number of them – they don't know why they are in prison. They are totally ignorant of the law and why they have been caught."[40] In the sense that the workshops helped the women demystify their own predicament, they were extremely popular. The prisoners began "critically analyzing" Sudanese laws and their own sentences.[41] But when a news article appeared in Sudan that discussed the training, the prison's warden directed the NGO to stop or face removal.[42] The organization responded with a threat of its own. The coordinator told the warden that if he pulled the plug on their legal-empowerment operation, the NGO would stop all of its work in the prison, including providing food for the inmates' babies. "When they threatened us, we said ... we will not feed the children, and they will die."[43] Without the public resources to feed the infants, rather than risk broader exposure of the conditions in his prison, the warden acquiesced to the NGO's demands.

A second popular legal development approach among NGOs in Sudan is training small groups of residents in rural or impoverished areas where there are no lawyers to act as lay attorneys, or "paralegals." These training sessions are an offshoot of the legal awareness workshops. Instead of focusing on broad principles, these courses aim to teach participants the basics of criminal law and procedure. People learn how to file basic court documents, such as bail papers, and how to advocate on behalf of individuals subjected to arrest for common offenses, such as brewing and selling alcohol. The hope is that with

[39] Interview with Samira, NGO director, in Khartoum, Sudan (June 2005).

[40] Interview with Abdullah, NGO program manager, in Khartoum, Sudan (June 2005).

[41] Ibid.

[42] Interview with Waleeda, Legal Aid Advocate, in Khartoum, Sudan (June 2005).

[43] Interview with Samira, NGO director, in Khartoum, Sudan (June 2005).

sufficient knowledge, paralegals will help prevent arbitrary arrests of war-displaced persons by the police and help connect disadvantaged Sudanese with actual lawyers in serious cases.

I asked a number of paralegal activists why they felt it was so important to learn and teach the nuances of legal procedure. One nonlawyer said,

> It is very important to have … legal awareness because the [Sudanese] people are … ignorant about their rights, even sometimes [getting arrested for] crimes that they didn't know [were crimes]. I'm not a lawyer, but I'm involved [because] legal work can be done by non-legal personnel. This is why I train paralegals.... People should know about … the law.[44]

A Sudanese lawyer who has trained hundreds of displaced persons to act as paralegals in Darfur said that such training is an effective strategy for grassroots empowerment. "The cases of IDPs [internally displaced persons] are not complicated. You don't need lawyers. You don't need these Latin words, or English words. It's simple. Everyone can do it."[45]

The third major demand-side program to encourage legal development in Sudan focuses on creating a network of justice centers in major towns and encampments for displaced persons throughout Sudan. Labeled "Justice and Confidence Centers," they have been built inside crisis zones in Darfur and in postconflict settings in southern Sudan where civil war raged for decades. Between 2004 and 2006, fourteen such centers were constructed as part of a national "Legal Aid Network" funded by UNDP.[46] The resources available vary from center to center, but the centers are meant to be places where individuals can access library materials, use the Internet, and speak with volunteer paralegals about legal matters. The centers are often housed in rented buildings. Some are new constructions, depending on available funds and location. They are typically run by volunteer Sudanese staff supervised by a foreign aid contractor (usually a program officer with an international NGO that

[44] Interview with Sohir, NGO director, in Khartoum, Sudan (June 2005).

[45] Interview with Maher, legal aid attorney, in Khartoum, Sudan (June 2005).

[46] Aicha Elbasri, "Working toward Equal Access to Justice for All: The Legal Aid Network Launched in Sudan," Joint Press Release of the United Nations Development Programme, People's Legal Aid Center, International Rescue Committee, and Ministry of Justice Legal Aid Department, Khartoum, Sudan (March 14, 2007). Available: www.sd.undp.org/Presspdf/launchoflegalaidnetwork-inSudan.pdf (accessed January 9, 2013).

received funds from UNDP to set up the center). Drop-in legal assistance is provided at the centers, sometimes by attorneys, though more often by nonattorney paralegals. They conduct legal-awareness-raising workshops related to human rights, voting, domestic violence, or women's rights. Other workshops focus on English-language legal terminology or on management skills. Given the international aid community's overarching interest in human rights, centers have strongly emphasized helping victims file human rights complaints.

In 2007 and again in 2010, I visited the Justice and Confidence Center in Juba, the regional capital of southern Sudan before South Sudan's independence. The center was established following the 2005 Comprehensive Peace Agreement, under the direction of an international NGO funded by the United Nations Development Programme. With the Juba center, the NGO also sponsored the creation of a "rule-of-law promotion" group, supervised by NGO staff and made up of volunteer Sudanese community leaders, including a pastor and a teacher. The group sought to solicit and document human rights grievances in the community and, if possible, to provide assistance for addressing those grievances.

Looking at the activities and outcomes of the Juba Center over a three-year period, it is clear that the project's success has been hampered by a preoccupation with human rights. On both of my visits, volunteers said that they received few complaints of human rights abuses but instead received a large number of mundane labor and employment claims or requests for legal assistance with property titles. (Landownership issues surfaced after the end of the civil war, as people returned to their homes only to find them occupied by new residents who held titles that were in many cases sold illegally during the war.) Rather than help people with their immediate needs and then shift the conversation to human rights, Juba Center leaders were unable to assist people with property claims and thus generally declined to do so. While the volunteers dutifully held weekly meetings on Wednesday afternoons to plan workshops for local sultans and church leaders on human rights, the center's connection to the larger community was limited. An expatriate representative of the international NGO overseeing the Juba Center acknowledged its shortcomings:

> What hasn't taken off is people coming to the ... center as such. People with money, who could afford a lawyer, have come, saying they need legal advice. [But they are not our target groups.] A State

Assembly person came by, but he's someone with more means. We want indigenous populations.[47]

In 2010, I asked the volunteers to describe their successes during the previous three years. They said that more people were aware of the center and that more unique visitors were coming in each week. They also said that they had begun providing limited assistance with property and labor and employment claims, in some cases by walking people to the labor office or local court. But they had been unable to convince their foreign backers to sponsor an on-site attorney or to purchase vehicles to help take people to relevant government offices.

Most strategic, budgetary, and policy decisions in these humanitarian-inspired legal development programs are made by non-Sudanese bureaucrats in international aid agencies, though local Sudanese personnel are arguably in a better position to determine what sort of outreach will be most effective. Among other consequences, this arrangement creates an incentive for local NGOs to shift their approach and rhetoric to suit donor interests. I encountered volunteers with various environmental protection organizations, for example, who were conducting legal awareness workshops in encampments for displaced persons, despite the tangential connection to their organizations' core missions. A large health organization I visited links legal awareness workshops with food and medicine delivery to the desert camps; doing so generates additional funding to help them promote health and empowerment. Some local NGOs look for ways to respond to the urgent humanitarian needs of displaced persons, while still leveraging the international community's passion for rights-based legal development.

Sudanese NGOs abide by this arrangement for two reasons: because they must and because they believe. Most Sudanese NGOs rely on Western donor nations and aid groups for operating funds, so they preach the requisite gospel of rights-based development. It is not an exaggeration to say that Sudan's most important independent NGOs would cease to exist without international support. According to Sudanese civil society activists, there are several reasons why NGOs must rely on international rather than domestic donations. The director of one human rights organization explained:

> We don't have this culture of NGOs funded by governments. The community is poor. And the [executives] here with big companies

[47] Interview with Sebastian, North American lawyer and aid worker, in Juba, South Sudan (April 2007).

have no interest to support civil society. They're not intellectuals, just merchants and businessmen. What good will it do them to make a donation? If you've got money, [the government] will facilitate your business. But if you give civil society the money, it won't help your business.[48]

Another local leader replied tersely, when asked why sophisticated Sudanese NGOs get their funding from outside the country, "Because to get it inside, you have to be pro-government."[49]

While funding is a critical motivator and legal development a logical route given the existence of international sanctions, many activists I met also support the priorities of their international backers. They have come to share their funders' faith that the law will save Sudan's poor and oppressed and firmly believe that building awareness of human rights is essential for Sudan's liberation from oppression. They believe that the law never really existed at all for the poor in Sudan and that introducing it through judicial training, legal empowerment workshops, legal assistance centers, and new prison architecture will modernize Sudan and its population. For adherents to the rights-first ideology, running the workshops, conducting the trainings, and constructing the justice centers are the best ways to engage with target populations. "There were some in [our NGO] who wanted to [write] reports on humans rights ... documenting cases of violence," said one human rights trainer. "But to us, that is meaningless. We want to teach people their rights. These are the basic essentials in life."[50]

CONCLUSION

The preceding description of the history and current trends of Sudanese civil society makes clear that legal politics has long been a central focus in efforts to promote peace and stability in Sudan. From the colonial era through Bashir's consolidation of power in the 1990s, Sudanese civil society activists and those abroad who have sought to educate them have regarded the rule of law as a touchstone for their ideological and strategic approaches. And with a set of international sanctions in place that privilege human rights promotion over other types of programs,

[48] Interview with Daoud, lawyer and NGO director, in Khartoum, Sudan (November 2006).
[49] Interview with Sunduq, NGO executive director, in Khartoum, Sudan (November 2006).
[50] Interview with Intisar, lawyer, in Khartoum, Sudan (December 2006).

civil society has increasingly become committed to and centered on a rights-based model of legal politics and development.

Building on the descriptive data provided here, the next chapter attempts a preliminary analysis of the progress and potential of humanitarian legal politics in Sudan. Charged with the monumental tasks of empowering a truly destitute and traumatized population and toppling a ruthless and sophisticated authoritarian regime, both Sudanese civil society and the international aid community are averse to asking whether rights-based politics is actually capable of achieving results. While local NGOs must produce progress reports for funders on their activities, in the English language, with which they have limited capacity, these studies are narrow in scope and often ignored. Little big-picture analytical work has been done to understand the consequences of rights-based programs in Sudan or within authoritarian states in general. In the next chapter, I address the conceptual and practical difficulties of pursuing a rights-first approach to humanitarian legal politics and provide a preliminary account of its intended and unintended consequences in a war-wracked, authoritarian state.

CHAPTER 6

HUMANITARIAN LEGAL POLITICS IN AN AUTHORITARIAN STATE, 2005–2011

ignorance

INTRODUCTION

The international aid community's promotion of law as a form of development, particularly in volatile states, comes from a sincere desire to empower some of the world's most downtrodden people. But it is based largely on a conception of rights and a theory of political empowerment that may have limited applicability for the poor in Sudan. One of the most significant factors in determining the success of any international development initiative is whether it is created with a clear understanding of a recipient country's specific political, social, and cultural realities and tailored to fit that unique local context. More often than not, foreign aid groups develop a single programmatic template and then try to use it across many different locations.

In 2005, I attended a workshop for Sudanese civil society activists in Khartoum, sponsored by the United Nations Mission in Sudan. The workshop took place shortly after the signing of the Comprehensive Peace Agreement that ended the Sudanese civil war earlier that year. The UN had just approved the peacekeeping mission to enforce the ceasefire. At the workshop, a senior UN official explained the mission's core goals in English to the Sudanese attendees. The representative lectured about the need for postconflict governments to sign international human rights treaties and submit themselves to the authority of international law. When the talk was over, a Sudanese woman sitting next to me turned her head and shook it. She told me the presentation was not relevant for the people of Sudan. I understood what she meant: the speaker had mentioned Sudan twice in thirty minutes and seemed ignorant of the fact that Sudan had already ratified major human rights treaties in the 1980s, including both the International Covenant on Civil and Political Rights and the International Covenant on Economic, Social, and Cultural Rights. Bashir's government also ratified the Convention on the Rights of the Child in 1991, even as it was systematically attacking the legal profession in Sudan. The UN official also mentioned specific human rights provisions that should be included in a "new constitution" without acknowledging that a new constitution had just been adopted in Sudan, that the terms of the ceasefire granted the Comprehensive Peace Agreement legal supremacy over any constitution, or that a new civil war was raging in Darfur. To some of the Sudanese activists present, the neatly packaged PowerPoint presentation was so general in its scope and its off-the-shelf platitudes that it had little or no connection to their daily experiences of authoritarian rule under the Bashir regime.

As described in the previous chapter, nonstate actors in Sudan have focused a great deal of attention on building up Sudan's legal infrastructure, particularly after the signing of peace accords in 2005. But demand-oriented forms of humanitarian legal politics – aimed at empowering and inspiring the poor to accept and use legal discourses like human rights – achieved at best limited success in the face of the preexisting and formidable authoritarian legal politics in Sudan. Aid programs were rarely tailored to the Sudanese context, and the narratives of law and rights they used reoriented and segmented the experiences of war-displaced persons from those of the civil society elites working with foreign partners and sponsors. The two pillars of humanitarian legal politics in Sudan have been a concept of human rights rooted in political liberalism and the power of rights to alleviate the suffering of the poor. But legal-awareness-raising activities in Sudan repeatedly disregarded, or at times fundamentally conflicted with, varying local conceptions of rights and of the role of the individual in society.

The portrayal of rights as inherently transformative was largely unconvincing to the poor in Sudan, who faced a daily reality rooted in authoritarian legal politics, including monitoring and questioning by police and security officers under the Bashir regime. While the merits of humanitarian legal politics are certainly real, the beneficial impacts of the interventions flow from their side effects and not from the core content of human rights themselves. Rights talk segregated civil society activists, who used the language of rights to create abstractions out of specific problems, from the impoverished persons they assisted, who narrated their problems and needs in more concrete ways.[1] In this way, human rights become an attractive discourse for domestic civil society elites and their funders engaging in humanitarian legal politics in an authoritarian context, but not for poor people whom those elites purport to represent. Rights talk ultimately may expose both groups – civil society elites and the poor – to dangerous risks under an authoritarian regime threatened by domestic criticism.

In this chapter, I first discuss challenges faced by promoters of humanitarian legal politics in a state in which significant forms of authoritarian legal politics already exist. One of the primary challenges is a philosophical disconnect between the different understandings of rights among elites and the poor in Sudan, affecting the endurance of humanitarian forms of legal politics. I then enumerate some of the consequences of humanitarian legal politics in the country. I conclude that an approach to legal politics rooted in rights discourse provides important material and symbolic benefits to those who accept it. But it also faces great challenges to achieving the long-term political goal of shifting the balance of power in war-ravaged states like Sudan.

CONTEMPORARY HUMANITARIAN LEGAL POLITICS AT WORK

As I witnessed them in Sudan, development programs aimed at training the poor to be aware of their rights were rooted in Western political liberalism and rights theory. Human rights were seen as the basic rights, freedoms, and protections to which all people are entitled simply by virtue of their being human, regardless of race, ethnic group, sex, religion, or other identities. Implicit in this concept of universally held natural rights was an emphasis on the individual as primary and sufficient and on the state as the exclusive actor with the obligation to protect those universal rights. In this way, human rights constituted a set of legal rules that bind state actors, ultimately disrupting the sovereignty those actors would otherwise enjoy by aiming to punish their conduct that violates international law.[2]

---

[1] See also Harri Englund "Towards a Critique of Rights Talk in New Democracies: The Case of Legal Aid in Malawi," 15 *Discourse and Society* (2004): 527–51.

[2] See also Richard Claude and Burns H. Weston, *Human Rights and the World Community: Issues and Action* (Philadelphia: University of Pennsylvania Press, 2006), p. 4.

This perception of human rights animating contemporary aid programs presumes that a state exists, and it creates in that state an affirmative duty to protect the dignity of the person. On their best behavior, state actors – including elected (and unelected) officials, police, and judges – not only would respect human dignity, but also would do so because of a perceived obligation to international human rights.[3]

But human rights occupy a contested terrain in international relations and in the relations between states and their citizens. For vociferous critics of the notion that human rights constitute legal rules, human rights are seen as a set of norms, guiding principles, or rhetorical propositions that at best have little if any influence over the decisions that states make.[4] For that reason, when states fail to respect human rights, the burden of protecting those rights begins to shift from the state violator to the violated individual – or his or her family, advocates, and supporters – to publicize the state's failures and create an agenda for change.

Humanitarian forms of legal politics stem from a conception of rights that follows a model known as "framing and shaming." Nonstate actors such as activists and NGOs build awareness of the discourse of individual human rights among indigenous populations so they may use that rhetoric to frame grievances and shame repressive governments into compliance with human rights norms. By publicizing human rights abuses through the media or contact with international aid groups, they hope that recalcitrant governments will be moved to save face by demonstrating a respect for human rights.[5]

Several conditions pertain where these Western-led frame-and-shame initiatives are most effective. First is a functioning government. In order to mobilize people to make human rights claims, a government must be present to petition. The state must also be stable enough and sensitive enough to respond to grievances other than with obfuscation, delay, or repression. Second, the government must be susceptible to pressure from domestic and/or international public opinion. Without that, there is no capacity to create shame. Third,

---

[3] See Harold Hongju Koh, "How Is International Human Rights Law Enforced?" 47 *Indiana Law Review* (1999): 1397–1417.

[4] See Jack Goldsmith and Eric Posner, *The Limits of International Law* (Oxford: Oxford University Press, 2005).

[5] See Margaret E. Keck and Kathryn Sikkink, *Activists beyond Borders: Advocacy Networks in International Politics* (Ithaca, NY: Cornell University Press, 1998).

the people must be willing to believe that embracing a concept of individually held rights will lead to material change in their daily lives or a net reduction in their suffering. But to the extent that individual determination is its goal, the internal logic of humanitarian legal politics tends to collapse when individuals identify with the collective above all else.

On a summer day in 2005, the temperature well above 50 degrees Celsius, I met with a group of women in a small tent in an encampment for displaced persons in the desert about an hour's drive from Khartoum. They had agreed to talk with me about their lives and their exposure to aid agencies (Sudanese and foreign) that had visited their community. During our conversation, I asked what they knew of "human rights." One of the women nodded and shrugged her shoulders. She turned and looked away. It was as if I had asked her what she thought about the planet Mars. "If I haven't seen an apple, then I won't know what it is," explained a Sudanese lawyer I later met, when asked about conceptions of law and rights in the country. "If I haven't seen rights, then I won't know what they are."[6]

Among the Sudanese I met – the people displaced by decades of war, the residents of tent cities who survive daily exposure to the excruciating Saharan heat – rights did not seem obvious, inalienable, or conferred upon every individual. Their conception of rights seemed to be shaped by their experiences of authoritarian legal politics; of oppression, violence, and chaos at the hands of the state military and non-state militias; and by a deep connection to religion as the source of their convictions. Sudanese lawyers versed in common law, intellectuals educated abroad, and civil society activists trained by foreign aid groups often expressed to me a different view of rights and liberties, rooted not in the ills of violence or the salvation of religion but in the belief that the state both has obligations to its citizens and – with greater awareness and stable or democratic political development – the capacity to meet those obligations. But outside this intelligentsia based in Khartoum (and in Juba after the war) local conceptions of rights seemed largely incompatible with this model. This is not to say that displaced persons did not understand human rights laws or treaties; many of them, particularly those educated in legal awareness workshops, had a sophisticated understanding of the core concepts of human rights and democracy, just as their trainers had intended. But those I met did not

---

[6] Interview with Yoosef, legal aid attorney, in Khartoum, Sudan (June 2005).

trust in the secular rights concept of humanitarian legal politics, shared with them by their teachers, that promoting a belief in international human rights treaties would eventually result in a change in the state's behavior toward them or end their suffering.

None of the impoverished Sudanese I met spoke about rights guaranteed by the government as an inherent part of their personhood. A universal conception of natural rights that underlies much of modern international human rights discourse largely did not seem to exist among the displaced persons I met in Sudan. For them, rights are bestowed as a result of full membership in a community or of submission to religious faith, not by virtue of being an individual or of relying on the government. Many of the religious, communal, and non-state-centric aspects of daily life are rooted in Sudan's history of diversity and in its deep-rooted ethnic cleavages, both in the context of a weak state struggling to stabilize itself. Much of rural (and urban) experience in Sudan is still oriented to the family or ethnic group, rather than around the individual's relationship to the state as international rights-based approaches would expect.

Certainly individuals have worked for decades within their local communities and accessed the local courts promoted by Bashir or previous administrations to resolve their disputes (often related to private property and involving marriage dissolution, inheritance disagreements, or theft). These kinds of legal cases are important because they shape the state's relationship with its citizenry and its capacity to exert authority through legal strategies.

But accessing the courts in these private disputes is largely unconnected to the concept of human rights, and doing so has not translated into a broader expectation that the government would protect people from public harms such as torture or provide them with clean food and water. Said one young man born into the civil war in the South, "The army has all the power to decide" someone's fate.[7] In this context, people have little hope that courts of law or that the discourse of rights imparted to them by aid donors and local activists will help them when guns seem to matter as much as the law, and when the regime controls the legal system. Aid workers are also well aware of this detachment of rights from reality: "Human rights means holding government actors

[7] Interview with Lok, civil society network director, in Juba, South Sudan (April 2007).

and institutions accountable, but the [Bashir government] has used these institutions to oppress this place."[8]

The gulf between the laudable philosophical goals of humanitarian legal politics and the reality of authoritarian legal politics in daily life in Sudan has practical consequences for local or national political mobilization. For example, while urban Sudanese commonly resort to Bashir's courts to resolve property-related disputes, it is taboo – and dangerous – to bring a human-rights claim against an arm of the government. Said one lawyer of human rights, "We never [use] those words [in court]. There's no way you can [safely] mention them."[9] A civil society activist echoed these comments: "If you said 'human rights,' that's when you are in a problem with [Sudanese state] security…. You're assumed automatically to have a link with the outside world."[10]

Even more confounding to Western development programs is the particular way religion has come to be practiced in Sudan. For many Sudanese whom I met, rights are not inalienable standards guaranteed by the state. Instead, rights are from God.[11] Thus, when rights are provided, it is through the will of God, not the state. When rights are limited or nonexistent, it is also through the will of God, not the state. The loss of rights is a fate ordained by God, and endless assaults on rights become part of God's plan. One Sudanese activist told me of a woman, displaced by the civil war to a desert shantytown, who was later falsely accused of stealing a mobile telephone. The woman said, "Allah, Allah, Allah!" the activist told me. She continued, "So, if Allah wills it, it's not necessary to follow-up the case in the court. This is one of the concepts of the people. They start by saying, 'God did this. God wanted this.'"[12] For many Muslims in Sudan, *shari'a* is not just a set of rules that structure society and personal relationships; it is the expression of devotion to God, arising out of the work of God and largely unchangeable by human hands.

When the existence or absence of rights is considered the will of God, it may have the effect of absolving human leaders of some culpability.

---

[8] Interview with Deborah, aid worker with the United Nations, in Juba, South Sudan (April 2007).

[9] Interview with Lina, lawyer, in Khartoum, Sudan (April 2007).

[10] Interview with Shadi, lawyer, in Khartoum, Sudan (April 2007).

[11] Interview with Najib, environmental-legal activist and NGO chairperson, in Khartoum, Sudan (June 2005).

[12] Interview with Nawal, nonlawyer director of legal services organization, in Khartoum, Sudan (June 2005).

Under these conditions, injured people are less likely to mobilize against the government, regardless of its human rights abuses, because the government is not seen as ultimately responsible. Through my observations and conversations, I found that impoverished Sudanese persons certainly thought poorly of their government, particularly with regard to its actions during the civil war. But they were also disinclined to move from voicing their grievances to demanding change.

Building on a deep religious piety, many Sudanese I met expressed their relationships to their communities more in terms of duties than of rights. They sought to understand their roles as devout men or women, or as members of a family or tribe, and expected that certain treatment from their families or tribes would result from fulfilling those roles properly. Duties are "part of our traditions and norms," said one activist.[13] "You have duties to protect [and] to fight for your tribe," echoed another.[14] "Sudanese culture," a women's rights activist in Sudan seemed to lament to me, is "loaded with ideas of duties and reciprocity in relationships, with no serious sanctions and accountability" when rights are violated.[15] This concept of duties to one's family or tribe, then, can prevent displaced persons from believing or hoping that rights may at some time be guaranteed by the state. Their displacement resulting from the state's war against them has been so lengthy – lasting generations and through both democratic and authoritarian governments – that they do not believe that any political leadership in Khartoum, no matter how democratic, will safeguard rights and freedoms.

As in other contexts abroad, rights among those I met in Sudan also tended to be understood and felt most closely on procedural grounds rather than substantive ones.[16] John Locke's theory of natural rights and social contract that undergirds much of human rights discourse and Western political liberalism states that the government is the guarantor of certain rights.[17] But Sudanese human rights lawyers I met described the free exercise of rights as simply the ability to petition the government to allow what political liberalism says government ought to guarantee. "Rights doesn't mean 100 percent implementation," said

[13] Interview with Habiba, women's rights activist, in Khartoum, Sudan (June 2005).

[14] Interview with Najib, environmental activist, in Khartoum, Sudan (June 2005).

[15] Interview with Nahda, women's rights activist, in Omdurman, Sudan (June 2005).

[16] See Tom R. Tyler, *Why People Obey the Law* (Princeton, NJ: Princeton University Press, [1990] 2006).

[17] John Locke, *Two Treatises on Government*, 1680–90 (Ian Shapiro, ed.) (New Haven, CT: Yale University Press, 2003).

one activist. "Once I am aware that I have the chance to do something, it's the start of the fight."[18]

The notion of inalienable and individual rights embedded in humanitarian legal politics does not fit easily in Sudan. But the second pillar of humanitarian legal politics – that knowledge of law and rights is inherently transformative – may be even less workable among the destitute in an authoritarian state. This theory of transformative rights, developed in the context of international human rights treaties in the aftermath of World War II, states that large numbers of indigenous poor properly armed with awareness of their rights will organize, mobilize, demand political reform, and perhaps even force the wholesale remaking of government.[19] But studies in democratic nations over the last several decades have made scholars wary of overstating the transformative potential of rights. Certainly, rights are a common frame for claims of injury in Western nations.[20] They hold symbolic value in political discourse and in managerial settings in organizations.[21] And providing rights to persons who have not previously experienced them creates new discourses they can draw upon, which may reconfigure their relationships and interactions with others.[22] But evidence also suggests that knowledge of rights alone is insufficient for achieving social change even in robust democracies.[23] Outcomes rest on access to resources and support structures, and positive institutional responses to rights-based

---

[18] Interview with Habiba, women's rights activist, in Khartoum North (Bah'ri), Sudan (June 2005).

[19] See Paul Gordon Lauren, *The Evolution of International Human Rights: Visions Seen*, 2nd ed. (Philadelphia: University of Pennsylvania Press, 2003). See also Frances Fox Piven and Richard A. Cloward, *Poor People's Movements: Why They Succeed, How They Fail* (New York: Vintage Books, 1979).

[20] On social-movement frames, see Robert D. Benford and David Snow, "Framing Processes and Social Movements: An Overview and Assessment," 26 *Annual Review of Sociology* (2000): 611–39; David Snow et al., "Frame Alignment Processes, Micromobilization, and Movement Participation," 51 *American Sociological Review* (1986): 464–81.

[21] Patricia J. Williams, *The Alchemy of Race and Rights: Diary of a Law Professor* (Cambridge, MA: Harvard University Press, 1991); Lauren B. Edelman et al., "Internal Dispute Resolution: The Transformation of Rights in the Workplace," 27 *Law & Society Review* (1996): 497–534.

[22] Michael McCann, *Rights at Work: Pay Equity Reform and the Politics of Legal Mobilization* (Chicago: University of Chicago Press, 1994).

[23] Stuart Scheingold, *The Politics of Rights: Lawyers, Public Policy, and Political Change*, 30th Anniversary ed. (Ann Arbor: University of Michigan Press, 2004).

claims.[24] Those who face unlawful discrimination, for instance, need sufficient time, socioeconomic resources, and often a willingness to accept a posture of victimhood in order to pursue grievances effectively as violations of legal or human rights.[25]

Do these limits on the transformative power of rights in democratic states hold in authoritarian states as well? Ethnographic work on human rights promotion and discourse is rarely conducted in authoritarian political contexts. Instead, research on law in despotic or authoritarian states has largely focused on legal institutions such as courts, rather than on discourses of legal empowerment championed by aid agencies to the poor.[26] Perhaps the criteria for the success of rights-based activism are different in authoritarian states. Most of the legal development work by lawyers, activists, international aid agencies and financial institutions, and foreign governments certainly seems to assume that rights awareness will have a distinct and significantly positive impact in nondemocratic settings. The conventional wisdom is that humanitarian forms of legal politics rooted in human rights discourse are counterhegemonic and can empower the poor in the context of authoritarianism.[27] This

[24] See Richard L. Abel and Philip S. C. Lewis, eds., *Lawyers in Society: Comparative Theories* (Berkeley: University of California Press, 1988); Charles Epp, *The Rights Revolution: Lawyers, Activists, and Supreme Courts in Comparative Perspective* (Chicago: University of Chicago Press, 1998); Marc Galanter, "Why the 'Haves' Come Out Ahead: Speculations on the Limits of Legal Change," 9 *Law & Society Review* (1974): 95–160; Terence Halliday and Lucien Karpik, eds., *Lawyers and the Rise of Western Political Liberalism* (Oxford: Clarendon Press, 1998); Terence Halliday et al., eds., *Fighting for Political Freedom: Comparative Studies of the Legal Complex and Political Liberalism* (Oxford: Hart, 2007); Robert A. Kagan, *Adversarial Legalism: The American Way of Law* (Cambridge, MA: Harvard University Press, 2001); Gerald Rosenberg, *The Hollow Hope: Can Courts Bring About Social Change?* 2d ed. (Chicago: University of Chicago Press, 2008).

[25] Kristin Bumiller, "Victims in the Shadow of the Law: A Critique of the Model of Legal Protection," 12 *Signs* (1987): 421–39.

[26] Tom Ginsburg and Tamir Moustafa, eds., *Rule by Law: The Politics of Courts in Authoritarian Regimes* (Cambridge: Cambridge University Press, 2008); Tamir Moustafa, *The Struggle for Constitutional Power: Law, Politics, and Economic Development in Egypt* (Cambridge: Cambridge University Press, 2007); Terence Halliday et al., eds., *Fates of Political Liberalism in the British Post-Colony: The Politics of the Legal Complex* (Cambridge: Cambridge University Press, 2012); Martin Shapiro, *Courts: A Comparative and Political Analysis* (Chicago: University of Chicago Press, 1981).

[27] Commission on Legal Empowerment of the Poor, *Making the Law Work for Everyone.* Vol. 1 (New York: United Nations Development Programme, 2008); Stephen Golub "The Legal Empowerment Alternative," in T. Carothers, ed., *Promoting the Rule of*

notion of rights *as* development – that human rights awareness is the first step toward liberation and salvation of the poor – is the governing logic behind the international aid programs I witnessed in Sudan.

In general, there is reason to be skeptical of the proposition that empowering people to be aware of rights will lead to political change in authoritarian states more reliably than it does in democratic states. Indeed, the problems of institutionalizing the rule of law are even more acute under authoritarian governments, which are defensive and domineering and which already create and marshal legal resources to suit their purposes. When trying to explain supply-oriented legal development programs, the Sudanese I met seemed to have more questions than answers. Is it possible to train an authoritarian government to hand over its authority on political matters to independent courts? What effect does training have on judges or police officials who must act in accordance with regime interests or risk their contracts not being renewed? Why would a military regime give in to demands for human rights? According to one Sudanese lawyer:

> I criticize my colleagues working with UN organizations here. Why are you organizing workshops to provide knowledge and training for the police? They don't violate human rights because of their ignorance.... This is the oxygen they breathe, violating human rights. Every totalitarian regime that wants to stay in power will find itself forced to violate human rights. So you can't change people through these workshops. You need another approach.[28]

In terms of demand-oriented legal development programs, how will disenfranchised and destitute populations be able to influence policy by being made *aware* that certain rights exist in theory? Why would oppressed people in authoritarian nations not need the same resources as those in democratic states to undertake effective action?

The Bashir administration prevents local NGOs and international aid agencies that it sees as threats from operating effectively in Sudan. It conducts routine surveillance of all organizations and activists involved in internationally backed rights campaigns. Personnel in the largest civil society groups in Sudan are monitored almost constantly by state security officials. Both the Sudanese government and aid agencies

Law Abroad: In Search of Knowledge (Washington, DC: Carnegie Endowment for International Peace, 2006), 105–36.

[28] Follow-up interview with Nabil, lawyer, in Khartoum, Sudan (January 2007).

operating in Sudan require all local NGOs to register with the government in order to be eligible to receive international funding. And as part of the registration process, NGOs must agree to have their assets confiscated if a local official believes their activities represent a public threat. In practice, according to NGO sources, if an independent organization receives "too much" funding or appears "too powerful," the government seizes its funds and shuts it down.[29] A woman who runs a reproductive health clinic in the Khartoum area said that security forces tried to close her clinic:

> They said that if we teach [people] to use condoms, we are teaching them to commit adultery.... They threatened our workers with Kalashnikovs. A few days later we re-opened [the clinic] ... because we know our rights. We have our right to keep it open. This government, they use force to test whether we know our rights.[30]

"In the 1990s, things were very bad," recalled another activist. "If you talk[ed] about human rights, people would run away from you. They'd tell you, 'I have children to raise. Why do you want to endanger my life?' Because ... if you talked about [human rights], you'd be captured."[31]

In the most extreme cases of authoritarian legal politics, the government closes independent legal organizations and then opens government-controlled groups under the same name. This is what happened to the Sudan Human Rights Organization, formed by a group of lawyers and activists to call attention to human rights abuses in Sudan in the mid-1980s following Nimeiri's ouster. In the early 1990s, when Bashir's crackdown on civil society was at its peak, the government imprisoned the leadership of the Sudan Human Rights Organization and ended its operations. Shortly afterward, the government launched a new group, also called the Sudan Human Rights Organization, that was answerable to Bashir's government.[32]

The Bashir administration's strategy of authoritarian legal politics has taken advantage of the public nature of NGOs to try to undermine their work. In the same way that the government played up divisions

---

[29] Follow-up interview with Samira, NGO director, in Khartoum, Sudan (May 2007).

[30] Interview with Nahda, women's rights activist, in Omdurman, Sudan (July 2005).

[31] Interview with Balima, human rights activist, in Khartoum, Sudan (March 2007).

[32] Adam M. Abdelmoula, "The 'Fundamentalist' Agenda for Human Rights: the Sudan and Algeria," 18 *Arab Studies Quarterly* (1996): 1–28.

within the legal community over the role of Islamic law, it has tried to exploit fault lines among NGOs: the government has sponsored the development of hundreds of loyalist NGOs, creating uncertainty among civil society activists over who is an ally or an opponent. Pervasive fear complicates the ability of rights-based NGOs to network and organize. Rather than engaging in collective action, members of such NGOs are often on guard against infiltration and betrayal. According to one activist, "Even training in human rights, we'd do it in secrecy! And you have to be very selective about your target group. You must make sure your target group is people who share the same opinion as you. You can't target anybody. You'd get into trouble."[33] To protect their personal safety, those who promote humanitarian legal politics and agitate for human rights can preach only to a limited extent beyond those already converted.

The Bashir administration also broadly targeted international workers for harassment. According to a former BBC News correspondent in Sudan, "During the two-and-a-half years I lived in Sudan, expatriates were regularly targeted by the authorities. Aid workers who provided information about human rights abuses ... were often arrested or expelled as spies."[34] Among the most severe punishments for a foreign aid worker is to be deemed *persona non grata* by the Sudan government. The government banned many aid workers from the country, including high-ranking UN officials. After a widely publicized International Criminal Court warrant for his arrest in 2009, Bashir expelled the staffs of ten foreign nongovernmental aid groups with operations in Darfur.[35]

The government also used the threat of force to intimidate its citizens even after the civil war ended and the peace agreement was signed. A Sudanese lawyer who works with displaced people says that his clients are afraid to speak up about their rights because the government does not seriously listen to rights-based claims from the people. His clients ask, "How can I [have] my rights if the government has a gun ... and has the right to demolish my house and force me to go

[33] Interview with Balima, human rights activist, in Khartoum, Sudan (March 2007).

[34] Jonah Fisher (2007). "Sudan Leaders Court Western Rage." *BBC News*. Available: http://news.bbc.co.uk/2/hi/africa/7122007.stm (accessed January 9, 2013).

[35] Sudanese staff who remained collected employment benefits from these foreign aid groups under Sudanese law, equivalent to months (in some cases years) of annual income, based on the number of years employed prior to the organization's expulsion.

to another place?"[36] Indeed, simply talking about rights means putting oneself on the government's radar and inviting scrutiny. Agitating for rights makes one visible and vulnerable.

One afternoon, I met with a woman named Gladys, who lives in an encampment for displaced persons outside Khartoum. She was driven out of her village in southern Sudan when she was nineteen. Sixteen years later when I met her, she was a thirty-five-year-old grandmother still living and working in the same "temporary" camp. Gladys worked in the local health clinic, a desert hut without electricity or running water, where malnourished mothers take their dying babies. She talked to me about the plight of displaced women and their children and told me of the many war widows who illegally brew and sell inexpensive alcohol in the encampments to be able to buy food for their hungry children. "They don't want to make beer," Gladys told me, "because they [know they] will be arrested." But their only option is to "go to the house of the Arabs to clean." To do that, the women must endure a long commute in desert traffic and leave their infants and children unattended in the camps "until seven or eight at night." So they can protect their children, the women stay in the camps and sell alcohol. It is hard to imagine an individual with more cause to demand her rights, but a widowed civil-war survivor illegally selling alcohol to earn money to feed her children is among the least able to defend herself if she attracts the ire of the state.

In addition to overt repression, the political realities of authoritarian legal politics in Sudan also undermine humanitarian legal politics and rights-based development programs. It is difficult to convince people that rights are an inherent part of being human when around them is evidence that rights seem to be commodities to be bought, sold, and traded. Gladys said that women who sell alcohol in the camps understand nothing of inalienable rights; they have as much freedom as they can afford.

> [Gladys]: [If the police] find you brewing alcohol, they collect everything in the house. And you will be taken, arrested. Sometimes two months in the prison. [But] if you have money, and if you give them, they will leave you.
>
> [Interviewer]: How much do you have to give them?
>
> [Gladys]: Give them something reasonable. Give them anything reasonable, and they will leave you.

[36] Interview with Maher, legal aid attorney, in Khartoum, Sudan (June 2005).

194

"Something reasonable" is the price of a displaced woman's freedom. Police, too, must make themselves subservient to the regime, as they lack their own political and economic power. The result is that rights are marketable and often relinquished to police officers (themselves often impoverished) in exchange for short-term freedom from ongoing persecution.

In this culture of commodification, rather than learning to demand rights collectively, people learn to manipulate the system to protect their property interests. The policy director of an NGO told me about a woman who had gone to them for assistance because the government wanted to build a high-tension electrical wire above her house. One of her neighbors started to build an additional floor on his house, to elevate it just enough to block the path of the high-tension wire. He had a friend inside the National Electricity Corporation, who was able to convince the government to pay an inflated price for the otherwise dilapidated and half-constructed house, to allow line construction to proceed. "This is the only way to get your rights," said the policy director, "to play games with the government."[37]

I asked why the woman did not file a case against the government, as the aid community was encouraging people to do with regard to human rights abuses, and as other Sudanese had done in similar cases of financial loss. "It's very difficult to ... take a case [against government] in the court. The court is the government also."[38] She went on to describe how a family contact in a relevant government office is usually the more effective and preferred option to litigation. The current judicial system is designed to absorb, delay, and obstruct any grievances that may be filed. Indeed, displaced persons who have been trained by NGOs and have then attempted to make claims against the government about unsafe drinking water, lack of electricity, or inadequate educational facilities have been roundly discouraged. Told on successive visits to return another day, speak with another person, file another form, wait for another person to return from a trip, those seeking redress finally give up. Effectively asserting one's rights requires political influence or, more often than not, family, neighborhood, or village connections within the various levels of the bureaucracy.[39]

[37] Interview with Jameela, NGO program manager, in Khartoum, Sudan (November 2006).

[38] Ibid.

[39] Even tenuous connections can create bridges of trust into the government bureaucracy. I enjoyed similar connections when I knew someone who was the neighbor of

The Bashir regime is particularly difficult to pressure through the promotion of humanitarian legal politics because of its ostensible alignment with Islam. It has persuaded many of Sudan's devout Muslims that its rule is in accordance with God's law. The belief that Bashir's rule is God's will promotes an attitude of acceptance (or resignation) among Sudan's most oppressed people and provides cover for some of the regime's brutal actions. Another by-product of its ostensible religious affiliation is that anyone who does dare to challenge the legitimacy of the government can easily be depicted as criticizing Islam itself and the immutability of God's work. The sin of questioning *shari'a* is a crime punishable by death.[40] This manipulation of religious devotion enabled Bashir to silence his most committed critics among the progressive intelligentsia:

> Once the *shari'a* was introduced [formally in 1983], it became a big problem for Sudanese modern academics or intellectuals. Because [since then] if you suggest we should use another rights framework, implicitly you're saying there's something wrong with *shari'a*, that it's not just. They have a difficult time. It's a debate they don't want to get into. And if they do join the debate, they will lose.[41]

Most vexing, however, is that even if a small group of internationally backed activists are able to create a workable rights framework; overcome repression, corruption, and religious dogma; and organize the people of Sudan, the primary leverage they have against the government is exposure of continued human rights abuses. And the fact is, by 2011 after years of legal intervention efforts by aid groups, that Bashir still did not care. Or, rather, he had little left to lose. Though certainly facing internal party pressure and cleavages, his rule had survived more than two decades of the combined impact of civil war, harsh economic sanctions, and legal action by the International Criminal Court (ICC). (The court charged Bashir with the most serious international crimes, including genocide, which would prevent Bashir from traveling to

---

a man who was the cousin of one of the police guards outside a ministry office where I was waiting for a permit to be processed.

[40] As detailed in Chapter 4 of this book, the leader of the Republican Brotherhood, Mahmoud Mohamed Taha, was executed for apostasy in 1985 under President Nimeiri. Though not a crime at the time, apostasy was criminalized in 1991 under President Bashir.

[41] Interview with Muhammad, NGO project manager, in Khartoum, Sudan (June 2005).

most ICC signatory countries. Bashir, however, traveled to a number of countries in the region and abroad to Asia, to drum up support for trade with Sudan.)

Sudan's primary economic partners, notably China, Malaysia, India, and Saudi Arabia, are fully aware of conditions within Sudan, yet they have continued to invest in and import from Sudan. Despite reports of atrocities from Darfur, the border with South Sudan, and other regions, China alone invested at least USD 15 billion in Sudan's petroleum industry after 1996, largely counteracting the negative impact of American sanctions. Oil production in Sudan increased to 500,000 barrels per day during the 2000s, boosting government revenue and largely making international opinion irrelevant to Bashir.[42] Sudan's oil, now mostly located in South Sudan, gave it strategic value abroad and provided funding for the Bashir regime to continue to promote authoritarian legal politics and resist international calls for reform and arrest.[43] Petrodollars also helped Bashir to construct new roads, supply new buses in Khartoum to alleviate traffic congestion, and erect new bridges over the Nile to connect Khartoum with outlying regions.

Since programs inspired by humanitarian visions of legal politics are designed to encourage legal mobilization to end President Omar al-Bashir's regime, why did his government allow these rights-based empowerment projects to occur at all? Bashir and his deputies, if nothing else, have demonstrated a keen understanding of Sudan's internal legal and political dynamics. They may not have believed legal empowerment posed enough of a credible threat to Bashir's power to end the training programs sponsored for judges or the destitute.

When humanitarian legal politics confronts authoritarian legal politics, it may not catalyze immediate or lasting political change. Humanitarian legal politics also does not make its intended impact at the deepest level among the poor. But it nevertheless forms the building blocks of engagement among nonaligned lawyers, civil society elites, and academics. While the poor certainly receive some important material and psychosocial benefits tied to education, beneficial impacts

---

[42] "No Strings: Why Developing Countries Like Doing Business with China," *The Economist* (Special Report on China's quest for resources), p. 14 (March 15, 2008). See also "Background: Sudan's Oil Industry," *Al-Jazeera* (July 2, 2011). Available: http://english.aljazeera.net/indepth/spotlight/southsudanindependence/2011/07/20117216441419555.html (accessed January 9, 2013).

[43] See generally Terry Karl, *The Paradox of Plenty: Oil Booms and Petro-States* (Berkeley: University of California Press, 1997).

accrue primarily to international and Sudanese elites, who receive aid funding to conduct these interventions with the poor.

A full account of legal interventions across the global South would require substantially more time on the ground across multiple settings. In the following section I expose the consequences as already experienced by Sudanese activists and their target communities during the interim period between the end of the civil war and South Sudan's secession, particularly in light of the number, range, and financing of these interventions in Sudan during that time.

THE IMPACTS OF HUMANITARIAN LEGAL POLITICS

The previous section addressed some of the situational constraints on humanitarian legal politics in Sudan. But, given the long-term investment in these programs, their outcome should be an empirical question. Even though the international aid community spent at least USD 30 million between 2005 and 2010 to build rights awareness among Sudan's most destitute populations, there has been no systematic effort to gather evidence of the effects or trajectory of these programs. What follows is a preliminary attempt to catalog the consequences of rights-based development work concentrating on the destitute in Sudan. While further study is required to assess the full potential of this strategy in Sudan, this discussion is intended to serve as a guide to understanding its near-term effects, particularly of legal awareness workshops.

Despite the variety of obstacles faced by those seeking to build up Sudanese society by instilling a rights consciousness among the poor, legal awareness workshops and training sessions provide a number of remarkable benefits. For the poor in particular, these benefits include a much-needed education and access to social services, particularly in the context of the many challenging settings in which they live, including encampments for war-displaced populations, rural villages, and prisons. At one workshop I attended in a desert encampment outside Khartoum, the facilitator asked participants about their educational backgrounds. Most said they had been taught by organizations conducting legal awareness workshops within the encampment – only a few mentioned the state educational system. In this way, rights-based development programs are important vehicles for the provision of basic education. They are also an important opportunity for NGOs to provide literacy training, food aid, and microloans. While legal awareness is the nominal goal, participants also appreciate the sandwiches and other food they receive during the session breaks or at the end of each day's workshop.

Legal awareness workshops also spread knowledge of Sudanese and international laws; they are a sort of free law school for displaced persons. Some trainers who followed up with those trained said that they had requested more workshops, especially among women who were unaware of their rights in marriage. A Khartoum-based lawyer who trained displaced women in Darfur told me that she kept in contact with those women from Darfur: "They were happy with what they learned. Also, [some] of them formed into a group to study these things more" on their own.[44] At some workshops, trainees even received copies of pertinent international laws in Arabic. I met several attorneys who said they know more trainees than government officials who can recite international human rights treaties.[45] In one encampment, I met Salma, a divorced mother of two who had received human rights training when she had earlier been in the women's prison. During the training, she said, she realized for the first time that a divorced woman has "rights to go and complain [in court] … if she has children, and the husband [has] not [been] helping her."[46] Nisreen, another displaced woman who had received training in prison, said, "We know now that after the peace agreement women have rights."[47] The main purpose of the workshops, according to one facilitator, is simply to advance this knowledge of rights among displaced people.[48]

Facilitators and participants said that, despite the challenges they faced, the training programs can actually change people's perceptions of rights – in a sense, transnationalizing their knowledge and reorienting their legal consciousness to one rooted in human rights. Teaching marginalized persons about relevant human rights norms enables them to speak the language of rights and to internalize the basic premise that rights are fundamental and inalienable. Imparting knowledge about rights can encourage this symbolic or psychological liberation from the bonds of oppression. These workshops may be the first place people

[44] Interview with Salaam, lawyer, in Khartoum, Sudan (November 2006).
[45] Interview with Maha, lawyer and legal awareness workshop facilitator, in Khartoum, Sudan (December 2006).
[46] Interview with Salma, internally displaced person near Omdurman, Sudan (June 2005).
[47] Interview with Nisreen, internally displaced person in Haj Yoosef, Sudan (June 2005).
[48] Interview with Zakaria, lawyer and legal awareness workshop facilitator, in Khartoum (May 2007).

hear about legal protections, and the first time they understand themselves as humans deserving of legal rights, not merely as survivors of war or of fate. In this sense, human rights awareness can help build the mental structures necessary for liberation.

The workshops can become discursive forums for displaced persons to talk openly about topics once considered *muharramat* (forbidden), such as religious conversion, the secession of southern Sudan, or children's rights. During some of the workshops I observed, participants became quite animated, eager to ask questions about rights they had not previously known they possessed. After one discussion about religious freedom, a non-Muslim man asked the workshop facilitator, "Does this mean I still have to shut down my business on Friday [the Islamic day of prayer and rest]?"

The workshops also provide much-needed encouragement that participants can have agency over their own lives and community. "We're always trying to explain to the villages [what services] they can expect from the government," said one aid worker. "The rest [we say] you have to do for yourselves. You have to organize yourselves so you [can] pay your one teacher and your [one] health worker."[49] In particular, the training of paralegals is intended to empower war-displaced persons to take care of themselves and one another to prevent arbitrary arrests where there are no trained lawyers. Legal awareness workshops serve the important function of "training people to ask government [for their rights], instead of [taking their rights] by force."[50] In this way, law and rights are promoted as alternatives to violence.

Civil society organizations obtain mainly material benefits from the relationships they develop with the international aid community to conduct these rights trainings. A women's rights activist I met put it most succinctly: "If I [could] summarize [my experience], most of the organizations where I volunteer get their funds from either Western embassies or international NGOs."[51] A perspective widely held among activists I met is that funding to local NGOs "depends on donors. Internationals are more concerned with human rights [than with other areas].... So they put [their money] into that field."[52] In addition, local businesses or party bosses are more likely to commit scarce resources

[49] Interview with Adelle, European aid worker, in El Obeid (May 2007).
[50] Follow-up interview with Samira, NGO director, in Khartoum (October 2006).
[51] Interview with Habiba, women's rights activist, Khartoum North (June 2005).
[52] Interview with Tamir, Sudanese NGO director, Khartoum (May 2007).

to government officials – in the form of taxes, payments, or incentives to obtain permits, lucrative contracts, and licenses – rather than to donate money to organizations that might be seen as hostile to the government or ruling party. The relationships between international groups and local civil society replace domestic contribution patterns typically found in robust or emerging democracies, as capital flows from foreign aid groups to help advance an independent civil society neither rooted in opposition political parties nor beholden to business interests connected to the regime.

Local discursive uses of human rights are signals to the international aid community that an organization and its staff are independent or nonaligned (whether or not this is actually the case). Some NGOs frame programs in international human rights language to obtain funding from high-impact donors such as the UN; not doing so would convey unfamiliarity with UN values.[53] In some circumstances, civil society leaders accept lucrative contracts to join international NGOs or the UN as "national staff." Employment with such organizations provides prestige, higher salaries than local NGOs, and experience working both in the English language and with substantial budgets and resources.

But legal knowledge may not be nearly sufficient to enable war-displaced Sudanese to mobilize their rights or ultimately force real change in their country. In part because the workshops are built around a largely new and, at times, unrecognizable vision of rights, they may not provide the impetus for mobilization. The success of human rights education programs is predicated on the hope that large numbers of poor people, when aware of their rights and fearless enough to seek protections of their rights from authoritarian governments, can one day organize to influence administrative decisions and ultimately create "bottom-up" change in regime actions, perhaps even in the makeup of the government itself. But the clash between the views of rights in Sudanese civil society (typically shared by Western aid agencies who fund them) and the different views in the encampments can constrain effective political action among the poor.

Pluralism also presents an obstacle to organizing. Those displaced by war are a fractured group.[54] They fled different villages across a

---

[53] See also José Antonio Lucero "Representing 'Real Indians': The Challenges of Indigenous Authenticity and Strategic Constructivism in Ecuador and Bolivia," 41 *Latin American Research Review* (2006): 31–56.

[54] I thank David Abernathy for drawing my attention to this issue in Sudan and in Africa more generally.

thousand-mile radius and ended up together in encampments surrounding Khartoum; they have different ethnic, tribal, cultural, and
linguistic traditions and are left with little choice but to live in these
camps with others from groups with whom they may have been in conflict. Darfuris, for instance, have been displaced by the thousands to the
camps around Khartoum, joining the millions of southern Sudanese
already there. The Sudanese government often employed Darfuris as
its foot soldiers in the twenty-two-year war against southern Sudan. It
is improbable that such disparate and impoverished groups, once at war
with one another, will organize together as a cohesive, empowered unit
to determine and demand common rights from an authoritarian government. This fragmentation is one reason why the Sudanese regime
might allow UN-funded rights training to take place, recognizing that
it is unlikely to affect opposition to the regime.

Even Sudanese who embrace international human rights norms find it
difficult to imagine exercising those rights, particularly in relation to the
Bashir administration's aggressive control of law and legal institutions.
When I asked a longtime women's rights activist in Sudan about how
she would use human rights, she replied, "In writing [to a foreign donor],
not in a [Sudanese] court. When you are in a court, you cannot talk
about human rights. They are deaf and mute about [human rights]."[55]
Disadvantaged populations in Sudan are reluctant to take claims of discrimination to the courts and disinclined to be seen as victims. A school
administrator explained, "Say there's a woman mistreated at work. Very
rarely do they sue. They're scared of being criticized. If you go to court,
it's a long process, and you have to pay in terms of time and money."[56]

The risk of inspiring a desire for human rights in a state as chaotic
and undemocratic as Sudan is that rights will take on a mythical quality; they will become unattainable ideals rather than lived principles.
Like a belief in God, knowledge of rights may provide comfort and
hope. But hope is an abstraction. It is unclear whether an education
in human rights, or a workshop reviewing epic poetry or contemporary nonfiction, such as the U.S. president Barack Obama's *Dreams
from My Father,* might arouse similar feelings of comfort, awareness, or
empowerment. That is, material and symbolic benefits arising from the
promotion of law to displaced persons, while real, do not necessarily

[55] Interview with Habiba, women's rights activist, in Khartoum North (Bah'ri), Sudan (June 2005).
[56] Interview with Leila, school administrator, in Omdurman, Sudan (June 2005).

Table 6.1. Consequences of humanitarian legal politics

	To Civil Society	To Displaced Persons
Intended benefits	Empowerment to mobilize rights and challenge regime	Empowerment to mobilize rights and challenge regime
Actual benefits	Material: prestige, upward mobility	Material: education, food
Costs	Dependence; co-optation	Illusion of hope; legitimizing the regime's legal investments and infrastructure

Source: Compiled by the author.

result from the core content of human rights. These benefits also do not reflect the intended consequences of humanitarian legal politics and rights-based approaches to development (Table 6.1).

Humanitarian actors promoting legal politics in Sudan come face to face with an authoritarian state also putting forward a vision of legal politics as the solution to Sudan's deep-rooted ills. Despite a variety of power-sharing protocols and peace agreements with liberation movements across Sudan, Bashir remains Sudan's longest-ruling president, leaving his legacy on the development and the activities of civil society. His government made substantial investments in the national network of police and security forces, *al-amn*. Laws in Sudan remain ostensibly Islamic in areas the regime controls, including the encampments around Khartoum. Corporal punishments for *huduud* offenses against Islamic law also remain common, particularly against non-Muslims who are poor and displaced.[57] In 2009, Sudanese women made international headlines after a group of them were arrested, flogged, and fined for wearing trousers.[58] One NGO trainer said, "these measures ... are a show of power ... to scare [the displaced] people."[59]

Desert encampments and squatter communities are not lawless areas. Rather, they are heavily monitored by legal authorities because of the large number of persons residing there who were displaced by the wars

[57] Chapter 4 of this book analyzes the administration's use of Islamic law in further detail.

[58] "Pants Pants Revolution," *Foreign Policy*, August 5, 2009, http://www.foreignpolicy.com/articles/2009/08/05/pants_pants_revolution (accessed January 9, 2013). The author of this *Foreign Policy* article chose to remain anonymous "due to security concerns" in Sudan.

[59] Interview, Najima, NGO founder, in Khartoum, Sudan (February 2007).

against President Bashir's regime and its policies. Security checkpoints abound on major roadways to the camps. Legal documents are required for passage through these government installations. Sporadic fighting takes place in the camps between displaced persons and the police, often when the police arrive to clear encampments in order to make way for new development projects. These confrontations between the regime and its most destitute have led to large numbers of casualties and intensified the regime's surveillance measures.[60]

I met many war-displaced persons who had received rights training and proudly displayed their workshop *shihadaat* (certificates of completion). While their participation in the programs was a source of great pride, most were still uncertain about what to do with the knowledge. As if they had studied Chaucer or ancient Greek, the education they received was significant, but it did not seem to them to be directly applicable to their daily lives. The fact that participants leave their classes with no action plan, no tools for organizing themselves, and no cohesion may suggest a missed opportunity. But doing anything more than raising awareness may also catch the eye of Bashir's security apparatus. As one NGO leader told me:

> Many NGOs are implementing the same things – raising awareness blah blah blah [sic] and what is the end result? Nothing! There is no clear vision, no strategy. They don't know to where this will lead. Okay, after you raise [legal] awareness of people, what are you going to do? That's why it's important to have a real network among these NGOs, to have a strategic plan to see, [to outline] the next steps.[61]

Local civil society activists in Sudan also sometimes demonstrate uncertainty about how to use their newfound legal knowledge. I attended an action meeting in 2006 held by an NGO and its supporters regarding their efforts to force the state government of Khartoum to conduct an environmental impact assessment before breaking ground on Khartoum's largest urban development project ever – a USD 4 billion commercial district with hotels and high-rise buildings at the confluence of the White Nile and Blue Nile rivers in central Khartoum. To the activists (some of them local traffic officers still in uniform after a long day's work), it was clear that the government was

---

[60] See Rogaia Mustafa Abusharaf, *Transforming Displaced Women in Sudan: Politics and the Body in a Squatter Settlement* (Chicago: University of Chicago Press, 2009), 23–6.

[61] Interview with Najima, NGO founder, in Khartoum, Sudan (February 2007).

violating national environmental legislation passed in 2000 by not conducting an environmental assessment. Almost all attendees wanted to file a case in the Constitutional Court seeking to prohibit development. The lone Sudanese attorney in the group tried twice to remind his colleagues that the Constitutional Court, whose justices were all appointed by Bashir, would not solve their problem and that any legal battle should be one small part of what should be a broader media campaign to convince their fellow citizens of the importance of environmental protection. When I met with the activists the following year, many were still wholly focused on pursuing a legal case. By 2010 the legal case had not gone forward, while development and renovation of the region were ongoing.

Sudanese NGOs built on a model of rights-based development may also fall into the trap of becoming dependent on foreign financial support and foreign ideas but being simultaneously powerless to engage their foreign backers in meaningful dialogue. Instead of being implementing "partners" as they are called, they risk simply doing their sponsors' bidding. Leaders of Sudanese NGOs often complain that the information they provide to international aid agencies is unnoticed and unheard. They submit periodic reports about how the NGO spent its money and details of outreach efforts but rarely hear back from their contacts at funding agencies.

> Before you submit [your report], they annoy you: "Where is your progress report?" Then you submit it, and they don't read it. They didn't read our report. When I went [to see our contact person at the United Nations], she was searching and couldn't even find it. I asked them to read our report and give feedback. Since June [four months earlier] we have not received our second [payment].... You know, they're just concerned with money – how much did you spend, where are the receipts?[62]

Several civil society activists I met described the amount of money and lack of oversight provided by donor groups as perpetuating what they felt was a culture of profiteering. The founder of a new NGO funded by the U. S. National Endowment for Democracy that conducts human rights training across Sudan said, "The problem is this: The [foreign] money is going to [Sudanese NGOs], who say [to the donor],

---

[62] Follow-up interview with Samira, NGO director, in Khartoum, Sudan (October 2006).

'I'll write you a really nice report.' And nothing is happening on the ground."[63] I spoke with another legal aid activist at a two-day conference on women and justice funded by the United Nations who told me, "UN funds and donor funds should be monitored; they need evaluation. A hell of a lot of money is coming to Sudan, but where is it going? This conference alone cost USD 43,000!"[64]

There is also some danger that humanitarian forms of legal politics may have unintended positive benefits for the Bashir administration, already accustomed to using any available legal tools and resources for political gain. To the extent that international aid agencies and their Sudanese employees provide basic aid and services, they also relieve the government of responsibility for caring for Sudan's millions of displaced persons. To the extent that rights-based programs in the encampments allow Bashir to overlook state duties to displaced persons, he is able to re-allocate funds to military and security that he might otherwise have to spend on education, subsidies, or other forms of development.

Moreover, teaching people to pursue grievances through the legal system potentially legitimizes the regime as a fair arbiter of justice and reinforces the regime's power over its citizens. This was precisely the regime's legal action strategy during and since the 1990s of making courts more accessible to the people by "shortening the judicial shadow" (taqsir al-zhul al-qada'i). In the chaotic, war-torn environment of Sudan, demands made for human rights provide another opportunity for the government to say no. "When they come to arrest you, you can say, 'This is against my human rights,'" said the director of an NGO. "But the police will still arrest you. You can fight with police. But in the end, you are still put in jail."[65]

CONCLUSION

Human rights, central to humanitarian legal politics in Sudan, provide a valuable topic of discourse for marginalized people to name both their oppression and their aspirations. Indeed, talking about rights can be psychologically liberating for survivors of war, displacement, and

[63] Interview with Tofeeq, NGO founder and human rights educator, in Khartoum, Sudan (June 2005).
[64] Interview with Intisar, lawyer, in Khartoum, Sudan (December 2006).
[65] Follow-up interview with Samira, NGO director, in Khartoum, Sudan (October 2006).

discrimination, as it reminds them of their own humanity and individual worth. Rights-based approaches to development can also be a vehicle for basic education and literacy training in desperate environments like Sudan's camps for the internally displaced.

While rights discourse provides important symbolic and material benefits, it faces challenges in achieving long-term political goals in an authoritarian state. The aid community's one-size-fits-all solutions tend to ignore local cultural, religious, and authoritarian political realities, limiting their credibility on the ground. As one NGO director said, "We don't work with the UN. You know why? It's not that we don't have confidence in their capacity. [It's because] they always want something from their perspective, not from ours."[66] Generic programming efforts that fail to acknowledge complex local context and local ways of thinking may not succeed in mobilizing local populations.[67] They may also generate a host of negative unintended consequences in authoritarian states, from putting activists in danger of harsh retribution to reinforcing a nondemocratic government's power.

In a fragile state riven by war, it is unclear that training people to understand their rights leads to actual mobilization of those rights, particularly from an authoritarian bureaucracy that uses law and legal institutions to absorb, defuse, and stymie grievances. Other resources beyond rights awareness may be necessary to empower oppressed populations and allow the international aid community to support grassroots development. Given the resources currently being invested in rights-based programs in Sudan and elsewhere, broad evaluation of the impacts and potential of these initiatives is needed. In Sudan, humanitarian forms of legal politics have led to some unmistakable benefits and constructed a broader politics of using law promotion within civil society as a tool of liberation.

The impacts on the poor of humanitarian legal politics are not the ones intended by activist proponents of human rights. Rather, for the ostensible target populations of efforts to promote law among the poor, the content of human rights is rather empty. In the process of

---

[66] Interview with Tofeeq, NGO founder and human rights educator, in Khartoum, Sudan (June 2005).

[67] See Sally Engle Merry, *Human Rights and Gender Violence: Translating International Law into Local Justice* (Chicago: University of Chicago Press, 2006). Merry argues that human rights is the only internationally recognizable language of emancipatory social justice, but that as a body of law, human rights also tends to serve the powerful.

conducting legal awareness workshops, it is certainly true that connections are made and relationships are built between the UN and
local civil society elites.[68] However, claims that human rights and legal
empowerment ultimately benefit the poorest and most vulnerable in a
society are not borne out by my research with Sudanese survivors of war
from Darfur and South Sudan.[69] Instead, human rights discourse may
produce dangerous expectations that the regime will listen or change.
But neither is the contrary and extreme argument – that human rights
are "civilizational" justifications for neocolonial interventions – borne
out by my study.[70] Costs derive from new stratifications created in civil
society, as local actors and interests are subordinated to foreign donors
and UN agencies that promote law.

From the perspective of the world's most poor, law is neither a grand
savior nor an absolute nemesis. Survivors of civil war displaced to live
under the jurisdiction of their adversaries have experienced the brute
force of authoritarian law enough to disconnect the challenges they face
every day from the liberating rhetoric of human rights promoters. That
is, legal discourse may not provide them clean water from their government, nor will the language of liberation embedded in transnational
ideas of human rights release them from the grip of the authoritarian
regime's national security forces that closely monitor their activities
to ensure compliance with repressive domestic laws. Benefits, instead,
are more tangible and mundane, the side effects of an internationally
connected civil society's attempts to assist impoverished war survivors:
psychosocial support and solace from local NGOs, a free meal at the
workshop, and documentary evidence of educational attainment (a
certificate and small graduation ceremony at the end of a weeklong
workshop).

Humanitarian forms of legal politics help provide elite jobs to elite
locals and a respite from immediate needs, such as education and food,
to poor persons. The costs of these projects, however, may run much
deeper, particularly in fragile states: creating expectations even among
aid practitioners that teaching of rights can lead to organizing or

[68] See Englund (2006); Merry (2006).
[69] See Golub (2006); UNICEF (2004); United Nations (2008).
[70] See, for example, Laura Nader, "Introduction," in *The Practice of Human Rights:
Tracking Law between the Global and the Local,* ed. M. Goodale and S. Merry
(Cambridge: Cambridge University Press, 2007); David Kennedy, "The International
Human Rights Movement: Part of the Problem?" 15 *Harvard Human Rights Journal*
(2002): 101–26.

mobilization; putting participants in danger from an authoritarian government's security apparatus designed to eliminate detractors, including human rights promoters; and causing NGOs and the displaced persons they assist to adopt the language of human rights, even cynically, to ensure their existence and livelihoods.

The impacts of humanitarian legal politics result largely from the interventions themselves. My data suggest a great deal of material and discursive disadvantages. With other scholars of the global South, I find areas of resistance to human rights by independent NGOs.[71] As this resistance fades, local relationships with the international aid community deepen. Little happens to poor people as a result: they neither receive benefits one would hope from human rights nor suffer the extreme consequences that some of the most critical literature might make us believe. Rather, they cannot and often do not call for human rights from government, as daily life runs its course and surveillance and arrests continue in their encampments.

My data on legal politics in Sudan suggest a number of implications for studying the politics of rights. First is the need to pay close attention to the political context or type of regime in which legal politics is promoted. Second is that the export of law as a model of development aid, particularly in states of war, creates benefits and costs. To analyze them, one must disaggregate civil society elites who are paid to teach about rights from those who are trained by those elites. Third, human rights education programs and other forms of humanitarian legal politics provide empirical evidence for expanding sociolegal theory concerning rights: the positive effects of rights-based strategies in the case of a chaotic and authoritarian state do not result from rights discourse itself, but rather from the fulfillment of more urgent material and symbolic needs. The educational model, however, is potentially dangerous when delivered into authoritarian contexts absent full knowledge of the national political context within which rights operate. Finally, sociolegal theory must confront the extent to which pluralism influences how disparate and divided groups can organize to mobilize collective rights.

Some scholars suggest that, to move beyond skepticism and critique, human rights as a moral philosophy must be recovered by decoupling

---

[71] See also Balakrishnan Rajagopal, *International Law from Below: Development, Social Movements, and Third World Resistance* (Cambridge: Cambridge University Press, 2003).

it from deeply troubling contemporary projects.[72] My purpose has been a step in this direction: to lay out the costs and benefits of humanitarian forms of legal politics in an authoritarian context for those scholars who investigate rights in their variety of settings, including a political and geographic context as complex as the authoritarian state in Sudan. There are advantages to promoting rights discourse among the poor – psychological liberation – and more practical benefits – improved knowledge, encouragement of nonviolent dispute resolution, and education about transnational norms that link disadvantaged communities with salient transnational discourses of rights, generating funding for civil society. But in chaotic, war-torn, and authoritarian environments like Sudan, humanitarian legal politics may also risk creating nonessential abstractions and added risks in the daily suffering of displaced persons.

[72] Helen Stacy, *Human Rights for the 21st Century: Sovereignty, Civil Society, Culture* (Stanford, CA: Stanford University Press, 2009).

CHAPTER 7

REFLECTIONS ON LEGAL POLITICS

I want to see a legal renaissance in this country.

– Lawyer in Khartoum[1]

Law is really broad. You can do anything.

– Law student at the University of Khartoum[2]

During an interview, a retired senior judge in Sudan said to me, "Some [Sudanese] people are sorry that the British left." He paused, reflecting on the comment, which seemed to surprise him, and continued, "That is sad that [our] national government should be even worse than the colonial government [had been]."[3] Promotion of the rule of law in Sudan began almost immediately after the 1898 colonial invasion of Sudan and was an essential feature of British operations. According to a British administrator, "One of the fundamental principles laid down by Bonham-Carter as the first legal secretary was that justice should be not only just, but quick and seen to be fair. That principle of the rule of law, associated with justice ... ran through [our approach] from the very start."[4]

Despite conscious political and rhetorical efforts to distinguish themselves from the colonial past, postcolonial governments in Sudan have

---

[1] Interview with Salaam, lawyer, in Khartoum, Sudan (November 2006).

[2] Interview with Ibtisam, law student, in Khartoum, Sudan (April 2007).

[3] Follow-up interview with Hassan, retired senior judicial official, in Khartoum, Sudan (April 2007).

[4] Interview with Sir Donald Hawley, former Chief Registrar of Sudan Judiciary (1953–5), in Wiltshire, England (January 2007).

been strikingly similar to one another and to the colonial administration – particularly in policies, institutional designs, leaders' uses of and dealings with the law, and their commonly held view that robust legal institutions can help bring about social stability and legitimize their rule. From colonial rule through the Bashir regime, resources have been expended to promote legal innovations. Building courts, law schools, and mosques – the British tasked the colonial legal department to oversee construction of mosques as part of a broader effort to monitor Sudanese activity – was meant to legitimize undemocratic rule. This process of law building ultimately extends the reach of the government through its grafting of state law onto religion and custom. The fragile state, then, still resembles the colonial regime in striking ways. British administrators in the first half of the twentieth century and every government since that time have sought the assistance of the law to maintain control. They have fought wars using not only soldiers but also lawyers, judges, and administrative personnel, who apply the laws and institutions of authoritarian leaderships like that of President Bashir to imprint on the fragile society a sense of permanence and durability.

This book has argued fundamentally that the practice of promoting law – and ultimately the law itself – is a social and political process. It is an evolving, layered set of activities in which different actors – state and nonstate – use different aspects of law, the legal order, and the rule of law to meet a variety of political, social, moral, and economic ends. Each time an actor uses the law, creates a legal institution, seeks a judicial ruling, or accepts the assistance of human rights specialists – each time legal politics is enacted – the shape of the law and the legal order changes. In this chapter I reflect on the multiple faces of legal politics that I found across periods and for different actors in Sudan.

The example of colonial legal politics demonstrated two of these faces of legal politics from the Anglo-Egyptian Sudan: one that legitimizes a colonial administration and one that helps to supersede it. Perceiving a legal vacuum when they invaded Sudan, the British immediately sought to build respect for the rule of law. They saw themselves as a class of "benevolent despots" and educated themselves in the law. They wanted to be seen as sources of social order, facilitators of economic development, and neutral arbiters of people's disputes with one another. They heard and accommodated grievances filed against them through channels they created and monitored. The rule of law they promoted, while ultimately weak and nondemocratic, helped them in the process to criminalize opposition, manage and co-opt religion and traditional authority, and create a class of elite Sudanese who would make careers out of the application of English common law. But colonial legal strategies could sustain the British grip on power in Sudan only for a limited time. The Sudanese used the common law and legal institutions that subjugated them to their advantage, ultimately to define their national identity and win political independence. Courts once used for surveillance became spaces for agitating against colonialism, and criminal prosecutions of emerging Sudanese political leaders (themselves trained in law by the British at Gordon College) helped to build sympathy among the masses.

After the departure of British colonial administrators, a variety of postcolonial authorities followed their example by seeking out the assistance of the law. They spent what little political capital they had to promote new legal theories and make dramatic changes in the law. In the 1950s and 1960s, the Sudanese judiciary helped to prop up the nation in spite of power vacuums in the legislative and executive branches. In the 1970s, President Jafaar Nimeiri and his deputy, the former chief justice Babiker Awadalla, reconfigured the Sudanese legal system from common law to civil law in order to leave a "legal" legacy. Having failed to engineer a Sudanese union with Egypt, and following a series of disastrous economic policies, Nimeiri imposed Islamic law in 1983 in a futile attempt to save his failing presidency.

President Omar al-Bashir, Sudan's longest-serving president, made the largest investment in courts and legal infrastructure that the nation had ever seen. Having learned from earlier failed military regimes, Bashir sought unprecedented control over lawyers, judges, and legal academics. He invested substantial resources in building up an authoritarian regime with the tools of legal politics – constructing new courts and law schools and engineering a rapid growth in the number of Sudanese lawyers to perpetuate his legal ideology. In doing so he projected an image of legal integrity while he facilitated massacres in southern Sudan and Darfur.

But legal politics cuts two ways. Authoritarian legal politics in Sudan coexisted and has been forced to contend with a growing vision of humanitarian legal politics. State actors not only promote law in their efforts to manufacture and maintain authority; the subjects of that authority also see legal tools and resources as a way to limit that authority. Nonstate actors in Sudan, alike captivated by the lure of law, adopt legal means to pressure an otherwise recalcitrant state and build up the potential for democracy. These nonstate actors have ranged

213

from foreign foundations sponsoring European and North American law professors to teach in Sudan during the 1950s and 1960s to foreign aid agencies and the grassroots operations they funded in the 2000s. They rely on a legal program intimately associated with the promotion of democracy and human rights. But like the struggle of Sudan's state authorities to maintain power, their efforts to win the hearts and minds of the Sudanese people also employ what they call law. The soldiers they conscript into their humanitarian-inspired missions to reform Sudan increasingly come from the vast populations of war-displaced persons in the desert. Having escaped to government-monitored tent cities, they are encouraged to feel empowered by law and to instigate the most restricted of revolutions inspired by the articulation of narrow, (human) rights-based claims. Together, the cases of actors presented in this book – colonial administrators, a succession of struggling post-colonial governments, and civil society actors and the international aid community that funds them – provide evidence that law and legal strategies are the building blocks of statehood – even fragile statehood. Two overlapping regimes of formal law, national and international, give legal politics its salience in a state otherwise plagued by violence and civil war.

While I use the case of Sudan to understand the role of law in build-ing a state, many of the elements associated with colonial, authoritar-ian, and humanitarian legal politics are not unique to fragile states. Democratic states, both robust and weak, and elite actors within them also continually seek to build up law and courts, to guarantee that judges are responsive and efficient, and to ensure that laws are understood and followed. (Indeed, law comprised the building blocks of eighteenth- and nineteenth-century American political development.)[5] As in frag-ile or authoritarian states, activists in democratic polities encourage the poor to understand law and rights discourse as a liberator from oppres-sion and to turn to state courts to resolve disputes and create politi-cal, social, or economic change. The case of Sudan reveals how these elite legal strategies are processes in constant flux. They shape political struggle as legal institutions are built up or broken down, while ordi-nary people draw from the law what they can, to manage their affairs or ameliorate their suffering. Law's significant role in fragile states like Sudan, as in stable democracies, reveals the broad pull of the law and,

[5] See Lawrence M. Friedman, *A History of American Law* (New York: Simon and Schuster, 1973).

ultimately, how the inner morality of the law is shaped by the goals of the actor creating or using its different facets.

BUILDING LAW AND AUTHORITY

The rule of law is typically seen as a force for positive change in an authoritarian state. It has been held up as a way to moderate repressive authority, foster the development of democratic institutions, and promote economic and social development. In short, the rule of law symbolizes a normative desire to promote a democratic, well-functioning state as much as it implies an agenda of legal development.

In practice, however, the activities of legal politics that constitute a program to promote the rule of law – training judges, police, and prison wardens to abide by human rights and educating survivors of war to demand those rights – are inseparable from activities that also strengthen law in a given country. While the two concepts are analytically distinct, it has practically proved challenging if not impossible to build the *rule* of law without building the *law* itself. The cases in this book suggest that forms of legal politics that reinforce the authority and power of legal institutions are more likely to sustain an authoritarian state than to usher in a new era of democratic rule, at least in the short term.

In Sudan, legal politics through law promotion by state elites has supported colonial and authoritarian rule through four primary channels: (1) the imposition of new legal ordinances, (2) the enforcement of the state's ability to punish, (3) the domination of the legal order, and (4) the management of grievances against the regime.

First, a state can pass laws that directly reinforce its control and shape constitutional authority to allow it to do so behind a façade of legitimacy. Even Sudan's democratically elected Parliament in the mid-1960s, fearing the rising influence of the Communist Party, voted to disband it. Parliamentarians designated the High Court's ruling against them a declaratory judgment, thinking that doing so would safeguard the country. Instead, ignoring the Court's authority set in motion a series of events that would lead to a military coup in 1969 led in part by the deposed chief justice, Babiker Awadalla. Decades later, the Comprehensive Peace Agreement and Interim National Constitution of 2005 were among the principal laws animating Bashir's political survival during an uncertain transition out of decades of civil war. The peace agreement marked the beginning of a six-year interim period, Sudan's third transition since its colonial independence. After signing the accords, Bashir became Sudan's first autocratic ruler to retain national control during a transition. He nevertheless maintained an aggressive, offensive posture toward civil society and opposition groups, with the help of new laws that entrenched the political, legal, and educational structure that his regime had spent the better part of the 1990s building. Many of Sudan's laws remained in direct violation of the Interim National Constitution of 2005. (The minister of justice publicly stated in 2007 that about sixty such laws were inconsistent with the Constitution.) But the Constitution also stipulated that existing laws would remain binding until repealed – even if they abrogate the reformist Bill of Rights: "All current laws shall remain in force ... unless new actions are taken in accordance with the provisions of this Constitution."[6] Parliament, predominantly appointed by Bashir's party, was unsurprisingly slow to act in the 2000s, particularly as southern Sudanese politicians focused precious energy on building up their new nation rather than on attempting to displace Bashir in Khartoum.

Further examples of governments using law to enforce domestic control and authority are found outside Sudan. In Chile authoritarian rule that began under General Augusto Pinochet in 1973 was perpetuated through a series of new laws building up to the 1980 constitution that remained in force after Pinochet's ouster.[7] In South Africa's darkest moments of violence under apartheid, successive administrations simultaneously sought to respect the principles of the law and to develop a state apparatus built on oppression.[8]

Second, law promotion also invites state control by exposing individuals to state-enforced punishment. The British strengthened their colonial authority not only by building institutions associated with the rule of law and encouraging Sudanese to use them, but also by increasing the administration's capacity to criminalize threats against it. Summary criminal convictions grew by nearly a third (from about twenty-five thousand to thirty-three thousand per year) under the new laws passed in the two years following a 1924 Sudanese revolt against the British

---

[6] Interim National Constitution of 2005, Section 226.5.

[7] Jens Meierhenrich, *The Legacies of Law: Long-Run Consequences of Legal Development in South Africa, 1652–2000* (Cambridge: Cambridge University Press, 2008), 304–9. See also Brian Loveman, *Chile: The Legacy of Spanish Capitalism*, 3rd ed. (Oxford: Oxford University Press, 2001).

[8] See Meierhenrich (2008). See also Stephen Ellmann, *In a Time of Trouble: Law and Liberty in South Africa's State of Emergency* (Oxford: Clarendon Press, 1992).

administration. In postcolonial Sudan, corporal punishments such as floggings, amputations, and cross-amputations have demonstrated regime authority, particularly during times of instability and unrest. Creating more courts and prisons extends the reach of the state toward its people at the same time – precisely Bashir's strategy in the 1990s to monitor and criminalize actions alleged to be threats to public order. By 2006, a year after the civil war ended, nearly half of Sudan's courts – most of which were constructed by the Bashir government during the war – were criminal courts. Building up legal authority through the criminal law directly expands the state's ability to govern.

Third, legal politics can bolster the authoritarian grip on political power through the legal order. This channel is less direct and transparent, because it extends beyond the legislature and court system. Nondemocratic governments in Sudan from the British to Bashir have gone to great lengths to control the legal order. In an effort to contribute to the broader pan-Arab politics of the time, President Nimeiri and then–Vice President Awadalla in the early 1970s completely realigned Sudan's state legal system from common law to civil law. Shortly after the end of Sudan's first civil war, South Sudan's first law school opened in Juba under President Nimeiri. Decades later, President Bashir – knowing that the Sudanese bar had helped to topple military regimes in 1964 and 1985 – expended capital to build a network of law schools and create a cadre of lawyers educated in the regime's approach to legal order and then monitored the legal profession closely to prevent "legal" attack. By ensuring that law students are indoctrinated in the regime's laws, the state limits the likelihood that they will challenge its existence. Consequently, consideration of how authoritarian governments use legal strategies as political resources – to secure and retain power – needs to look beyond courts and examine legal systems, legal education, legal personnel, and other aspects of the legal order.

Fourth, regimes manage grievances against them under the rubric of the rule of law. Employing the rule of law runs the risk of constraining a regime's ability to act. But accommodating complaints and resolving disputes provide the appearance of moderation, which makes even a defective form of the rule of law useful and helps regimes to gain at least the tacit consent of the governed. To the extent that British district commissioners accommodated people's grievances, the Sudanese grew to expect their foreign rulers to act reasonably and in accordance with the legal system they carefully established and promoted. Decades later, Bashir's creation of public grievance boards that report directly to him, and his administration's acceptance and tacit encouragement of cases concerning harms committed by government ministries, similarly provide an outlet for citizen complaints against institutions of the regime. Like the British, Bashir portrays himself as a benevolent ruler ready to manage and confine government institutions that overstep their boundaries.

Paradoxically, the power of the law to sustain a nondemocratic regime partly stems from the normative content given to it by those who use it to limit that regime. Symbolized and reified as an ahistorical, apolitical institution, law is wielded by governors to achieve their willed ends. To advance his interests domestically and internationally, Bashir in the 2000s promoted an image of himself as a statesman who brought an end to Africa's longest civil war by signing the 2005 CPA and the Interim National Constitution of the same year. (In 1972 Nimeiri had also ended civil war while remaking the legal system to fit his image of political power.) These documents became the legal and constitutional façade on what continued to be an authoritarian regime, buying the Bashir administration at least six more years in power to preside over South Sudan's secession in 2011 and earning it some modicum of legitimacy as a reformed government willing to see South Sudan to its independence.

While it is impossible to know whether people's revolutions like those of 1964 or 1985 could emerge once again in Sudan (as they did in 2011 in Egypt and Tunisia, among other places), Bashir swept away for at least a short time the possibility of a widespread uprising after 2005. The signing of the peace agreement, witnessed by world leaders, focused attention on Bashir's ability to end war and to create legal reform. The Sudanese I met in 2006–7 and in 2010 were largely frustrated at what they felt was a lack of implementation of the peace deal and the provisions of the constitution – *kalaam fadi* (empty words), they called these documents. But such empty words have gone a long way to providing an aura of reform.

The legitimizing glow surrounding legal innovations also comes from the expansion of law into the private sphere, a tactic used by both colonial and postcolonial administrations in Sudan. Promoting law has extended the reach of the state and has helped regimes to gain legitimacy by being responsive to people's daily lives and reinforcing their moral codes and norms of behavior. Over time people began to turn to the colonial administration to resolve tens of thousands of disputes. By 2010, Bashir's courts were handling hundreds of thousands of cases brought each year by Sudanese citizens.

The symbolic authority provided by the elite promotion of law and other practices of legal politics, ultimately reinforcing existing structures of power and class, is far from limited to Sudan. Parallels can be found even to eighteenth-century England, where, by facilitating obedience in lower classes, the law protected the ownership rights of propertied classes. Investigating the law's dominion over class structures, Douglas Hay writes,

> The law ... became something more than the creature of a ruling class – it became a power with its own claims, higher than those of prosecutor, lawyers, and even the great scarlet-robed ... judge himself. To them, too, of course, the law was The Law. The fact that they reified it, that they shut their eyes to its daily enactment in Parliament by men of their own class, heightened the illusion. When the ruling class acquitted men on technicalities they helped instill a belief in the disembodied justice of the law in the minds of all who watched. In sort, its very inefficiency, its absurd formalism, was part of its strength as ideology.[9]

Examples of the symbolic power of the law are also to be found across states coping with war, brutality, violence, and suffering. In those places, as in Sudan, law has played a prominent part in the struggle for stability, even in the moments when the most astute observer might imagine law to be absent from harrowing accounts of violence, civil war, and survival. Despotic regimes have used and continue to use law to stabilize themselves and leave a legal legacy. As in Sudan, law is lived in a variety of unstable conflict-laden and postconflict political contexts – in post-Soviet Russia, Liberia, Bosnia following the collapse of Yugoslavia, Congo, Chad, and Somalia. The poor experience the blunt force of the law in their daily lives. It is a source of their suffering and of their confusion: they are being trained to see it as the key that unlocks the door to their liberation – as it simultaneously locks them in oppression. They encounter both authoritarian and humanitarian forms of legal politics at the same time. They do not live in a legal vacuum; rather, law frames both their suffering and how they are instructed to imagine their salvation.

In the early 1990s following the collapse of the Soviet Union, Western nongovernmental organizations rushed to a rapidly declining

---

[9] Douglas Hay, "Property, Authority, and the Criminal Law," in Hay, Linebaugh, Rule, Thompson, and Winslow, *Albion's Fatal Tree: Crime and Society in Eighteenth Century England* (London: Allen Lane, 1975), 33.

Russia to teach local women's groups about human rights and how to access Russian legal institutions.[10] Julie Hemment's ethnographic portrait of these interventions concludes, "It looked like the victory of ... civil society ... over states. However, these [legal] interventions of the supposedly post-ideological age were deeply ideological," propping up former Soviet elites and reorienting the goals and strategies of independent women's groups.[11]

During and immediately after Liberia's transition to democracy in 2003–6, local and international groups worked to raise awareness of new laws hastily being passed. They encouraged the poor to find lawyers and go to the courts for justice, though the legal system was imperfect, the courts were weak, the country's only law school was collapsing, and the Liberian Bar Association, with its 215 members, was uncoordinated and diffuse.[12] International aid groups encouraged the government to conduct consultations in this atmosphere of legal chaos. While it was largely superficial, the consultative legal process helped lend credibility to an otherwise unreliable government.

After the breakup of Yugoslavia, international aid workers and diplomats in Bosnia-Herzegovina sought to build up state capacity by focusing on the enactment of new laws, particularly a national election law. Their elite-level work was built on an appeal to Bosnians to adopt a more "European" identity and vision of the rule of law. Local political leaders, however, were concerned with how the rule of law could "maintain power and the status quo."[13] The legal development strategies of the aid community were thus detached from the reality of elites

[10] Julie Hemment, *Empowering Women in Russia: Activism, Aid and NGOs* (Bloomington: Indiana University Press, 2007).

[11] Ibid., 139.

[12] See *Liberia: Resurrecting the Justice System*, Africa Report No. 107, International Crisis Group, April 6, 2006. See also "Executive Challenges Members of Liberian Bar Association," Press Release of the Government of the Republic of Liberia, January 23, 2009. Available: http://www.emansion.gov.lr/press.php?news_id=1046 (accessed January 9, 2013). See also Till Blume, "Security and Justice Institutions in Liberia: From State Collapse toward Institutions," unpublished research paper presented to London School of Economics Crisis States Research Centre, May 24, 2007, p. 9 (copy on file with author).

[13] See Kimberly Coles, "Ambivalent Builders: Europeanization, the Production of Difference, and Internationals in Bosnia-Herzegovina," 25 PoLAR (2002): 1–18, 7–8. See also Kimberly Coles, *Democratic Designs: International Intervention and Electoral Practices in Post-War Bosnia-Herzegovina* (Ann Arbor: University of Michigan Press, 2007).

seeking to maintain their authority after the transition, and largely immaterial to the Bosnian poor, whose identities had no connection to the European-focused marketing campaigns for the election law.

In 2010 when Somalia was ranked the world's most failed state by the Fund for Peace (edging out Sudan), the United Nations Development Programme trained more than five hundred police officers to apply the country's penal and traffic codes. UNDP proclaimed, "Courts registered 6500 cases in 2010 compared to 500 in 2008 due to UNDP's capacity building efforts. Furthermore, 54 male[s] and 33 females graduated ... from the Faculty of Law at the University of Hargeisa [in semiauto-nomous Somaliland]. Eleven males and fourteen females in this group benefited from a UNDP scholarship."[14] More cases in the courts, and more lawyers in the streets – more law – has become a proxy for build-ing the rule of law. This strategy has also been the central focus of Bashir's authoritarian legal politics in Sudan for at least two decades, just as it was the core of colonial legal politics in Sudan and Britain's other colonial outposts.

Beneath the shattered streets and shallow graves almost ubiquitous in states tortured by civil war and political violence, the law is pres-ent and articulated as a form of salvation. Where aid agencies tread, they find and fund local lawyers and civil society activists who replicate their interests in building up the law, perhaps just as their weak gov-ernments hoped they would. In Sudan, on every page one turns in the history books blackened by the charred remains of immolated villages and bloodied by the millions of victims of warfare, one finds governing powers wielding law as if it were a gun facilitating their theft of politi-cal or national wealth. Legal strategies repeatedly helped to promote a strong central authority's illegitimate claims to power. The actions of Turco-Egyptian colonialists of the nineteenth century, British colo-nialists of the twentieth century, and the Bashir military regime of the twenty-first century reveal how central authorities have sought to employ legal power as an instrument for consolidating control over diverse groups. State-controlled procedures and state-sponsored outlets for grievances buttress the state's claims to legal authority and legiti-macy. Law in this sense strengthens a state's power, its hegemony, and its ability to tyrannize. For Sudan's most oppressed minorities – those

---

[14] UNDP Somalia, "The Rule of Law and Security (ROLS) 2010 Project Achievements." Available: http://www.so.undp.org/index.php/The-Rule-Of-Law-and-Security-ROL S-2010-project-achievements.html (accessed January 9, 2013).

displaced by war to live out their days in desert encampments – human rights becomes an unlikely ideological tool to put in the legal toolkit. Any hope that human rights offer for liberation must be tempered by the realities of the regime under which people live.

THE REACH OF THE LAW

At best, the extension of law's reach and the development of legal institutions have done little to realize the broader social goal of a lasting peace and poverty alleviation, as aid workers hope. At worst, law has served as one of the instruments that authoritarian governments use to consolidate their rule. However, this discussion should not be taken to mean that law itself somehow has an inherently harmful quality, simply because the assumption underlying rights-based approaches to development – namely, that law's benevolent, democracy-inspiring influence would lead to positive political and social change – does not stand up to empirical scrutiny. Rather, the cases from Sudan presented in this book demonstrate that the normative content of the law – and, by extension, the rule of law – is shaped by the actors who use it.

For not only the Bashir regime and its predecessors have sought to use law, legal personnel, and institutions. The international aid community and the activists and lawyers they fund in Sudan have been similarly tempted by the law, seeing it as an instrument for reform and a bulwark against chaos and collapse. They have sought to impose a notion of law on the Sudanese that is rooted in Western values of political liberalism and in the centrality of the individual. Although this notion of law has little traction beyond the local civil society groups paid to promote legal solutions, it remains the predominant approach to legal development and empowerment in Sudanese civil society.

Elites seek to create legal solutions to deliver themselves and others from the harms they confront. The appeal of law as an expression of values is certainly real, from conflicted states such as Sudan to the robust democracies of Western Europe and North America. The promotion of legal solutions by elite actors across the world reveals how society gives law its multifaceted nature, to combat society's ills and achieve its hopes.[15] The intuitive belief in the value of law is precisely what allows

---

[15] On law's immanence in social order, see Eugen Ehrlich, *Fundamental Principles of the Sociology of Law* (New Brunswick, NJ: Transaction Publishers, 2002 [Cambridge, MA: Harvard University Press, 1936]). See also Philip Selznick, "Sociology of Law,"

elite actors to embrace, distort, and manipulate law in times of failing politics. It is certainly not a categorical harm that elite actors promote law. Nevertheless, features of law and law promotion shadow the precarious paths toward political violence or salvation from it.

The symbolic power of the law gives it the illusion of stability while its very nature is unstable, capable of easy manipulation by elite actors, both domestic and foreign, state and nonstate. Thus, law has considerable psychic power not only for state actors who use it as the driving force behind their authority, but also for nonstate actors who use it to shake the foundation upon which that authority rests. Law has the same allure as religion. Law punishes, and it saves. Paul Kahn has written that "the issue is not whether the law makes us better off, but rather what it is that the law makes us."[16] In conflicted societies like Sudan, struggling governments use the law to make their rule more stable, but ironically law's internal instability also allows civil society to employ it.

My data in this book call attention to the need for further research on law and society in insecure areas within and beyond the global South, and when it is safe for the researcher and for those interacting with the researcher. Specific areas of further investigation into the role of legal politics in fragile states include 1) the ways in which aid practitioners use law to transfer ideologies of hope to the poor and 2) the multidimensional and uneven relationship between international conceptions of rights and grassroots approaches to rights and resistance to authoritarian rule.[17] The unsettled and violent history of a nation at war cannot be understood without adequate attention to that nation's uneasy relationship with the law. In these contexts, the law is at once an instrument of tyranny and at the service of liberty, demonstrating the power (and puzzle) of law's rule.

Ending his study of law and class structure in eighteenth-century England, E. P. Thompson famously referred to the rule of law as an "unqualified human good." Even when the law was used to instill fear in the poor, he argued, it was more than just a pliable instrument to

---

in *The Encyclopedia of Philosophy*, Vol. 7 (London: Macmillan, 1967), 478–80, as cited in Martin Krygier, *Philip Selznick: Ideals in the World* (Stanford, CA: Stanford University Press, 2012), 122–4, 208–10.

[16] Paul W. Kahn, *The Cultural Study of Law: Reconstructing Legal Scholarship* (Chicago: University of Chicago Press, 1999), 6.

[17] See Leila Kawar and Mark Fathi Massoud, "Symposium: New Directions in Comparative Public Law," 22(3) *American Political Science Association Law & Courts Section Newsletter* 32–36 (Fall 2012).

be wielded "this way and that" by whichever state actor held power.[18] While his study concluded that law existed on its own as an ideology to serve and to legitimize power tightly controlled by elites, he also demonstrated that law later served to constrain those powers. My findings about colonial law in Sudan come to a similar conclusion.

THE POLITICS OF THE LEGAL PROFESSION

The fact that law's normative content proceeds from those who use it challenges the view that building law will lead to a robust rule of law or a reduction in political repression. Such a conclusion is less surprising when one considers that law is primarily shaped by the people who constitute the legal profession – in Sudan, a cadre of individuals trained to work under the law, though many seek to advance deep political convictions and aspirations. Rather than constituting a distinct segment of the society, the profession has permeable boundaries with the government and civil society elites.

Modern Sudan is a critical case providing evidence of how the legal profession, when under control, can itself become an instrument of a central authority's tyrannical objectives. Most notably, Babiker Awadalla, Sudan's most prominent chief justice and proponent of the rule of law, joined a military coup in 1969 and proceeded to tear down the legal structures he had carefully built up for the better part of two decades. In Sudan, lawyers and judges under democratic administrations have been just as active in the fight for political stability as military and sectarian elites have been. (Civil war has raged during every democratic and military administration in Sudan.) Many of these military and sectarian elites are themselves legally trained or closely advised by lawyers, as in the case of Babiker Awadalla's relationship with President Nimeiri, and Hassan al-Turabi's relationship with President Bashir. Government ministers and officials often shift into and out of positions in private practice or the judiciary or legal academia before or after their time in state administration.

The boundary of the legal profession is also permeable to aid agencies and civil society organizations that ostensibly work against the regime's interests. But here, the goals of the individual lawyers can be focused as much on personal advancement as on social change. For

---

[18] E. P. Thompson, *Whigs and Hunters: The Origin of the Black Act* (New York: Pantheon Books, 1975), 266.

civil society elites, human rights work offers the assurance of career mobility. Sitting on a small bench just outside the law faculty of the University of Khartoum, a student looking forward to her graduation commented to me that if she does not find a job "in banking, it will be in human rights." She concluded, "I enjoy human rights."[19] Like the financial industry, the field of human rights promises relatively stable employment, skills attainment, economic gain, and the future opportunity to leave Sudan and work abroad. International agencies that promote human rights in Sudan arrive armed with promises to the Sudanese of on-the-job training and a chance to implement the international community's goal of building the rule of law. But in entering Sudan, they stratify and separate elites who profit from human rights from the poor who have less to gain from a new ideology.

TOWARD A RESPONSIVE LAW

At the twilight of colonialism, European powers began to endow select local elites with ruling capacity, handing to them the colonial project of lifting countries of the global South out of "backwardness" and into the "civilized" world. These local elites, usually from a single ethnic or religious group, labored under colonialism, but they also benefited from their relationships with foreigners.[20] Meanwhile, a political underclass was maintained – the groups of "backward" individuals unable to gain from the transnational-local interactions of colonial legal politics. Decades later, the United Nations would similarly encourage Sudanese people to interact with it and the state by creating a network of court-like centers in towns and villages throughout Sudan. Much in the same way, transnational-local interactions rooted in humanitarian legal politics do not benefit the targets in the manner intended, although it is undeniable that rule-of-law programs unwittingly produce educational benefits. But funding mechanisms create a new category of local elites, who grow wealthier and shift into and out of jobs with international aid groups or United Nations agencies. International relationships translate into increased salaries. While a higher salary yields obvious benefits, it also widens an economic gulf, making local civil society elites appear more like their international counterparts than like the

---

[19] Interview with Nayima, law student, in Khartoum, Sudan (April 2007).

[20] See Heather Sharkey, *Living with Colonialism: Nationalism and Culture in the Anglo-Egyptian Sudan* (Berkeley: University of California Press, 2003).

225

domestic poor people whom they purportedly assist and represent. This stratification challenges the notion that education about law and human rights reaches the deepest roots where effects are intended.

The problem facing a fragile nation like Sudan is not one of a lack of law. Rather, it is the balance of power in the use of law: law becomes one more weapon in the arsenal. The challenge is not to fill the vacuum, but to understand who will turn to legal strategies and when they will try to use legal strategies. Though certainly a source of hope and education for civil society, formal law is less likely to be used by the poor, for whom it also creates a form of subjugation rather than liberation.

The rule-of-law ideology, like a cloth draped over an aggressive animal, is an attempt by nonstate actors to subdue autocratic leaders. But constructing an elaborate judicial system may not be the best way to deal with authoritarian regimes or collapsing states. Political authorities in Sudan have been struggling since the colonial administration to construct a judicial system responsive to political rulers' need for social support. So, under what circumstances might legal politics create space for regime change, as happened in late colonial Sudan? The preliminary answer from Sudan suggests that the path to the rule of law may be as political, violent, and chaotic as civil war itself. It also suggests that a regime's perception of its durability matters as much as its strategies matter. The colonial regime saw itself as in the service of the British Crown and also to a limited extent of the people of Sudan. But it was facing not only an increasingly vocal group of Sudanese who sought to unite with Egypt, but also a broader decline in the British imperial project. Knowing that their days were numbered, the British sought to leave the Sudanese with knowledge of the rule of law and the rules of parliamentary government. To preserve the Crown's relationship with Sudan, administrators helped rush the Sudanese to independence.

In Sudan and other states confronting colonial, authoritarian, and humanitarian legacies, law emerges and is exploited in the context of catastrophe. In the most tragic of these circumstances, state and nonstate actors fumble to control it, but few succeed. The poor remain poor – in Sudan, Somalia, Chad, Liberia, post-Soviet Russia, apartheid South Africa, and Pinochet's Chile. As Sudan's brightest civil society activists leave in search of opportunities elsewhere, or as they die out, who will replace them? As a result of the Arabization policies of the 1990s, many young Sudanese from elite families do not speak English (unlike their parents or grandparents). Civil society's interdependent relationship with the international donor community requires a command of

English to write proposals and reports to secure and maintain funding. Even in non-English-speaking societies like Sudan, English prevails as the modern language of human rights. The lack of English-language fluency among civil society activists will hinder their development for at least a generation, further isolating the Sudanese from transnational advocacy groups and human rights networks. Meanwhile, government ministries continue to fund intensive English-language training programs for senior government officials and bureaucrats. Understanding the emergence of any future civil society in Sudan means recognizing the many roles that the language of law plays in oppression and in liberation, in constructing identity and legal personhood and in destroying it, and in giving civil society activists a purpose for existence (to educate others about law and to change "lived law") while limiting the scope of their goals through the government's watchful security apparatus.

The January 2011 plebiscite, in which southern Sudanese decided to form a new nation, passed by an overwhelming 99 percent. Six months later, the world welcomed South Sudan as its newest country. The fate of those living in both Sudans, however, remains tenuous. If history is any indication, urban stability may only be achieved at the price of one-party rule, failed democracies, and war. Rural areas may continue to suffer. Encampments for displaced persons may become permanent fixtures in the desert. And legal strategies will continue to be employed by elite actors in the unstable cycle of war, chaos, and transition.

Contrary to Martin Krygier's notion that "the law does not rule in a failed state,"[21] Sudan presents a case where the state would not exist in its current form without the chaotic and tragic mismanagement of the law throughout its history. I do not take issue with Krygier's four outcomes of the rule of law: a reduction of domination, of fear, of indignity, and of confusion.[22] I cannot long for these four outcomes to be realized in Sudan any more than Gladys or Nisreen or Salma can long for them. These three women continue to live in the stark and miserable desert outside Khartoum under the watchful eye of Bashir's network of police,

---

[21] Martin Krygier, "Approaches to the Rule of Law," in *The Rule of Law in Afghanistan: Missing in Inaction*, ed. Whit Mason (Cambridge: Cambridge University Press, 2011), 17.

[22] Martin Krygier, "Four Puzzles about the Rule of Law: Why, What, Where? And Who Cares?" in *Getting to the Rule of Law*, ed. James Fleming, NOMOS 54 (New York: New York University Press, 2011).

while I write these words only recollecting the miseries they privately shared with me.

But Gladys, Nisreen, and Salma may never experience the other face of the law that can potentially save them. For them to experience a reduction in their suffering, Sudan must be transformed from a state in which law serves the violent interests of the powerful to one in which it secures the dignity of each person and his or her community. Even in the nation's most decisive democratic transformations in 1956, 1964, and 1985, the poor received no such relief. They remain waiting; their hope returns each morning to greet the rising sun.

I do not in these reflections on legal politics in Sudan reject the concept of law as justice. After all, what did Sudanese nationalists in the 1950s – and Gandhi in India a decade earlier – use to liberate their people except the very British law that had been oppressing so many of them? I carry from my untroubled and expectant years of legal education my own ideal aspirations of what the law must be. Disenchanted by my historical observations of Sudan, however, I must temper my aspirations with knowledge of the ways in which law has been suborned to serve the cause of despotism. In seeking to understand the law, I have illuminated its contours and facets, its myriad uses in the service of war and of tyranny, of peace and of liberty. Law provides a diverse set of tools for all those conscious of their weaknesses – from struggling despots to aspiring subjects.

The realities of power are not disguised in law. Rather, my longitudinal study of Sudan has shown that legal practices reveal these realities of power openly. But nonstate actors bewilder themselves by focusing energy on law's uses as an instrument for human rights – often at the expense of delivering actual services and with the by-product of preventing large-scale protests in favor of institutionalized strategies that will ultimately be controlled and stymied by the regime. The malleability of law helps state power to sustain itself while legal strategies mystify nonstate actors into adopting narrower forms of rhetoric and mobilization rooted in rights consciousness. And for the most indigent ethnic and religious minorities displaced by war who have never experienced the luxury of justice – and who may never experience it if Sudan (North and South) continues down its historically chaotic path – the ideal of human rights has become a tool of ugly politics.

This book has revealed that in a state as embroiled in civil war and authoritarian rule as Sudan, the law (and the process of building the rule of law) is not an unqualified human good. This does not mean that we who believe in justice should give up the struggle against bad laws or "disarm ourselves before power."[23] It means that, in this century, in the face of bulging bureaucracies, inefficient courts, and recurrent warfare, law is not the powerful weapon of the weak to push states to protect what decent people call human rights. Nor is law powerful enough to engage activists in a radical reassessment of how states operate. Effective nonviolent critiques and revolutions begin the old-fashioned way, when groups of people – crowds – stand together in the streets, not in courtrooms; sit in together, protest together, risk their lives together at the hands of unjust rulers for the kind of justice in which they believe.[24] This kind of people power in 2011 toppled recalcitrant governments in Egypt and Tunisia and has been, in the more than fifty years since Sudan's independence, the country's only effective catalyst for democracy. The most effective critiques of the Sudanese state have come from nonviolent movements within that state – from the poor and wealthy, nonlawyer and lawyer.

Like E. P. Thompson before me, I have stepped out onto my precarious ledge. But like Thompson's study of property law in England, "even this study does not prove that all law as such is bad."[25] Legal empowerment provides a host of unintended benefits, often unrelated to the law and insufficient to achieving its intended goal of justice, but necessary nonetheless to provide some relief from decades of displacement.

But in a divided society and volatile state, the activities of state and nonstate actors risk refashioning legal tools into weapons. Weapons are wielded both to kill and to protect, according to the intent of the actor who carries them. But a weapon must be regulated and controlled. Its power and potential for misuse must be understood. In this century, law is used perilously, and the protection of human rights is subverted to justify various military interventions across the Middle East and Africa. But this study has shown how even in the extreme context of Sudan, state and nonstate actors have turned toward the law. Those subjected to it and those who subject them to it all believe in law's power.

In early-modern England, ruling classes ultimately surrendered to this power of the law, rather than "shatter their own self-image and

---

[23] Thompson (1975), 266.

[24] See Erica Chenoweth and Maria J. Stephan, *Why Civil Resistance Works: The Strategic Logic of Nonviolent Conflict* (New York: Columbia University Press, 2011).

[25] Thompson (1975), 267.

repudiate 150 years of constitutional legality."[26] In Sudan's divided, multicultural, multiethnic, multilingual context – a state so tragically different from E. P. Thompson's eighteenth-century England – Bashir's government has nevertheless found itself able to maintain power for more than two decades despite lacking steady social support. The Sudanese who suffer cannot wait for "constitutional legality" to deliver them from injustice at some unknown time from now, only to be tyrannized again by another autocrat. True legality can provide hope, but hope must accompany needed services, like health clinics, schools, clean water, and electricity.

For those of us, like Thompson, who have dreamed of seeing a world in which law prevents poverty, in which law serves the poor as much as it mystifies them, in which law truly liberates the oppressed, modern Sudan presents a vexing case. If any moment existed in which law constrained power (and certainly such moments existed), it has surely been overshadowed by the dark times when a ruling despot wielded law like a criminal positions a bullet into his gun.

Like the power of drink enticing an alcoholic, the pathological attraction to controlling law suggests that law itself controls the subject who seeks to control it. Given law's use as an instrument of oppression, it is unlikely that it can be transformed forever into an instrument of liberation – the tension between these goals is what makes law the set of protean tools that it is and will continue to be in war-torn states. At its extremes, like a weapon, law is both the great destroyer and the great liberator. Perhaps, then, it is law whose influence must be monitored and controlled.

[26] Ibid.

APPENDIX A: METHODOLOGICAL DETAIL

The findings in this book rely on a variety of methods, including archival research, interviews with key informants, and ethnographic observations. The purpose of this appendix is to supplement the methodological description found in Chapter 1. Here, I provide further detail on the archival, interview, and data-analysis components of this study, particularly for scholars and students considering projects that involve comparative and historical research in Sudan or other volatile settings.

ARCHIVAL RESEARCH

This section details my research in several archives in England, Egypt, and Sudan.

England

Hundreds of thousands of pages of classified documents and private correspondence – in addition to more than thirty thousand photographs – are meticulously categorized and kept in files and boxes at Durham University's Sudan Archive.[1] Documents are gathered in collections,

---

[1] *See* M. W. Daly and L. E Forbes, *The Sudan: Photographs from the Sudan Archive, Durham University Library* (Reading, UK: Garnet, 1994); Heather J. Sharkey, "Beyond the Sudan Archive: A Guide to Doing Research on the Sudan in Durham," 13 *Sudan Studies* (January 1993): 10–19; L. E. Forbes, "The Sudan Archive, Durham, as a Source for the Study of Modernization in the Sudan" in *Modernization*

organized by box and file numbers. Collections bear the surnames of their donors – British colonial administrators from the Anglo-Egyptian Sudan, for example, Robertson, Udal, Luce, and Hawley. The archive also holds copies of government documents from the Anglo-Egyptian Condominium, including ordinances and the *Annual Reports on the Finances, Administration, and Condition of the Sudan*, published between 1902 and 1952. These serve as the self-reported institutional memory of the colonial administration and provided both the crucial quantitative data for the trend charts and evidence for the argument I construct about colonial legal politics in Chapter 2.

The archivists who cataloged the documents into collections assisted me in finding the most relevant collections to my study of the role of law in Sudan. I narrowed the many thousands of pages of documents to roughly four thousand to five thousand pages relevant to my study of law. To ensure that I was not missing important information, I supplemented my work with the archivists with index searches of words that included "law," "ordinance," and related terms. Building on the work of the historian Heather Sharkey, I hypothesized that law played a key role in creating a Muslim elite in Khartoum and that law simultaneously enabled and disabled their struggle for nationalism during the latter part of Condominium Sudan. Michael McCann's work in law and society also suggested that labor or trade unions would play an important role in legal development.[2] So I searched the archive's index for nonlegal terms to complement my existing searches, including "trade union," "labour," "ethnic," "Muslim," "nationalism," and related words. I noted the results and requested hundreds of files, three at a time. Further reading helped me to refine my searches and conduct additional rounds of document review. Using bibliographic computer software, I annotated about five hundred of the most relevant documents into searchable and digitized "libraries" that included relevant quotations and their sources. In this book, I cite Sudan Archive sources as the archive categorizes them, using their box, file, and page numbers (for example, 863/4/23–25).

in the Sudan: Essays in Honor of Richard Hill, ed. M. W. Daly (New York: Lillian Barber Press, 1985), 161–70; E. S. B. Cory and L. E. Forbes, "Resource for Sudanese Studies: The Sudan Archive of the University of Durham," 31 *African Research and Documentation* (1983): 1–11.

[2] Michael McCann, *Rights at Work: Pay Equity Reform and the Politics of Legal Mobilization* (Chicago: University of Chicago Press, 1994).

Secondary literature provides an essential check on the accuracy of hypotheses generated from examining primary historical records (and vice versa). In order to complement my study of original sources from the Sudan Archive, I conducted a literature review of relevant sources at the library of the School of Oriental and African Studies (SOAS), University of London, which holds one of the most extensive collections of books on Sudan. I worked closely with the custodians of the law collections and Sudan collections to find those most relevant to the role of law in the colonial enterprise, nationalist struggles, and strategies of postcolonial governance and foreign humanitarian development.

Egypt

The bond between Sudan and Egypt is the "most ancient" of Sudan's foreign relationships.[3] And because of Sudan's sensitive and unsettled relationship with the Western world, Egyptian and Arabic-language scholars have had more success than Western scholars (though not total success) in getting visas to, researching in, and writing scholarly works about Sudan. For these reasons I traveled to Egypt to access historical records as well as books on Sudan, at the National Archives in Cairo, and dissertations and other documents on Sudan, at the American University of Cairo.

Because Britain colonized Sudan nominally with Egypt and utilized Egyptian technical, logistical, and financial support, I did a close reading of Egyptian historical accounts to check the reliability of the data I had gathered at Durham University's Sudan Archive, which had been written from the perspective of the British colonial administrators. At *Dar al-Kutub al-Masri* (Egyptian National Archives) I began the Egyptian component of my archival research by conducting a computer-based search of books and documents with "Sudan" in the title. I narrowed to the relevant citations related to law and politics (and not, say, agriculture), requested each of them, and took notes by hand and later translated and digitized them into my bibliographic software. I accessed relevant books and documents on the development of the legal system in Sudan. These included Arabic-language books on the historical relationship between Egypt and Sudan[4] (a relationship that shaped Sudan's

---

[3] John O. Voll and Sarah P. Voll, *The Sudan: Unity and Diversity in a Multicultural State* (Boulder, CO: Westview Press, 1985).

[4] Abdullah Abd Al-Razaq Ibrahim and Showqi Al-Jamal, *Tarikh Masr Wa al-Sudan al-Hadith Wa al-Mu'aasar [Contemporary and Modern History of Egypt and Sudan]*

struggle for nationalism and the independent nation's legal system, illuminated in Chapter 3), as well as scholarship on Sudanese democratic movements,[5] religiosity,[6] and civil society.[7] Computer-based searches in Egypt were a remarkable contrast to the handwritten paper indices I had to use in Sudanese archives and libraries.

At the American University of Cairo, I accessed a number of more contemporary secondary sources on Sudan, including human rights reports related to Sudan's legal and prison systems[8] and dissertations written by Sudanese nationals, providing an additional perspective to the works I studied elsewhere.[9]

Sudan

Archival research in Sudan afforded me the opportunity to collect historical data and records produced after colonial independence. During my time in Sudan, I was able to obtain permission to enter and collect written records from the following six sources: *Dar al-Watha'iq al-Qowmi* (National Records Office), the Ministry of Justice, and the following four libraries: the University of Khartoum Law Library, the Sudan Library, the Judiciary Library, and the Ahfad University for Women library. I also made use of English-language scholarly books on Sudanese history, available at the British Council Library.

After a lengthy process to obtain permission to enter the National Records Office, I used the only available index, the handwritten *masadir al-dirasat al-sudaniyya* (Sources of Sudanese Studies) in order to

(Cairo: Dar al-Thaqafah lil-Nashr wa al-Towze'a,1997). *See also* Showqi Ata Allah Al-Jamal, *Tarikh al-Sudan wa Wadi al-Nil wa Alaqat Misr* [*History of the Sudan, the Nile Valley, and Relations with Egypt*] (Cairo: Anglo-Egyptian Library, 1980).

[5] Zaki Al-Bahiri, *Al-Haraka al-Demokratiyya Fi al-Sudan 1943–1985* [*The Democratic Movement in Sudan 1943–1985*] (Dar Nahdat al-Sharq, Cairo University, 1990).

[6] Mahjoub Al Tijani, *Al-Din Wa al-Dowla Fi al-Sudan* [*Religion and the State in Sudan*] (Cairo: Legal Studies and Information Center on Human Rights, 1990).

[7] Heidr Ibrahim Ali, *Al Mujtama al-Madani Wa al-Tahawul al-Demokrati Fi al-Sudan* [*Civil Society and Democratic Transformation in Sudan*] (Cairo: Ibn Khaldoun Center Press, 1995).

[8] Africa Watch (1991), *Sudan – Inside Al Bashir's Prisons: Torture, Denial of Medical Attention and Poor Conditions* (Washington, DC: Lawyer's Committee for Human Rights, 1996); Rone (1996).

[9] See M. O. O. El-Faki, *Islam and Human Rights: A Case Study of the National Islamic Front (NIF) in the Sudan*. MA Thesis, Sociology and Anthropology. Cairo: American University of Cairo, 1995.

find appropriate copies of newspapers, magazines, and other sources on independent Sudan. Many of these sources evidenced both government opinion (e.g., through the nationalized press) and that of the intelligentsia in Khartoum (e.g., local "zines" or periodicals put out by socialists or literary groups in the short-lived democratic period of the 1960s).

At the University of Khartoum's Faculty of Law, I accessed copies of the annual *Sudan Law Journal and Reports* (*SLJR*), a combined case reporter (a record of important written judicial opinions) and law review (articles by law professors and other legal scholars). The *SLJR* debuted in English, with most articles written by European or American law professors who taught at the University of Khartoum during the 1950s and 1960s. Since the 1970s, it has been published primarily in Arabic. At the Sudan Library of the University of Khartoum, I accessed dissertations and books documenting legal work, trade union organizing, and civil society development in Sudan. At the library of the Sudan Judiciary administration, I accessed historical records and documents about the development of Sudan's legal system. At Ahfad University for Women, I accessed materials on minority rights, women's rights, and legal aid campaigns in Sudan. These historical and contemporary materials cannot be found elsewhere and served as a check on what lawyers, civil society activists, and government officials had told me during my interviews with them.

Gathering sensitive or hidden data depends on building rapport and trust with relevant officials who keep these data secure. While I was in Sudan, many of the lawyers and judges I met had spoken to me about what they felt was an increasing quantity of courts and lawyers alongside a decreasing quality of these legal institutions and the legal profession – indicators of changes in the function and character of law in Sudan. But no one seemed to have information on exactly how many courts and lawyers existed in Sudan, nor the ability to measure change over time. It was a series of uncorroborated but consistent "hunches." After months of promises and return trips, I succeeded in locating quantitative data on the growth in numbers of courts and lawyers in Sudan from the time of independence, part of the essential evidence for my argument about how military administrations use legal tools and resources to build consent for their rule and legitimate their authority. Many of these data had been unpublished and kept in the dusty bottoms of locked file cabinets.

IN-DEPTH INTERVIEWS

Interviews with state officials and civil society activists focused on gathering facts dealing with behaviors as well as perceptions of the functions of law and legal strategies. Interviewees were asked different questions based on their relative positions. Members of the legal profession spoke frankly and broadly about the differences they experienced in their work as attorneys or judges during the various political administrations in power, the relationship between the bench and bar, judicial independence, and the roles of religion and custom. (Much of this research appears in Chapter 3 and Chapter 4.) Civil society activists spoke to me about their motivations, as well as about their personal and organizational goals, leadership, campaigns, and strategies, particularly legal or court-based strategies. I also asked them about key issues they faced in their work, challenges and obstacles to achieving their goals, why they chose to work in civil society, and the extent to which their families and communities have supported their decisions. These questions helped me to understand their efforts, particularly the legal strategies they chose and their perceived usefulness. Finally, I asked them about their relationships with international donors and aid agencies and how these connections affect their work. (Much of this research on humanitarian legal politics appears in Chapter 5 and Chapter 6.) Each interview lasted from half an hour to eight hours, with an average of about seventy-five minutes. To protect confidentiality, I translated and transcribed data into English on my own. I kept all data in encrypted, password-protected files.

ANALYSIS AND CODING

I coded all documents I created (more than two hundred of them) using the Text Analysis Mark-Up Software (TAMS) Analyzer program. I developed, checked, and used more than three-hundred-and-fifty codes and subcodes; for example, "colonialism>effects>religious," "courts>procedure," and "NGOs>strategies>networking." Using these codes I analyzed individual themes as they appeared across interview transcripts and field notes. I also developed "metacodes" to allow me to search transcripts by demographic data.

Triangulation helped me to confirm the validity of each piece of information I gathered. For instance, I collected materials from government archives in Sudan as well as from sources in England and Egypt.

I compared statements by government actors with those of activists and opposition leaders. Triangulation is "a vehicle for cross validation when two or more distinct methods ... yield comparative data."[10] I analyzed the empirical data through systematic translation, transcription, and computer-aided coding and analysis of my interview transcripts, field notes, and historical materials.

[10] Todd D. Jick, "Mixing Qualitative and Quantitative Methods: Triangulation in Action," 24(4) *Administrative Science Quarterly* (1979): 602–11, at 602.

APPENDIX B: INTERVIEW LIST

Note: The author conducted all interviews, except numbers 172–5 in this list, which were conducted by a research assistant under the author's supervision. Fifteen of these 175 interviews are repeat interviews, listed accordingly. Unless otherwise indicated, all interview names in this list are pseudonyms.

1. Interview with Mustafa, NGO director, in Khartoum, Sudan (May 2005).
2. Interview with Samira, NGO director, in Khartoum, Sudan (June 2005).
3. Interview with Waleeda, school teacher and volunteer, in Khartoum, Sudan (June 2005).
4. Interview with Muhammad, NGO project manager, in Khartoum, Sudan (June 2005).
5. Interview with Habiba, women's rights activist, in Khartoum, Sudan (June 2005).
6. Interview with Farid, NGO executive director, in Khartoum, Sudan (June 2005).
7. Interview with Najib, NGO chairperson, in Khartoum, Sudan (June 2005).
8. Interview with Elias, law professor, in Khartoum, Sudan (June 2005).
9. Interview with Salma, internally displaced person in Haj Yoosef, Sudan (June 2005).
10. Interview with Nada, internally displaced person in Haj Yoosef, Sudan (June 2005).

11. Interview with Nisreen, internally displaced person, in Haj Yoosef, Sudan (June 2005).

12. Interview with Yoosef, legal aid attorney from Darfur, in Khartoum, Sudan (June 2005).

13. Interview with senior official, Sudan Bar Association, in Khartoum, Sudan (June 2005).

14. Interview with Majda, women's rights activist, in Khartoum, Sudan (June 2005).

15. Interview with Sohir, NGO director, in Khartoum, Sudan (June 2005).

16. Interview with Abdullah, NGO program manager, in Khartoum, Sudan (June 2005).

17. Interview with Tofeeq, NGO founder and director, in Khartoum, Sudan (June 2005).

18. Interview with Najwa, health awareness educator, in Mayo camp for displaced persons, in Khartoum, Sudan (June 2005).

19. Interview with Leila, school administrator, in Omdurman, Sudan (June 2005).

20. Interview with Raouf, human rights activist, in Khartoum, Sudan (June 2005).

21. Interview with Amina, NGO program manager, in Khartoum, Sudan (June 2005).

22. Interview with Wahib, NGO information officer, in Khartoum, Sudan (June 2005).

23. Interview with Maher, legal aid attorney from Darfur, in Khartoum, Sudan (June 2005).

24. Interview with Nahda, women's rights activist, in Omdurman, Sudan (June 2005).

25. Interview with Adil, lawyer and member of Parliament, in Khartoum, Sudan (July 2005).

26. Interview with Nabil, lawyer, in Khartoum, Sudan (July 2005).

27. Interview with law professor and judicial-training consultant, in England (September 2006).

28. Interview with Sir Donald Hawley, former Chief Registrar of Sudan Judiciary (1953–55), in Durham, England (October 2006). Note: pseudonym not used.

29. Interview with former law professor of the University of Khartoum, in London, England (October 2006).

30. Interview with Haroob, former law dean, in Khartoum, Sudan (October 2006).

31. Interview with Malika, lawyer, in Khartoum, Sudan (October 2006).

32. Follow-up interview with Samira, NGO director, in Khartoum, Sudan (October 2006).

33. Follow-up interview with Waleeda, school teacher and NGO volunteer, in Khartoum, Sudan (October 2006).

34. Interview with Daoud, human rights lawyer, in Khartoum, Sudan (November 2006).

35. Interview with Omer, human rights lawyer, in Khartoum, Sudan (November 2006).

36. Interview with Salaam, lawyer, in Khartoum, Sudan (November 2006).

37. Interview with Tawfik, NGO associate director, in Khartoum, Sudan (November 2006).

38. Interview with Sunduq, NGO executive director, in Khartoum, Sudan (November 2006).

39. Interview with Taha, NGO director and Sudanese legal consultant to the United Nations, in Khartoum North, Sudan (November 2006).

40. Interview with Shamsiyaa, women's rights activist, in Khartoum, Sudan (November 2006).

41. Interview with Huda, lawyer, in Khartoum, Sudan (November 2006).

42. Interview with Zaki, civil servant, Ministry of the Environment, in Khartoum, Sudan (November 2006).

43. Interview with Jameela, NGO program manager, in Khartoum, Sudan (November 2006).

44. Interview with Bashir, former government minister, in Khartoum, Sudan (November 2006).

45. Interview with Gasim, former government minister, in Khartoum, Sudan (November 2006).

46. Interview with Warren, European lawyer working in Khartoum, Sudan (November 2006).

47. Interview with Ahmed, lawyer, in Khartoum, Sudan (November 2006).

48. Interview with Muhannad, civil society activist, in Khartoum, Sudan (November 2006).

49. Interview with senior judicial official 1, in Khartoum Sudan (December 2006).

50. Interview with senior judicial official 2, in Khartoum, Sudan (December 2006).

51. Interview with Maha, lawyer and legal awareness workshop facilitator, in Khartoum, Sudan (December 2006).

52. Interview with Intisar, lawyer, in Khartoum, Sudan (December 2006).

53. Interview with Hind, civil society activist, in Khartoum, Sudan (December 2006).

54. Follow-up interview with Sir Donald Hawley, former Chief Registrar of Sudan Judiciary (1953–55), in Wiltshire, England (January 2007). Note: pseudonym not used.

55. Follow-up interview with Nabil, lawyer, in Khartoum, Sudan (January 2007).

56. Interview with Fatima, lawyer, in Khartoum, Sudan (January 2007).

57. Interview with Asma, lawyer, in Khartoum, Sudan (January 2007).

58. Interview with Abdul Gadir, lawyer and civil society activist, in Khartoum, Sudan (January 2007).

59. Interview with senior judicial official 3, in Khartoum, Sudan (January 2007).

60. Follow-up interview with senior judicial official 3, in Khartoum, Sudan (January 2007).

61. Follow-up interview with Abdul Gadir, lawyer and civil society activist, in Khartoum, Sudan (January 2007).

62. Interview with Najima, NGO founder, in Khartoum, Sudan (February 2007).

63. Follow-up interview with Samira, NGO director, in Khartoum, Sudan (February 2007).

64. Interview with retired senior judicial official 1, in Khartoum, Sudan (February 2007).

65. Interview with Mansour, lawyer and former government minister, in Khartoum, Sudan (February 2007).

66. Interview with Aarif, government lawyer, in Khartoum, Sudan (February 2007).

67. Interview with Abdullahi, senior judicial official, in Khartoum, Sudan (February 2007).

68. Interview with Babiker Awadalla, former Speaker of Parliament, Chief Justice, and Prime Minister, in Khartoum, Sudan (February 2007). Note: pseudonym not used.

69. Follow-up interview with Malika, lawyer, in Khartoum, Sudan (February 2007).
70. Interview with Sadiq, lawyer, in Khartoum, Sudan (February 2007).
71. Interview with Abdul Moneim, lawyer, in Khartoum, Sudan (February 2007).
72. Interview with Hassan, retired senior judicial official, in Khartoum, Sudan (February 2007).
73. Interview with Balima, human rights activist, in Khartoum, Sudan (March 2007).
74. Interview with Abu Musa, lawyer, in Khartoum, Sudan (March 2007).
75. Interview with Watani, lawyer, in Khartoum, Sudan (March 2007).
76. Interview with senior government official in Khartoum, Sudan (March 2007).
77. Interview with Nahid, lawyer and founder of NGO, in Khartoum, Sudan (March 2007).
78. Interview with Gazila, lawyer and NGO program manager, in Khartoum, Sudan (March 2007).
79. Interview with Noura, lawyer and NGO program manager, in Khartoum, Sudan (March 2007).
80. Interview with Sarah, NGO program assistant, in Khartoum, Sudan (March 2007).
81. Interview with Samir, NGO director, in Khartoum, Sudan (March 2007).
82. Interview with Sandino, judge formerly based in southern Sudan, in Khartoum, Sudan (March 2007).
83. Interview with Safia, police official, in Khartoum, Sudan (March 2007).
84. Follow-up interview with Gazila, lawyer and NGO program manager, in Khartoum, Sudan (March 2007).
85. Interview with Talal, lawyer, in Khartoum, Sudan (April 2007).
86. Interview with Ibtisam, law student, in Khartoum, Sudan (April 2007).
87. Interview with Nayima, law student, in Khartoum, Sudan (April 2007).
88. Follow-up interview with Hassan, retired senior judicial official, in Khartoum, Sudan (April 2007).

89. Follow-up interview with Sohir, NGO director, in Khartoum, Sudan (April 2007).
90. Interview with Tayyib, lawyer, in Khartoum, Sudan (April 2007).
91. Interview with Suleiman, lawyer, in Khartoum, Sudan (April 2007).
92. Interview with Ibn Khalifa, lawyer, in Khartoum, Sudan (April 2007).
93. Interview with Hashim, lawyer, in Khartoum, Sudan (April 2007).
94. Follow-up interview with Suleiman, lawyer, in Khartoum, Sudan (April 2007).
95. Interview with Mukhtar, senior judicial official, in Khartoum, Sudan (April 2007).
96. Interview with Ismael, senior judicial official, in Khartoum, Sudan (April 2007).
97. Interview with Lok, civil society network director, in Juba, South Sudan (April 2007).
98. Interview with Maryann, expatriate aid worker, in Juba, South Sudan (April 2007).
99. Interview with Nicholas, expatriate aid worker and NGO director, in Juba, South Sudan (April 2007).
100. Interview with William, lawyer, in Juba, South Sudan (April 2007).
101. Interview with Corinne, United Nations official, in Juba, South Sudan (April 2007).
102. Interview with Thomas, expatriate lawyer and aid worker, in Juba, South Sudan (April 2007).
103. Interview with Deborah, aid worker with the United Nations, in Juba, South Sudan (April 2007).
104. Interview with Elizabeth, expatriate lawyer and aid worker, in Juba, South Sudan (April 2007).
105. Interview with George, church manager, in Juba, South Sudan (April 2007).
106. Interview with Suletra, former judge, in Juba, South Sudan (April 2007).
107. Interview with senior legal affairs minister in Juba, South Sudan (April 2007).
108. Interview with Johnson, United Nations staff program manager in Juba, South Sudan (April 2007).

109. Interview with Bajor, United Nations official, in Juba, South Sudan (April 2007).
110. Interview with senior judicial official 1 in the Government of South Sudan, in Juba, South Sudan (April 2007).
111. Interview with Isiah, NGO volunteer director, in Juba, South Sudan (April 2007).
112. Interview with Liza, NGO volunteer, in Juba, South Sudan (April 2007).
113. Interview with Michael, NGO volunteer, in Juba, South Sudan (April 2007).
114. Interview with David, NGO volunteer, in Juba, South Sudan (April 2007).
115. Interview with Job, international NGO program manager, in Juba, South Sudan (April 2007).
116. Interview with Charles, international NGO program manager, in Juba, South Sudan (April 2007).
117. Interview with Peter, Catholic priest, in Juba, South Sudan (April 2007).
118. Interview with Tok, lawyer, in Juba, South Sudan (April 2007).
119. Interview with Intrepa, lay Church community leader, in Juba, South Sudan (April 2007).
120. Interview with Luke, lay Church community leader, in Juba, South Sudan (April 2007).
121. Interview with senior judicial official 2 in the Government of South Sudan, in Juba, South Sudan (April 2007).
122. Interview with Daniel, European lawyer and aid worker, in Juba, South Sudan (April 2007).
123. Interview with Sebastian, North American lawyer and aid worker, in Juba, South Sudan (April 2007).
124. Interview with John, lawyer, in Juba, South Sudan (April 2007).
125. Interview with Alima, lawyer in the Ministry of Legal Affairs and Constitutional Development, in Juba, South Sudan (April 2007).
126. Interview with Anbar, lawyer in the Ministry of Legal Affairs Constitutional Development, in Juba, South Sudan (April 2007).
127. Interview with Naloj, senior official in the Ministry of Legal Affairs and Constitutional Development, in Juba, South Sudan (April 2007).
128. Interview with Roger, lawyer, in Juba, South Sudan (April 2007).
129. Interview with Phillip, lawyer, in Juba, South Sudan (April 2007).

130. Interview with Fadwa, NGO program officer, in Juba, South Sudan (April 2007).
131. Interview with Ilham, lawyer, in Juba, South Sudan (April 2007).
132. Interview with Rafiq, lawyer and opposition leader, in Khartoum, Sudan (April 2007).
133. Interview with Lina, lawyer, in Khartoum, Sudan (April 2007).
134. Interview with Theodore, church official, in Khartoum, Sudan (April 2007).
135. Interview with Shadi, lawyer, in Khartoum, Sudan (April 2007).
136. Interview with Hani, lawyer and Member of Parliament, in Khartoum, Sudan (April 2007).
137. Interview with Jeffrey, former judge in South Sudan, in Khartoum, Sudan (April 2007).
138. Interview with Michael, church leader, in Khartoum, Sudan (April 2007).
139. Interview with Kunok, lawyer, in Juba, South Sudan (April 2007).
140. Interview with Jamal, lawyer, in El Obeid, Sudan (May 2007).
141. Interview with Khalid, lawyer, in El Obeid, Sudan (May 2007).
142. Interview with Nadir, lawyer, in El Obeid, Sudan (May 2007).
143. Interview with Adelle, foreign aid worker, in El Obeid, Sudan (May 2007).
144. Interview with Yasir, Sudanese aid worker, in El Obeid, Sudan (May 2007).
145. Interview with Rahman, village sheikh, near El Obeid, Sudan (May 2007).
146. Interview with Kahlil, NGO director, in El Obeid, Sudan (May 2007).
147. Interview with Rana, NGO coordinator, in El Obeid, Sudan (May 2007).
148. Interview with Zacharia, lawyer and legal awareness workshop facilitator, in Khartoum, Sudan (May 2007).
149. Follow-up interview with Samira, NGO director, in Khartoum, Sudan (May 2007).
150. Interview with Tamir, NGO director, in Khartoum, Sudan (May 2007).
151. Interview with Lomot, Member of Parliament, in Omdurman, Sudan (May 2007).
152. Follow-up interview with Samira, human resources manager with an international NGO, in Khartoum, Sudan (June 2010).

153. Interview with Terrence, NGO director, in Khartoum, Sudan (June 2010).
154. Interview with Michael, NGO program director, in Khartoum, Sudan (June 2010).
155. Interview with Figaro, NGO director, in Khartoum, Sudan (June 2010).
156. Follow-up interview with Mansour, lawyer and former government minister, in Khartoum, Sudan (June 2010).
157. Interview with Ranya, NGO director, in Khartoum, Sudan (June 2010).
158. Interview with Baseema, NGO employee, in Khartoum, Sudan (June 2010).
159. Interview with Muatassim, NGO program coordinator, in Khartoum, Sudan (June 2010).
160. Interview with Maysa, NGO program coordinator, in Khartoum, Sudan (June 2010).
161. Interview with Tamara, NGO program coordinator, in Khartoum, Sudan (June 2010).
162. Interview with Iris, NGO program coordinator, in Khartoum, Sudan (June 2010).
163. Interview with Ghania, NGO program officer, in Khartoum, Sudan (June 2010). (Author's file reference number 164).
164. Interview with Omera, United Nations official, in Juba, South Sudan (June 2010) (Author's file reference number 165).
165. Interview with Gabriel, foreign aid worker with the United Nations, in Juba, South Sudan (June 2010) (Author's file reference number 184).
166. Interview with Destiny, Sudanese staff member with the United Nations, in Juba, South Sudan (June 2010) (Author's file reference number 188).
167. Interview with Joseph, foreign aid worker with the United Nations, in Juba, South Sudan (June 2010) (Author's file reference number 193).
168. Interview with Isiah, Sudanese NGO volunteer director, in Juba, South Sudan (June 2010) (Author's file reference number 194).
169. Interview with Patrick, Sudanese NGO volunteer, in Juba, South Sudan (June 2010) (Author's file reference number 195).
170. Interview with Hamid, Sudanese NGO volunteer, in Juba, South Sudan (June 2010) (Author's file reference number 196).

171. Interview with Jaden, South Sudan government official, in Juba, South Sudan (June 2010) (Author's file reference number 198).
172. Interview with Raw'ah lawyer, in Khartoum, Sudan (July 2010) (Author's file reference number 201).
173. Interview with Mina, lawyer, in Khartoum, Sudan (July 2010) (Author's file reference number 202).
174. Interview with Abdul-Haq, lawyer, in Khartoum, Sudan (July 2010) (Author's file reference number 203).
175. Interview with Dhakwan, lawyer, in Khartoum, Sudan (July 2010) (Author's file reference number 204).

BIBLIOGRAPHY

Sudan Archive, Durham University

Annual Report of the Finances, Administration and Condition of the Sudan, 1902–1952 [including *Annual Report of the Legal Secretary to the Sudan Government,* 1902–1952].

Arber, H. B. 1944. "The Typical Sudanese." Sudan Archive, Durham University. 715/9/43–45.

Arthur, A. J. V. 1951. "Letter to His Parents, May 25, 1951." Sudan Archive, Durham University. SAD 726/7/19.

———. 1982. "Memoir of a District Officer in the Sudan – 1949/54." A. J. V. Arthur Collection, Sudan Archive, Durham University.

Confidential Memorandum of the Office of the Legal Secretary, "Is It Desirable that the Sudan Government Should Introduce Legislation to Define the Persons to Whom the Term Sudanese Should Be Applied?" Robertson Collection, Sudan Archive, Durham University, 517/12/7.

Crole, G. B. Undated. "Lecture on Sudan," delivered at the General Meeting of the Elgin and District Branch of the Workers' Educational Association. Sudan Archive, Durham University, SAD 748/12/1–8.

Hawley, Sir Donald. 1982. "Law in the Sudan under the Anglo-Egyptian Condominium," Durham Sudan Historical Records Conference, Durham University, April 14–16. Sudan Archive, Durham University, HAW 43/6/45.

James, L. 1982. "The Sudan Police Force in the Final Years of the Condominium," Durham Sudan Historical Records Conference, Durham University, April 14–16. Sudan Archive, Durham University.

Kirk-Greene, A. H. M. 1982. *The Sudan Political Service: A Preliminary Profile,* [a 1982 paper from St. Antony's College, Oxford University, now on file at the Sudan Archive, Durham University].

Luce, Sir William. 1934. "Diary excerpts, February 20, 1934." William Luce Collection, Sudan Archive, Durham University. 829/12/42–43.

Undated manuscript, Luce Collection, Sudan Archive, Durham University, 830/1/82.

Martin, Paul. 1969. "Army Overthrows Sudan Cabinet," (British newspaper, unknown), May 25, 1969, K. D. D. Henderson Collection, Sudan Archive, Durham University 539/7/18.

Mayall, R. C. 1948. "Communication between Sir James Robertson, and R. C. Mayall," March 25, 1948. Mayall Collection, Sudan Archive, Durham University 521/11/17.

McDowell, William Crocket. Undated. "Memoir of Work and Career," McDowell Collection, Sudan Archive, Durham University, 815/8.

"Newspaper Cuttings," K. D. D. Henderson Collection, Sudan Archive, Durham University, 539/7/4.

Ridley, John. 1969. Opinion. *Daily Telegraph*, May 27, 1969. K. D. D. Henderson Collection, Sudan Archive, Durham University 539/7/20.

Robertson, James W. 1948. "Letter to Bishop Morris Gelthorpe, March 20, 1948." Robertson Collection, Sudan Archive, Durham University, 521/11/24–28.

1948 "Letters to Sudan Agent from 1948." Robertson Collection, Sudan Archive, Durham University, 521/11/65.

1951. "A Layman's Marginal Comments on the Draft Sudan Constitution Ordinance 1951." Sudan Archive, Durham University, 518/13/8.

1952. "Speech on Recent Constitutional Developments in Sudan," March 4, 1952. Robertson Collection, Sudan Archive, Durham University, 529/13/17–43.

Undated. "Letter to Mohammed Eff. Osman Yasin (Semi-official correspondence)," Robertson Collection, Sudan Archive, Durham University, 528/3/18–28

Undated. "Note to Marjory Perham, Times Newspaper." Sudan Archive, Durham University, 528/3/41.

"SECRET: Development of Ministerial Responsibility among Sudanese Members of Councils," Office of the Civil Secretary, Sudan Government. Robertson Collection, Sudan Archive, Durham University 518/13/1.

Sumner, Geoffrey. 1969. "Tomb is Key to Sudan," *Sunday Times*, June 1st, 1969. K. D. D. Henderson Collection, Sudan Archive, Durham University 539/7/26.

"Untitled manuscript." Undated. K. D. D. Henderson Collection, Sudan Archive, Durham University 539/7/29–47.

Wingate, F. R. 1910. "Letter from Wingate to Asser, Acting Sirdar and Governor-General in Cairo, 26 September 1910." F. R. Wingate Collection, Sudan Archive, Durham University, 297/3/161.

Cases

All are reported in *Sudan Law Journal and Reports*.

Dairat El Mahdi v. Abdel Gadir Abu Regeila, S.L.J.R. (*The Sudan Law Journal and Reports*) (1960) at 49.

Ali Abu Sam v. Kambal Osman, S.L.J.R. (1962) at 207.

Maeema Hassan v. Mursi Hassan, S.L.J.R. (1962) at 86.

Fatma Ibrahim v. The Attorney General, S.L.J.R. (1958) at 3.

Khartoum Municipal Council v. Michel Cotran, S.L.J.R. (1958) at 85.

Furmeister and Co. v. Abdel Ghani Ali Mousa, S.L.J.R. (1959) at 38.

Heirs of Naeema Ahmed Wagealla v. El Hag Ahmed Mohammed, S.L.J.R. (1961).

John Fairweather v. Gabriel Gabrielides, S.L.J.R. (1963) at 212.

Mohammed Adlan v. Sudan Government, Awad El Sid Abdullah and others, S.L.J.R. (1956) at 64.

Building Authority of Khartoum v. Evangellos Evangelledes. S.L.J.R. (1958) at 44.

Asma Mahmoud Mohamed Taha and Abdel Latif Amr Hisballah vs. the Sudan Government, S.L.J.R. (1986).

Books and Articles

Abbas, Ali Abdalla. 1991. "The National Islamic Front and the Politics of Education," *Middle East Report*, September–October 1991, No. 172, pp. 22–5.

Abd al-Rahim, Muddathir. 1969. *Imperialism and Nationalism in the Sudan*. Oxford: Clarendon Press.

Abd al-Rahim, Muddathir, Raphael Badal, Adlan Hardallo, and Peter Woodward, eds. 1986. *Sudan since Independence*. Hunts, UK: Gower.

Abdelmoula, Adam M. 1996. "The 'Fundamentalist' Agenda for Human Rights: the Sudan and Algeria," 18(1) *Arab Studies Quarterly* 1–28.

Abel, Richard L. and Philip S. C. Lewis, eds. 1988. *Lawyers in Society: Comparative Theories*. Berkeley: University of California Press.

Abusharaf, Rogaia Mustafa. 2009. *Transforming Displaced Women in Sudan: Politics and the Body in a Squatter Settlement*. Chicago: University of Chicago Press

Africa Watch. 1991. *Sudan – Inside Al Bashir's Prisons: Torture, Denial of Medical Attention and Poor Conditions*. Washington, DC.

Ahmed, Judge Mohammed Abuzeid. 2007. "The Public Grievances and Corrections Board (Ombudsman) of Sudan," Khartoum.

Al-Bahiri, Zaki. 1990. *Al-Haraka al-Demokratiyya Fi al-Sudan 1943–1985 [The Democratic Movement in Sudan 1943–1985]*.Cairo University: Dar Nahdat al-Sharq.

Al-Jamal, Showqi Ata Allah. 1980. *Tarikh al-Sudan wa Wadi al-Nil wa Alaqat Misr [History of the Sudan, the Nile Valley, and Relations with Egypt]*. Cairo: Anglo-Egyptian Library.

Al-Mufti, Hussein Sir Ahmed. 1959. *Tatowar Nizham al-Qadha Fi al-Sudan [The Development of the Judicial System in Sudan]*. Khartoum: Sudan Renaissance Library.

Al-Tijani, Mahjoub. 1996. *Al-Din Wa al-Dowla Fi al-Sudan [Religion and the State in Sudan]*. Cairo: Legal Studies and Information Center on Human Rights.

Ali, Heidr Ibrahim. 1995. *Al Mujtama al-Madani Wa al-Tahawul al-Demokrati Fi al-Sudan [Civil Society and Democratic Transformation in Sudan]*. Cairo: Ibn Khaldoun Center Press.

Amnesty International. 2013. "Sudan." Available: http://www.amnesty.org/en/region/sudan.

Andersson, Jens A. 2002. "Administrators' Knowledge and State Control in Colonial Zimbabwe: The Invention of the Rural-Urban Divide in Buhera District, 1912–80," 43(1) *The Journal of African History* 119–43.

Anonymous. "Pants Pants Revolution," *Foreign Policy*, 5 Aug. 2009. Available: http://www.foreignpolicy.com/articles/2009/08/05/pants_pants_revolution (accessed January 9, 2013).

Arbour, Louise. 2008. "Foreword," in *Claiming the Millennium Development Goals: A Human Rights Approach*. Geneva: United Nations Office of the High Commissioner for Human Rights HR/PUB/08/3. Available: http://www.unhcr.org/refworld/docid/49fac1162.html (accessed January 9, 2013).

Awad, Waktor Mohammed Al Din. 1970. *Qanoon al-'Ouqoobat al-Sudani [Sudan Penal Code, Annotated]*. Cairo: World Press.

"Background: Sudan's Oil Industry," *Al-Jazeera* (July 2, 2011). Available: http://english.aljazeera.net/indepth/spotlight/southsudanindependence/2011/07/20117216441419555.html (accessed January 9, 2013).

Beidelman, T. O. 1966. "Intertribal Tensions in Some Local Government Courts in Colonial Tanganyika: I," 10(2) *Journal of African Law* 118–30.

Benford, Robert D. and David Snow. 2000. "Framing Processes and Social Movements: An Overview and Assessment," 26 *Annual Review of Sociology* 611–39.

Benton, Lauren. 2002. *Law and Colonial Cultures: Legal Regimes in World History, 1400–1900*. Cambridge: Cambridge University Press.

Beset by Contradictions: Islamization, Legal Reform and Human Rights in Sudan, Lawyers Committee for Human Rights, 1996.

Beshir, Mohamed Omer. 1974. *Revolution and Nationalism in the Sudan*. London: Rex Collins.

Bickel, Alexander M. 1962. *The Least Dangerous Branch: The Supreme Court at the Bar of Politics*. Indianapolis: Bobbs-Merrill.

Blume, Till. 2007. "Security and Justice Institutions in Liberia: From State Collapse toward Institutions," unpublished research paper presented to London School of Economics Crisis States Research Centre, May 24. (Copy on file with author.)

"Briefing: Economics and the Rule of Law," *The Economist* (March 15–21, 2008), 84.

Bumiller, Kristin. 1987. "Victims in the Shadow of the Law: A Critique of the Model of Legal Protection," 12 *Signs* 421–39.

Burg, Elliot M. 1977. "Law and Development: A Review of the Literature and a Critique of 'Scholars in Self-Estrangement,'" 25 *American Journal of Comparative Law* 492.

Burr, J. Millard and Robert O. Collins. 2003. *Revolutionary Sudan: Hassan Al-Turabi and the Islamist State, 1989–2000*. Leiden: Brill.

Campbell, Robert. 1885. *Lectures on Jurisprudence or the Philosophy of Positive Law by the Late John Austin of the Inner Temple, Barrister at Law*. 5th ed. London: John Murray.

Caputo, Robert. 1982. "Sudan: Arab-African Giant," 161 *National Geographic* (March 1982) 346–79.

Carothers, Thomas. 2006. "The Rule of Law Revival," in Thomas Carothers, ed., *Promoting the Rule of Law Abroad: In Search of Knowledge*. Washington, DC: Carnegie Endowment for International Peace.

Chanock, Martin. 1985. *Law, Custom, and Social Order: The Colonial Experience in Malawi and Zambia*. Cambridge: Cambridge University Press.

Chavez, Rebecca Bill. 2004. *The Rule of Law in Nascent Democracies: Judicial Politics in Argentina*. Stanford, CA: Stanford University Press.

Chenoweth, Erica and Maria J. Stephan. 2011. *Why Civil Resistance Works: The Strategic Logic of Nonviolent Conflict*. New York: Columbia University Press.

Cichowski, Rachel. 2007. *The European Court and Civil Society: Litigation, Mobilization and Governance*. Cambridge: Cambridge University Press.

Claude, Richard and Burns H. Weston. 2006. *Human Rights and the World Community: Issues and Action*. Philadelphia: University of Pennsylvania Press.

Cohn, Bernard S. 1996. *Colonialism and Its Forms of Knowledge: The British in India*. Princeton, NJ: Princeton University Press.

Coles, Kimberly. 2002. "Ambivalent Builders: Europeanization, the Production of Difference, and Internationals in Bosnia-Herzegovina," *Political and Legal Anthropology Review* 25 (*PoLAR*) 1–18.

  2007. *Democratic Designs: International Intervention and Electoral Practices in Post-War Bosnia-Herzegovina*. Ann Arbor: University of Michigan Press, 2007.

Collins, Robert O. 2008. *A History of Modern Sudan*. Cambridge: Cambridge University Press.

Comaroff, John and Jean Comaroff. 1997. *Of Revelation and Revolution, Volume 2: The Dialectics of Modernity on a South African Frontier*. Chicago: University of Chicago Press, pp. 1–56.

2006. "Law and Disorder in the Post-Colony: An Introduction," in Comaroff and Comaroff, eds., *Law and Disorder in the Post-Colony*. Chicago: University of Chicago Press.

2009. *Ethnicity, Inc.* Chicago: University of Chicago Press.

Commission on Legal Empowerment of the Poor. 2008. *Making the Law Work for Everyone* (Vol. 1). New York: United Nations Development Programme.

Cory, E. S. B. and Forbes, L. E. 1983. "Resource for Sudanese Studies: The Sudan Archive of the University of Durham," 31 *African Research and Documentation* 1–11.

Dahl, Robert. 1957. "Decision-making in Democracy: The Supreme Court as a National Policy-maker," 6 *Journal of Public Law* 279–95.

Daly, M. W. 2008. *Darfur's Sorrow: A History of Destruction and Genocide.* Cambridge: Cambridge University Press.

Daly, M. W. and Forbes, L. E. 1994. *The Sudan: Photographs from the Sudan Archive, Durham University Library.* Reading: Garnet.

Deng, Francis. 1995. *War of Visions: Conflict of Identities in the Sudan.* New York: Brookings Institution Press.

Denzin, Norman K. and Yvonna S. Lincoln. 1994. "Introduction: Entering the Field of Qualitative Research," in *Handbook of Qualitative Research.* Thousand Oaks, CA: Sage.

de Waal, Alex. [1988] 2005. *Famine That Kills: Darfur, Sudan.* Oxford: Oxford University Press.

Dezalay, Yves and Bryant G. Garth. 2010. *Asian Legal Revivals: Lawyers in the Shadow of Empire.* Chicago: University of Chicago Press.

Douzinas, Costas. 2000. *The End of Human Rights: Critical Legal Thought at the Turn of the Century.* Oxford: Hart.

Dworkin, Ronald. 1986. *Law's Empire.* Cambridge, MA: Harvard University Press.

Edelman, Lauren B. et al. 1996. "Internal Dispute Resolution: The Transformation of Rights in the Workplace," 27 *Law & Society Review* 497–534.

Ehrlich, Eugen. [1936] 2002. *Fundamental Principles of the Sociology of Law.* New Brunswick, NJ: Transaction.

Elbasri, Aicha. 2007. "Working toward Equal Access to Justice for All: The Legal Aid Network Launched in Sudan," Joint Press Release of the United Nations Development Programme, People's Legal Aid Center, International Rescue Committee, and Ministry of Justice Legal Aid Department, Khartoum, Sudan. March 14. Available: www.sd.undp.org/ Presspdf/launchoflegalaidnetworkinSudan.pdf (accessed January 9, 2013).

El-Faki, M. O. O. 1995. *Islam and Human Rights: A Case Study of the National Islamic Front (NIF) in the Sudan.* MA Thesis, Sociology and Anthropology. Cairo: American University of Cairo.

El Tom, Mohamed El Amin Ahmed. 2006. *Higher Education in Sudan: Towards a New Vision for a New Era*, Friedrich Ebert Stiftung and Sudan Center for Educational Research.

Ellmann, Stephen. 1992. *In a Time of Trouble: Law and Liberty in South Africa's State of Emergency*. Oxford: Clarendon Press.

Englund, Harri. 2004. "Towards a Critique of Rights Talk in New Democracies: The Case of Legal Aid in Malawi," 15 *Discourse and Society* 527–51.

Epp, Charles. 1998. *The Rights Revolution: Lawyers, Activists, and Supreme Courts in Comparative Perspective*. Chicago: University of Chicago Press.

Eybin, Rosalind (Chief Social Development Advisor of British DFID). Undated. "How to Make a Rights-Based Approach to Development Work: A DFID Perspective," Overseas Development Initiative (on file with author).

Fadlalla, Ali Suleiman. 2006. "Law Reform in the Sudan: A Brief History," unpublished paper presented at United Nations Development Programme/ Ahfad University for Women workshop on law reform, September 2006, p. 3. Copy on file with author.

Failed States Index. 2012. *Foreign Policy*. Available: http://www.foreignpolicy. com/failedstates (accessed January 9, 2013).

Fanous, Safwat S. 2001. "UK Role in Influencing the Rise and Development of Sudanese Political Parties and Civil Society," *Conference on Sudanese-British Relations*. University of Khartoum Dept. of Political Science in collaboration with The British Council.

Fearon, James. 2011. "Governance and Civil War Onset," *World Development Report 2011 Background Paper*. Washington, DC: The World Bank.

Feinäugle, Clemens, Tilmann Röder, and Verena Wiesner, eds. 2006. *Max Planck Compilation of The Papers and Proceedings of the Heidelberg Seminar on Potential Disputes before the Sudanese Constitutional Court*, Max-Planck Institute for Comparative Public Law and International Law (draft on file with author).

Felstiner, William L. F., Richard L. Abel, and Austin Sarat. 1980–1. "The Emergence and Transformation of Disputes: Naming, Blaming, Claiming …," 15 *Law & Society Review* 631–54.

Fisher, Jonah. 2007. "Sudan Leaders Court Western Rage," *BBC News*. Available: http://news.bbc.co.uk/2/hi/africa/7122007.stm (accessed January 9, 2013).

Fluehr-Lobban, C. and H. B. Hillawi. 1983. "Circulars of the Shari'a Courts in the Sudan, 1902–1979," 27(2) *Journal of African Law* 79–140.

Fluehr-Lobban, Carolyn. 1987. *Islamic Law and Society in the Sudan*. London: Frank Cass.

Forbes, L. E. 1985. "The Sudan Archive, Durham, as a Source for the Study of Modernization in the Sudan" in M. W. Daly, ed., *Modernization in the Sudan: Essays in Honor of Richard Hill*. New York: Lillian Barber Press, pp. 161–70.

Ford Foundation. 2000. *Law: Ford Foundation Grantees and the Pursuit of Justice.* New York: Ford Foundation.

    2000. *Many Roads to Justice: The Law-Related Work of Ford Foundation Grantees around the World,* edited by Mary McClymont and Stephen Golub. New York: Ford Foundation.

Freedom House. 2012. *Worst of the World 2012: The World's Most Repressive Societies.* New York: Freedom House.

Friedman, Lawrence M. 1973. *A History of American Law.* New York: Simon & Schuster.

Fuller, Lon. 1969. *The Morality of Law.* New Haven, CT: Yale University Press.

    1978. "The Forms and Limits of Adjudication," 92 *Harvard L. Rev.* 353–409.

Galanter, Marc. 1974. "Why the 'Haves' Come Out Ahead: Speculations on the Limits of Legal Change," 9 *Law & Society Rev.* 95–160.

Gardner, James A. 1980. *Legal Imperialism: American Lawyers and Foreign Aid in Latin America.* Madison: University of Wisconsin Press.

Ginsburg, Tom and Tamir Moustafa, eds. 2008. *Rule by Law: The Politics of Courts in Authoritarian Regimes.* Cambridge: Cambridge University Press.

Ginsburg, Tom. 2003. *Judicial Review in New Democracies: Constitutional Courts in Asian Cases.* Cambridge: Cambridge University Press.

Goldsmith, Jack and Eric Posner. 2005. *The Limits of International Law.* Oxford: Oxford University Press.

Golub, Stephen. 2006. "The Legal Empowerment Alternative," in T. Carothers, ed., *Promoting the Rule of Law Abroad: In Search of Knowledge.* Washington, DC: Carnegie Endowment for International Peace, pp. 105–36.

Government of the Republic of Liberia. 2009. "Executive Challenges Members of Liberian Bar Association," Press Release. 23 January. Available: http://www.emansion.gov.lr/press.php?news_id=1046 (accessed January 9, 2013).

Greenhouse, Carol J. 1994. "Constructive Approaches to Law, Culture, and Identity," 28(5) *Law & Society Review* 1231–42.

Gretton, George. 1968. "The Law and Constitution in the Sudan," *The World Today: The Royal Institute of International Affairs,* August 1968, p. 319.

Guttman, Egon. 1957. "A Survey of the Sudan Legal System," S.L.J.R.

    1957. "Law Reporting in the Sudan," *International and Comparative Law Quarterly,* p. 687.

Hagan, John and Wenona Raymond-Richmond. 2008. *Darfur and the Crime of Genocide.* Cambridge: Cambridge University Press.

Hailey, Lord. 1951. *Native Administration in the British African Territories.* Part III. *West Africa: Nigeria, Gold Coast, Sierra Leone, Gambia.* London: Colonial Office.

Halliday, Terence C. and Lucien Karpik, eds. 1998. *Lawyers and the Rise of Western Political Liberalism*. Oxford: Clarendon Press.

Halliday, Terence, C., Lucien Karpik, and Malcolm M. Feeley. 2007. *Fighting for Political Freedom: Comparative Studies of the Legal Complex and Political Liberalism*. Oxford: Hart.

eds. 2012. *Fates of Political Liberalism in the British Post-Colony: The Politics of the Legal Complex*. Cambridge: Cambridge University Press.

Hamid, Mohammed Khalifa. 2006. *Al-Nizham al-a'i al-Sudani: Tarekhahu, Nizhumuhu, Tatowruhu, Istiqlaluhu, wa Atharahu fi al-Mujtama* [*The Sudanese Judicial System: Its History, Organization, Development, Independence, and Influence on Society*]. Khartoum: Khartoum Press.

Hamilton, Alexander. 1788. The Federalist No. 78. Available: http://www.constitution.org/fed/federa78.htm (accessed January 9, 2013).

Harding, Alan. 1966. *A Social History of English Law*. London: Penguin Books.

2002. *Medieval Law and the Foundations of the State*. Oxford: Oxford University Press.

Hart, H. L. A. 1997. *The Concept of Law*. Oxford: Oxford University Press.

Hawley, Donald. 1995. *Sandtracks in the Sudan*. Wilby, UK: Michael Russell.

Hay, Douglas. 1975. "Property, Authority, and the Criminal Law," in Douglas Hay, Peter Linebaugh, John G. Rule, E. P. Thompson, and Cal Winslow, eds., *Albion's Fatal Tree: Crime and Society in Eighteenth Century England*. New York: Pantheon Press, pp. 17–64.

Heckman, James J., Robert L. Nelson, and Lee Cabatingan, eds. 2010. *Global Perspectives on the Rule of Law*. New York: Routledge.

Helmke, Gretchen and Frances Rosenbluth. 2009. "Regimes and the Rule of Law: Judicial Independence in Comparative Perspective," 12 *Annual Review of Political Science* 345–66.

Helmke, Gretchen and Julio Ríos-Figueroa, eds. 2011. *Courts in Latin America*. Cambridge: Cambridge University Press.

Hemment, Julie. 2007. *Empowering Women in Russia: Activism, Aid, and NGOs*. Bloomington: Indiana University Press.

Hendly, Kathryn. 1996. *Trying to Make Law Matter: Legal Reform and Labor Law in the Soviet Union*. Ann Arbor: University of Michigan Press.

Hilbink, Lisa. 2007. *Judges beyond Politics in Democracy and Dictatorship: Lessons from Chile*. Cambridge: Cambridge University Press.

Hill, Richard. 1959. *Egypt in the Sudan, 1820–1881*. Oxford: Oxford University Press.

Hirschl, Ran. 2004. *Towards Juristocracy: The Origins and Consequences of the New Constitutionalism*. Cambridge, MA: Harvard University Press.

Holt, P. M. and M. W. Daly. 2000. *A History of the Sudan: From the Coming of Islam to the Present Day*, 5th ed. Essex: Pearson Education.

Human Rights Watch. 1999. *Democratic Republic of Congo: Casualties of War: Civilians, Rule of Law, and Democratic Freedoms.* New York: Human Rights Watch.

2013. "Sudan." Available: http://www.hrw.org/doc?t=africa&c=sudan (accessed January 9, 2013).

Humphreys, Stephen. 2010. *Theatre of the Rule of Law: Transnational Legal Intervention in Theory and Practice.* Cambridge: Cambridge University Press.

Hussin, Iza. 2007. "The Pursuit of the Perak Regalia: Islam, Law, and the Politics of Authority in the Colonial State," 32 *Law & Social Inquiry* 759–88.

Ibrahim, Abdullah Abd Al Razaq and Showqi al-Jamal. 1997. *Tarikh Masr Wa al-Sudan al-Hadith Wa al-Mu'aasar* [*Contemporary and Modern History of Egypt and Sudan*]. Cairo: Dar al-Thaqafah lil-Nashr wa al-Towze'a.

Ibrahim, Abdullahi Ali. 2008. *Manichaean Delirium: Decolonizing the Judiciary and Islamic Renewal in Sudan, 1898–1985.* Leiden: Brill.

Idris, Amir H. 2005. *Conflict and Politics of Identity in Sudan.* New York: Palgrave Macmillan.

International Crisis Group. 2006. "Liberia: Resurrecting the Justice System," *Africa Report* No. 107, April 6.

2013. "Sudan." Available: http://www.crisisgroup.org/en/regions/africa/horn-of-africa/sudan.aspx (accessed January 9, 2013).

International Development Law Organization. 2010. *Legal and Judicial Development Assistance Global Report 2010.* Rome: IDLO.

Jensen, Erik and Thomas Heller. 2003. *Beyond Common Knowledge: Empirical Approaches to the Rule of Law.* Stanford, CA: Stanford University Press.

Jeppie, Shamil. 2010. "The Making and Unmaking of Colonial Shari'a in Sudan," in Shamil Jeppie, Ebrahim Moosa, and Richard Roberts, eds., *Muslim Family Law in Sub-Saharan Africa: Colonial Legacies and Post-Colonial Challenges.* Amsterdam: Amsterdam University Press.

Jick, Todd D. 1979. "Mixing Qualitative and Quantitative Methods: Triangulation in Action," 24(4) *Administrative Science Quarterly* 602–11.

Johnson, Douglas. 2003. *The Root Causes of Sudan's Civil Wars.* Bloomington: Indiana University Press.

Kagan, Robert A. 2001. *Adversarial Legalism: The American Way of Law.* Cambridge, MA: Harvard University Press.

Kahn, Paul W. 1999. *The Cultural Study of Law: Reconstructing Legal Scholarship.* Chicago: University of Chicago Press.

Karl, Terry. 1997. *The Paradox of Plenty: Oil Booms and Petro-States.* Berkeley: University of California Press.

Kawar, Leila. 2009. *Defining Legal Frontiers: Immigrant Rights Adjudication in France and the United States.* Ph.D. dissertation, New York University.

Kawar, Leila and Mark Fathi Massoud. 2012. "Symposium: New Directions in Comparative Public Law," 22(3) *American Political Science Association Law & Courts Section Newsletter* 32–36 (Fall).

Keck, Margaret E. and Kathryn Sikkink. 1998. *Activists beyond Borders: Advocacy Networks in International Politics*. Ithaca, NY: Cornell University Press.

Kennedy, David. 2002. "The International Human Rights Movement: Part of the Problem?" 15 *Harvard Human Rights Journal* 101–26.

Khalid, Mansour. 1990. *The Government They Deserve: The Role of the Elite in Sudan's Political Evolution*. London: Kegan Paul International.

Kirk-Greene, A. H. M. 1982. "The Sudan Political Service: A Profile in the Sociology of Imperialism," 15(1) *International Journal of African Historical Studies* 21–48.

Knox-Mawer, R. 1958. "The Jury System in British Colonial Africa," 2(3) *Journal of African Law* 160–3.

Koh, Harold Hongju. 1999. "How Is International Human Rights Law Enforced?" 47 *Indiana Law Review* 1397–417.

Köndgen, Olaf. 2010. "Shari'a and National Law in the Sudan," in Jan Michiel Otto, ed., *Sharia Incorporated: A Comparative Overview of the Legal Systems of Twelve Muslim Countries in Past and Present*. Leiden: Leiden University Press, pp. 181–230.

Kramer, Mathew H. 2007. *Objectivity and the Rule of Law*. Cambridge: Cambridge University Press.

Krygier, Martin. 2001. "Rule of Law," in Neil J. Smelser and Paul B. Bates, eds., *International Encyclopedia of the Social and Behavioral Sciences*. Oxford: Elsevier Science, Vol. 20, pp. 13403–8.

   2011a. "Approaching the Rule of Law," in Whit Mason, ed., *The Rule of Law in Afghanistan: Missing in Inaction*. Cambridge: Cambridge University Press, pp. 15–34.

   2011b. "Four Puzzles about the Rule of Law: Why, What, Where? And Who Cares?" in James Fleming, ed., *Getting to the Rule of Law*, NOMOS 54 New York: New York University Press, pp. 64–106.

   2012a. *Philip Selznick: Ideals in the World*. Stanford, CA: Stanford University Press.

   2012b. "Rule of Law," in Michel Rosenfeld and András Sajó, eds., *Oxford Handbook of Comparative Constitutional Law*. Oxford: Oxford University Press, pp. 233–249.

Larson-Rabin, Leah. 2007. "Introduction to the 25th Anniversary Issue: Happenstance and Memory: A Legacy of Law and Development Scholarship and Policy in Legal Education," 25 *Wisconsin International Law Journal* 209.

Lauren, Paul Gordon. 2003. *The Evolution of International Human Rights: Visions Seen*, 2nd ed. Philadelphia: University of Pennsylvania Press.

Law, David and Mila Versteeg. 2013. "Sham Constitutions," 101 *California Law Review* (August 2013).

Layish, Aharon and Gabriel R. Warburg. 2002. *The Reinstatement of Islamic Law in Sudan under Numayrī: An Evaluation of a Legal Experiment in the*

Light of Its Historical Context, Methodology, and Repercussions. Leiden: Brill.

Lekha-Sriram, Chandra, Olga Martin-Ortega, and Johanna Herman, eds. 2011. *Peacebuilding and the Rule of Law in Africa.* New York: Routledge.

Locke, John. 2003. *Two Treatises on Government, 1680–90*, edited by Ian Shapiro. New Haven, CT: Yale University Press.

Lord Caradon, in the Introduction to Mahgoub, Mohammed Ahmed. 1974. *Democracy on Trial: Reflections on Arab and African Politics.* London: Andre Deutsch.

Loveman, Brian. 2001. *Chile: The Legacy of Spanish Capitalism*, 3rd ed. Oxford: Oxford University Press.

Lubman, Stanley. 1999. *Bird in a Cage: Legal Reform in China after Mao.* Stanford, CA: Stanford University Press.

Lucero, José Antonio. 2006. "Representing 'Real Indians': The Challenges of Indigenous Authenticity and Strategic Constructivism in Ecuador and Bolivia," 41 *Latin American Research Review* 31–56.

Lutfi, G. A. 1967. "The Future of the English Law in the Sudan," 12 *Sudan Law Journal and Reports* 219.

Macmichael, Sir Harold. 1934. *The Anglo-Egyptian Sudan.* London: Faber and Faber.

Mahgoub, Mohamed Ahmed. 1974. *Democracy on Trial: Reflections on Arab and African Politics.* London: Andre Deutsch.

Mamdani, Mahmood. 1996. *Citizen and Subject: Contemporary Africa and the Legacy of Late Colonialism.* Princeton, NJ: Princeton University Press.

Marshall, A. H. 1953. *The Position of Tribal Leaders in the Life of Sudan*, Report to the Foreign Office, PRO/150919 Public Records Branch Khartoum, July 16, 1953. Reprinted in *The British Documents on the Sudan: 1940–1956*, edited by Mahmoud Salih Omdurman, Sudan: Abdel Karim Mirghani Cultural Center, Volume VIII.

Marshall, Monty G. and Benjamin R. Cole. 2011. *Global Report 2011: Conflict, Governance, and State Fragility.* Vienna, VA: Center for Systemic Peace.

Mason, Whit, ed. 2011. *The Rule of Law in Afghanistan: Missing in Inaction.* Cambridge: Cambridge University Press.

Massell, G. J. 1968. "Law as an Instrument of Revolutionary Change in a Traditional Milieu: The Case of Soviet Central Asia," 2(2) *Law & Society Review* 179–228.

Massoud, Mark Fathi. 2006. "Rights in a Failed State: Internally Displaced Women in Sudan and Their Lawyers," 21 *Berkeley Journal of Gender, Law & Justice* 2–12.

2011. "Do Victims of War Need International Law? Human Rights Education Programs in Authoritarian Sudan," 45 *Law & Society Review* 1–32.

2012. "Lawyers and the Disintegration of the Legal Complex in Sudan," in Terence C. Halliday, Lucien Karpik, and Malcolm M. Feeley, eds., *Fates of Political Liberalism in the British Post-Colony: The Politics of the Legal Complex*. Cambridge: Cambridge University Press, pp. 193–218.

Mauddathiri, H. 1956. "A Memorandum for the Enactment of a Sudan Law Derived from the Principles of Islam," November 1956. Khartoum: Sudan Library (Sudan Library 8H Hassan).

McAdams, A. James, ed. 1997. *Transitional Justice and the Rule of Law in New Democracies*. Notre Dame, IN: University of Notre Dame Press.

McCann, Michael. 1994. *Rights at Work: Pay Equity Reform and the Politics of Legal Mobilization*. Chicago: University of Chicago Press.

Méndez, Juan, Paulo Sergio Pinheiro, and Guillermo O'Donnell. 1998. *The (Un)Rule of Law and New Democracies in Latin America*. Notre Dame, IN: University of Notre Dame Press.

Merry, Sally Engle. 1998. *Colonizing Hawai'i: The Cultural Power of Law*. Chicago: University of Chicago Press.

2006. *Human Rights and Gender Violence: Translating International Law into Local Justice*. Chicago: University of Chicago Press.

Merryman, John Henry. 1977. "Comparative Law and Social Change: On the Origins, Style, Decline and Revival of the Law and Development Movement," 25 *American Journal of Comparative Law* 457–91.

Moustafa, Tamir. 2003. "Law versus the State: The Judicialization of Politics in Egypt," 28 *Law and Social Inquiry* 883–930.

2007. *The Struggle for Constitutional Power: Law, Politics, and Economic Development in Egypt*. Cambridge: Cambridge University Press.

Mustafa, Zaki. 1971. *Common Law in the Sudan: An Account of the Justice, Equity and Good Conscience Provision*. Oxford: Oxford University Press.

Nader, Laura. 2007. "Introduction," in Mark Goodale and Sally Engle Merry, eds., *The Practice of Human Rights: Tracking Law between the Global and the Local*. Cambridge: Cambridge University Press, pp. 117–29.

Niblock, Tim. 1987. *Class and Power in Sudan: The Dynamics of Sudanese Politics 1898–1985*. London: MacMillan Press.

Nixon, Rob. 2011. *Slow Violence and the Environmentalism of the Poor*. Cambridge, MA: Harvard University Press.

Nonet, Philippe and Philip Selznick. [1978] 2001. *Law and Society in Transition: Toward Responsive Law*. New Brunswick, NJ: Transaction.

Noonan, John T. [1976] 2002. *Persons and Masks of the Law: Cardozo, Holmes, Jefferson, and Wythe as Makers of the Masks*. Berkeley: University of California Press.

"No Strings: Why Developing Countries Like Doing Business with China," *The Economist (Special Report on China's Quest for Resources)*, p. 14 (March 15, 2008).

Omer, Mohammed Abdel Khaliq. 1986. *Qanoon al-Murafa'at al-Masri Fi al-Sudan [Egyptian Law of Pleadings in Sudan]*. Cairo: Modern Technical Press.

Onoma, Ato Kwamena. 2010. *The Politics of Property Rights Institutions in Africa*. Cambridge: Cambridge University Press.

Osborn, Emily Lynn. 2003. "'Circle of Iron': African Colonial Employees and the Interpretation of Colonial Rule in French West Africa," 44(1) *The Journal of African History* 29–50.

Peerenboom, Randall. 2002. *China's Long March toward Rule of Law*. Cambridge: Cambridge University Press.

   ed. 2010. *Judicial Independence in China: Lessons for Global Rule of Law Promotion*. Cambridge: Cambridge University Press.

Perham, Marjory. 1954. "Delicate Transfer of Rule in the Sudan: Dangers Facing the New Regime," *The Times*, June 16, 1954.

Perry-Kessaris, Amanda, ed. 2010. *Law in the Pursuit of Development: Principles into Practice?* New York: Routledge.

Peters, Rudolph. 1994. "The Islamization of Criminal Law: A Comparative Analysis," 32 *Die Welt Des Islams: International Journal for the Study of Modern Islam* 246–74.

Piven, Frances Fox and Richard A. Cloward. 1979. *Poor People's Movements: Why They Succeed, How They Fail*. New York: Vintage Books.

Popova, Maria. 2012. *Politicized Justice in Emerging Democracies: A Study of Courts in Russia and Ukraine*. Cambridge: Cambridge University Press.

Rajagopal, Balakrishnan. 2003. *International Law from Below: Development, Social Movements, and Third World Resistance*. Cambridge: Cambridge University Press.

Rajah, Jothie. 2012. *Authoritarian Rule of Law: Legislation, Discourse and Legitimacy in Singapore*. Cambridge: Cambridge University Press.

Read, James S. 1979. "Studies in the Making of Colonial Laws: An Introduction," 23(1) *Journal of African Law* 1–9.

Roberts, Simon. 2005. "After Government? On Representing Law without the State," 68(1) *The Modern Law Review* 1–24.

Robertson, James. 1974. *Transitions in Africa: From Direct Rule to Independence*. London: C. Hurst.

Robinson, Mary, United Nations High Commissioner for Human Rights. 2001. "Bridging the Gap between Human Rights and Development: From Normative Principles to Operational Relevance," December 3, 2001, World Bank. Available: http://www.unhchr.ch/Huricane/Huricane.nsf/6 0a520ce334aaa77802566100031b4bf/2da59cd3ffc033dcc1256b1a0033f 7c3?OpenDocument (accessed January 9, 2013).

Rone, Jemera. 1996. *Behind the Red Line: Political Repression in Sudan*. New York: Human Rights Watch.

Rose, N. and P. Miller. 1992. "Political Power beyond the State: Problematics of Government," 43(2) *British Journal of Sociology* 173–205.

Rose-Ackerman, Susan. 2004. "Establishing the Rule of Law," In Robert Rotberg, ed., *When States Fail: Causes and Consequences*. Princeton, NJ: Princeton University Press.

Rosenberg, Gerald. 2008. *The Hollow Hope: Can Courts Bring about Social Change?* 2nd ed. Chicago: University of Chicago Press.

Salman, Salman. 1981. "Legal Profession in Sudan: A Study of Legal and Professional Pluralism," In C. J. Dias et al., eds., *Lawyers in the Third World: Comparative and Developmental Perspectives*. New York: International Center for Law and Development, pp. 226–47.

Scheingold, Stuart. 2004. *The Politics of Rights: Lawyers, Public Policy, and Political Change*. 30th Anniversary ed. Ann Arbor: University of Michigan Press.

Scheppele, Kim Lane. 2003. "Constitutional Ethnography: An Introduction," 38(3) *Law & Society Review* 389–406.

Schler, Lynn. 2003. "Ambiguous Spaces: The Struggle over African Identities and Urban Communities in Colonial Douala, 1914–45," 44(1) *The Journal of African History* 51–72.

Seidman, Robert B. 1972. "Law and Development: A General Model," 6(3) *Law & Society Review* 311–342.

Selznick, Philip. 1967. "Sociology of Law," in Paul Edwards, ed., *The Encyclopedia of Philosophy*, Vol. 7. London: Macmillan, pp. 478–80.

  1992. *The Moral Commonwealth: Social Theory and the Promise of Community*. Berkeley: University of California Press.

Shamir, Ronen. 1990. "'Landmark Cases' and the Reproduction of Legitimacy: The Case of Israel's High Court of Justice," 24(3) *Law & Society Review* 781–806.

Shapiro, Martin. 1981. *Courts: A Comparative and Political Analysis*. Chicago: University of Chicago Press.

Sharkey, Heather J. January 1993. "Beyond the Sudan Archive: A Guide to Doing Research on the Sudan in Durham," 13 *Sudan Studies* 10–19.

  2003. *Living with Colonialism: Nationalism and Culture in the Anglo-Egyptian Sudan*. Berkeley: University of California Press.

  2006. "Missionary Legacies: Muslim-Christian Encounters in Egypt and Sudan during the Colonial and Postcolonial Periods," in Benjamin F. Soares, ed., *Muslim-Christian Encounters in Africa*. Brill: Leiden, pp. 57–88.

Shklar, Judith. 1964. *Legalism: Law, Morals, and Political Trials*. Cambridge, MA: Harvard University Press.

Silverstein, Gordon. 2008. "Singapore: The Exception That Proves Rules Matter," in Tom Ginsburg and Tamir Moustafa, eds., *Rule by Law:*

The Politics of Courts in Authoritarian Regimes. Cambridge: Cambridge University Press, pp. 73–101.

Snow, David, et al. 1986. "Frame Alignment Processes, Micromobilization, and Movement Participation" (with E. Burke Rochford, Jr., Steven K. Worden, and Robert D. Benford), 51 *American Sociological Review* 464–81.

Stacy, Helen. 2009. *Human Rights for the 21st Century: Sovereignty, Civil Society, Culture.* Stanford, CA: Stanford University Press.

Stern, Rachel E. 2013. *Environmental Litigation in China: A Study in Political Ambivalence.* Cambridge: Cambridge University Press.

Stromseth, Jane, David Wippman, and Rosa Brooks. 2006. *Can Might Make Rights: Building the Rule of law after Military Interventions.* Cambridge: Cambridge University Press.

Sudan Government. 1898–1956. *The British Documents on the Sudan: 1940–1956,* Vol. 8, edited by Mahmoud Salih Omdurman. Sudan: Abdel Karim Mirghani Cultural Center.

Sudan Government. 1948 Ordinance No. 17.

Section 9, Civil Justice Ordinance, 1929.

Judgments (Basic Rules) Act of 1983.

Interim National Constitution of 2005.

2006. *Al-Iqtisad wa al-Mal* [Economics and Finance]. Sudan Judiciary Administration. February 13.

"Sudan Peace Project," Max Planck Institute for Comparative Public Law and International Law. Available: http://www.mpil.de/ww/en/pub/research/details/know_transfer/africa_projects/sudan_peace_project.cfm (accessed January 9, 2013).

"Sudan Says No to Hybrid Courts for Darfur Crimes," *Sudan Tribune,* September 21, 2009. Available: http://www.sudantribune.com/Sudan-says-no-to-hybrid-courts-for,32543 (accessed January 9, 2013).

Thompson, E. P. 1975. *Whigs and Hunters: The Origin of the Black Act.* New York: Pantheon Books.

Trimingham, J. Spencer. 1949. *Islam in the Sudan.* Oxford: Oxford University Press.

Trubek, David M. and Marc Galanter. 1974. "Scholars in Self-Estrangement: Some Reflections on the Crisis and Development Studies in the United States," *Wisconsin Law Journal* 1062–102.

Twining, William. 1959. "Law Reporting in the Sudan," 3(3) *Journal of African Law* 176–8.

Tyler, Tom R. ([1990] 2006). *Why People Obey the Law.* Princeton, NJ: Princeton University Press.

Udal, J. O. 1998. *The Nile in Darkness: Conquest and Exploration 1504–1862.* Norwich, UK: Michael Russell.

2005. *The Nile in Darkness: A Flawed Unity 1863–1899.* Norwich, UK: Michael Russell.

UNICEF. 2004. "The Human Rights-Based Approach: Statement of Common Understanding," in *State of the World's Children (Annex B)*. Available: http://www.unicef.org/sowc04/sowc04_annexes.html (accessed January 9, 2013).

United Nations. 2006. *Pathways to Justice: Access to Justice with a Focus on Poor, Women, and Indigenous Peoples*. UN Development Programme Cambodia.

"United Nations and the Rule of Law." Available: http://www.un.org/en/ruleoflaw/index.shtml (accessed January 9, 2013).

United Nations Department of Public Information. 2007. "Promoting Rule of Law 'Very Heart of the United Nations Mission,' Says Deputy Secretary-General, in Legal Committee Remarks," DSG/SM/346 GA/L/3327. Available: http://www.un.org/News/Press/docs/2007/dsgsm346.doc.htm (accessed January 9, 2013).

United Nations Development Programme and United Nations Population Fund. 2007. *Regional Program Document 2008–11: Latin America and the Caribbean*. New York: United Nations.

United Nations Development Programme Somalia. 2010. "The Rule Of Law and Security (ROLS) 2010 Project Achievements." Available: http://www.so.undp.org/index.php/The-Rule-Of-Law-and-Security-ROLS-2010-project-achievements.html (accessed January 9, 2013).

United Nations Security Council. 2004. *Report of the Secretary-General on The Rule of Law and Transitional Justice in Conflict and Post-Conflict Societies*. S/2004/616.

Vantini, Giovanni. 1981. *Christianity in the Sudan*. Bologna, Italy: EMI.

Vogler, Richard. 2005. *A World View of Criminal Justice*. Aldershot, UK: Ashgate.

Voll, John O. and Sarah P. Voll. 1985. *The Sudan: Unity and Diversity in a Multicultural*. London: Croom Helm. 1985.

Widner, Jennifer A. 2001. *Building the Rule of Law: Francis Nyali and the Road to Judicial Independence in Africa*. New York: W. W. Norton.

Williams, Patricia J. 1991. *The Alchemy of Race and Rights: Diary of a Law Professor*. Cambridge, MA: Harvard University Press.

Willis, Justin. 2005. "Hukm: The Creolization of Authority in Condominium Sudan," 46(1) *The Journal of African History* 29–50.

Wood, Jennifer and Clifford D. Shearing. 2007. *Imagining Security*. Cullompton, UK: Willan.

Woodward, Peter. 1990. *Sudan, 1898–1989: The Unstable State*. Boulder, CO: L. Rienner.

World Bank. 2011. *World Development Report: Conflict, Security, and Development*.

2013. "Law and Development Movement." Available: http://siteresources.worldbank.org/INTLAWJUSTINST/Resources/LawandDevelopmentMovement.pdf (accessed January 9, 2013).

INDEX

Surnames starting with al- are alphabetized by the subsequent part of the name.

Abboud, Ibrahim, 85, 94, 94n20, 101, 159

Adlan, Mohammed, 100–1

Adlan (Mohammed) v. Sudan Government, et al. (1956), 100–1, 103

Advisory Council for Northern Sudan (colonial era), 80

Advocacy Act (1983), amended under Bashir, 128

African Union, 129, *166t*

ajaweed (older persons as mediators), 19

alcohol-related offenses, *113n89*, 114, 127, *127n18*, 148, 150

Alier, Abel, *106n68*

American University of Cairo, 40

Anglo-Egyptian rule. *See* colonial era

Ansar religious sect, 91, *92t*, 102

apostasy, crime of, *37n43*, *113n89*, 115–16, 126–7, 196

appeals: in colonial era, 57–8, 59, 71; Constitutional Court, no appeal from decisions of, 130. *See also* High Court

Arabic language: author conducting research in, 40; Awadalla's resignation letter in, 103; Bashir's adoption of Arabic-only policies in education and government, 127; Cairo University-Khartoum branch teaching in, 100, 126; colonial *qadis* using in *shari'a* courts, 65; laws translated into, under Nimeiri, 112; lawyers' knowledge of, 123; legal education using,

136; SPS testing in, 54; translation of Sudanese law into, 112

Archer, Geoffrey, 62

authoritarian rule (generally): expansion of legal institutions under, 11; law-based strategies of, xiii, 4, 7, *8t*, 9–10, 26–7, 218; overview, 16; violating human rights, 25, 191. *See also* legitimacy

authoritarian rule in Sudan (1989–2011), 119–54; benefiting from religious view of God's will, 187–8; dangers of rights-based expression in, 163, 183–7, 193–5, 209; law-based strategies of, 206; and legal politics, 25, 121, 203. *See also* al-Bashir, Omar Hassan

Awadalla, Babiker: on Abboud regime, 101, 124; as Chief Justice, 103–10, *106n67*; legal education of, 73; and legal system reform, 117, 213, 217; and military coup (1969), 215, 224; political agenda of, 117, 118, 224; as speaker of parliament, 92–3

al-Azhari, Ismael, 86, 92

al-Bahiri, Zaki, *92n13*

bar association: adequate training to function at time of Sudan's independence, 95–6; under Bashir, 121–31, 217; categorized as trade union, 128; division created between older and younger lawyers, 143;

267

failed states: fallacy of legal vacuum in, 4, 164, 227; Fund for Peace on, *2n2*; legal order in, xiii, 4; Somalia as, 221; Sudan as, 2, *2n2*. *See also* fragile states
Failed States Index (2012), *2n2*
family law, 65. *See also* divorce
first period of independent Sudan (1956–64), 88–102; Abboud regime, 85, 94, 101; adequate training for legal system to function, 95–6; civil service posts in, 93; democracy during, 101–2; foreign intervention's focus in, 156; inadequate training for self-government, 91; initial lack of legislation, 93–4; legacy from colonial era, 84, 88–9, 156; legal structure in, 94–102; overview, 87; parliamentary system, 93–4; political parties in, 91, *92n13*; separation of *shari'a* from civil law, 97; Sudanization of government, 89–91
Ford Foundation, 158–9, *159n10*, 161
Foreign Policy on "failed" states, *2n2*
fragile states: akin to colonial states, 212; law not absent in, 26, 146, 214, 227; legal tools and strategies in, xiii, 3–5, 13, 20, 27–31, 226; limited knowledge of how law-based strategies are used in, 31; lived experience of the law in, 19–20, 28
"framing and shaming" practices of activists, 184–5
Freedom House rankings of countries for political rights and civil liberties, *2n2*
Fund for Peace on "failed" states, *2n2*

Garang, John, *106n68*
genocide, 33, 196
Gezira Scheme, 50, 111
"Global Knowledge Transfer" project, 172
God's will, 150, 187–8, 196
Gordon College Sheikhs' School, 72, 98, 156
government-oriented NGOs (GONGOs), 168, 192
grassroots empowerment, 10, 12, 170, 173, 176
grievance processing. *See* complaints against government officials

hadith (Prophet Muhammad's tenets), 128
Hamadien, Brigadier, 125
Hanafi school of Islamic law, 52, 126
Harding, Alan, *48n9*
Hawai'i, colonial law in, 50
Hawley, Donald, 44, *45n1*, 58, 59, 157

Hay, Douglas, 127, 219
Hemment, Julie, 220
High Court: in colonial era, 56, 83; judicial review, power of, 100–1; Nimeiri's removal of members of, 105, 106; precedents applied by, 98–9; refusal of parliament to implement order (1966–7), 102, 103–4, 215; reporting of decisions of, 100, 159; Taha case, 116
homicide cases, 69–70
huduud punishment. *See* corporal punishment
human dignity. *See* dignity of the person
human rights: authoritarian regimes in violation of, 25, 191; detachment of, from daily reality, 184–7, 204, 222; educating oppressed persons about, xiv, 4, 11, 27, 42, 170–1; grassroots legal culture of, 10, 12, 170, 173; and intimidation by government, 193; against Islamic concepts, 129; NGOs framing programs in language of to obtain funding, 201; not viewed as guaranteed in Sudan, 188–9; research on civil society actors' knowledge of, 42; scope of, 183; serving the powerful, *207n67*, 228; success of humanitarian interventions aimed at promoting, 156, 190; Sudan Human Rights Organization, 124; Sudanese civil society in Cairo focusing on, 162; theory of transformative rights, 189–90; UN emphasis in postconflict Sudan on, xiv, 39, 168–79; victimhood posture necessary to fight for, 189–90. *See also* humanitarian legal politics; rights-based approach to development
humanitarian actors, 17, 155–80; Bashir allowing due to unlikelihood of raising opposition, 192–4, 202; government-oriented NGOs (GONGOs), 168, 192; harassment and banning of international workers, 193, *193n35*; history of legal development initiatives, 156–64; information from, as self-serving, 32; international aid groups in Sudan (by type), 166, *166t*; as justice activists, 161–2, 179; lack of meaningful dialogue with, 205–6; law-based strategies of, *8t*, 9; and lawyers, 224–5; legal awareness workshops conducted by, xi, 173–4, 198–200; networks of NGOs, 167–8, *167n23*; non-Sudanese personnel making strategic, budgetary, and policy decisions

the poor: aid programs for, 164; authoritarian
and humanitarian legal politics
simultaneously in lives of, 219;
educating on legal and human rights
to empower, 42, 182, 190–1, 198;
humanitarian legal programs' failure
to alleviate suffering of, 12, 182–3,
197–8, 207–10, 225–6; obstacles in
accessing court system, 5, 9, 148, 186;
and theory of transformative rights, 189.
See also displaced persons
postcolonial Sudan: first period (1956–64),
87, 88–102; second period (1965–76),
87, 102–10; survival of state during, 85;
third period (1977–89), 87, 110–17
Powers of Nomadic Sheikhs Ordinance
(1922), 70
Powers of Sheikhs Ordinances (1927–8), 68
precedents, creation of, 98–100, 118
principal chief (*nazir*), 69
property law: British system, 62–3; in first
period (1956–64), 99; under Nimeiri,
65n75. *See also* land registry system
protestors, Bashir's criminal actions against,
149
Public Grievances and Corrections Board,
146–7, 218
punishment. *See* corporal punishment;
criminal law; Penal Code

qadis (judges), 51, 57, 65, 66, 72, 76
qanoon al-maheliyya ("law of the locality"),
67–8
qanoon september (September law), 113–14

Ranat, Abu (Chief Justice), 95, 96, 100–1
Registrar of Trade Unions, 128
religion: diversity in Sudan, 34–5; grafting
of state law to, 212; and human rights,
187–8; and legitimacy of Bashir regime,
150, 196. *See also* Christianity in Sudan;
Islamic law
Republican Brotherhood, 115
research design, 39–43; analysis and coding,
236–7; archival research, 231–5;
interviews, 40, 236, 238–47
revolts and coups: Bashir becoming
self-proclaimed leader, 117, 119; against
colonial power, 49, 60, 77; against
military regimes, lawyers' role in, 123–4;
Nimeiri deposed by coup, 11, 103–5;
Nimeiri leading coup, 103–5, 215

rights-based approach to development, xii,
39, 168–79; demand-oriented initiatives,
170, *170f*, 171, 173–7, 182, 191; effect
of non-Sudanese personnel in positions
of authority, 178–9; evaluation needed
for, 207; failure to tailor to Sudanese
situation, 182; judiciary support from,
171–3; Justice and Confidence Centers,
176–8; Omdurman Prison, rights
workshops at, 174–5; and paralegal
training, 175–6; rule of law programs,
171; supply-side initiatives, 170–1, *170f*,
191; and United Nations Development
Programme's initiatives, 171; viewing law
as form of development, 179, 181, 209.
See also humanitarian legal politics
Robertson, James W., *61n57*, 80, 91
Robinson, Mary, 169
Roll of Advocates, 100. *See also* bar
association
rule by law, defined, *21t*, 23
rule of law: in colonial era, 11, 44, 46,
47, 53, 59, 75, 211–12; considered
as force for positive change, 2–3, 7,
215; defined, *21t*, 22–3; humanitarian
actors integrating into their work, 2, 3,
161–2; ideology as gift of colonialism, 82;
institutionalization of, in fragile states,
13; legal education advancing, 72–4; and
moderation, 2, 48; role of, xii, 2–3, 42,
215; shaped by actors who use it, 5, 222
rural areas, 145, *145n61*, 175–6, 227
Russia and human rights for women, 220

sanctions against Sudan, 162–3
al-Sanhuri, Abd al-Razzak, 109, 128
School of African and Oriental Studies of the
University of London, 40
secession of South Sudan, 15, 36, 165, 198,
200, 218. *See also* South Sudan
second period of independent Sudan
(1965–76), 87, 102–10; court system
in, 105; democratic regime as chaotic
(1964–9), 102, 160; direct humanitarian
interventions in, 156, 159–60; Nimeiri's
coup, 103–5; transition from common
law to Egyptian civil law and back again,
102, 107–10, 213
Self-Government Statute (1953), 84, *95n22*
September law (*qanoon September*), 113–14
Shakir, Mohamed, 72
shari'a. See Islamic law

275

Sharkey, Heather, *73n100*
Shklar, Judith, *25n11*
"shortening the judicial shadow" (*taqsir al-zhul al-qada'i*), 120, *143–44n59*, 143–50, *144f*
SLJR. *See Sudan Law Journal and Reports*
"slow violence," 27
social stability. *See* stability created by legal system
Socialist Party, 104
Somalia and rule of law, 221
South Africa, 30, 47, 216
South Sudan: Bashir agreeing to separation of, 153, 218; civil society in, 161; common-law legal system in, *38n45*; English as language of law in, 152; interviews conducted by author in, 40; law school in, 217; ongoing conflict with, 33; statehood of, 15, 227
southern Sudan: British using different approach to native administration in, 70; Christian missionaries in, 34, *34n37*, 70, *94n20*; civil war with, xiv, 32; criminal laws enforced in, 150; direct humanitarian interventions in, 161; Islam promotion in, *94n20*; "Justice and Confidence Centers" in, 176–7; law of, outside scope of book, *38n45*; and university education, 74. *See also* civil war
Soviet Union and control of judges, 29
SPLM (Sudan People's Liberation Movement), 130, 163
SPS. *See* Sudan Political Service
stability created by legal system, 48–9, 59–63, 75, 83, 119, 223
stare decisis, 98–100, 118
state building, Western-style, 156, 214
strikes, 79, 101, 115, 124
Sudan: as "failed" state, 2, *2n2*; geographic and ethnocultural makeup, 34–5, *90n8*; historical background of, 15, 35–6; life expectancy in, xiv; as "most fragile" state, *2n2*; overview of conflict in, 32–3; research conducted in, 39; sanctions against, 162–3. *See also specific time periods and rulers*
Sudan Bar Association. *See* bar association
Sudan Human Rights Organization, 124, 192
Sudan Law Journal and Reports (SLJR), 100, 133, 159
Sudan Law Project, funded by Ford Foundation, 159

Sudan National Records Office (Khartoum), 39
Sudan People's Liberation Movement (SPLM), 130, 163
Sudan Plantations Syndicate, 50
Sudan Political Service (SPS, British colonial rule), 44; background of members of, 54, *54n30*; "benevolent despotism" of, 53–8, 119, 212; claims filed with, 64; on devolution of court system, 71–2; dual allegiance of, 61, *61n57*, 82; duration of posting in Sudan, *61n57*; and education, 74, *74n106*; governmental departments created by, 55–6, *56t*; local officials' powers under, 68–9; mind-set of, 54–5; and mosque administration, 66–7; and native administration, 68–9, 76; and *shari'a*, 56–7
Supreme Court of South Sudan, 171
Supreme Court of Sudan, 130, 132, 171. *See also* High Court
symbolic benefits of law-building programs, 12–13, 207, 209
symbolic power of law, 219, 223

Taha, Mahmoud Mohammed, *36n43*, 115–16, *196n40*
taqsir al-zhul al-qada'i ("shortening the judicial shadow"–expanding courts under Bashir), 120, *143–44n59*, 143–50, *144f*
taxation, 50, 68, 69, 145
tenancy rights, 50, *50n16*
Tenenbaum, Elcana, *157n3*
third period of independent Sudan (1977–89), 87, 110–17; autocratic rule of Nimeiri during, 113; direct humanitarian interventions in, 156; instability in, 116–17; Islamic law, imposition of, 88, 110, 112–13; transition to democracy (1985–6), 115–16. *See also* al-Mahdi, Sadiq
Thompson, E. P., 223–4, 229
top-down application of legal politics, 4, 10, 25, 27, 81, 153, 171
tort procedure: civil code redrafted in Egyptian style, 107; in colonial era, 59, 80, *80n123*; in first period (1956–64), 98; under Nimeiri, *65n75*
trade unions, 79, 101, 102, 104, 115, 124, 128, 160
al-Turabi, Hassan, 112, 117, 119, 131, 224
Turco-Egyptian rule (1821–84), 35, 52, *52n24*, 221

Umma Party, 86, 91, *92t*, 102, 112, 117
unions. *See* trade unions
United Nations: assistance for rule-of-
    law development, xii, 3, 19; on
    Darfur conflict, 33; and elites, 225;
    generic programming of, 171–2, 207;
    international aid groups in Sudan from,
    166–7, *166t*, *167n22*; NGOs framing
    programs in human rights language to
    obtain funding from, 201; rights-based
    development approach of, xii, 3, 39,
    168–79; Rule of Law Unit, 3; Sudan
    joining upon independence, *90n8*
United Nations–African Union Mission in
    Darfur (UNAMID), *167n22*
United Nations Development Programme, xi,
    39, 164, 167, 171, 173, 176, 221
United Nations Mission in Sudan (UNMIS),
    164, *167n22*, 181
University of Hargeisa, 221
University of Khartoum: and British
    legacy, 74, *80n123*, 98, 156;
    common-law-trained lawyers from,
    under Bashir, 138; curriculum, 135, 157;
    English common law as focus of, 98,
    100; faculty, 132, 157; legal profession
    influenced by, 122–3; library as data

source, 39; prestige of, *109n78*, 122;
    relationship with University of London,
    122, 157; teaching in Arabic, 136;
    tensions with graduates of *shari'a* schools,
    126
University of London, 122, 157
urf (customs) of Maliki school, 51
U.S. Agency for International Development
    (USAID), 158, *166t*
U.S. sanctions against Sudan, 162–3

violence and volatility: in authoritarian
    regimes, 36; law serving in spite of itself,
    10, 27; legal tools adopted in times of, 6;
    "slow violence," 27. *See also* revolts and
    coups

Watson, James, 62
women: corporal punishment for dress
    violations, 203; in displaced persons
    camps, 194–5; and legal awareness
    workshops, 199; Omdurman Prison,
    rights workshops at, 174–5; and
    reproductive health clinic, 192; women's
    groups in post-Soviet Russia, 220
Woodward, Peter, 118
World Bank assistance, xii, 3, 19, 39, *166t*

Other Books in the Series (*continued from page iii*)

A Sociology of Constitutions: Constitutions and State Legitimacy in Historical-Sociological Perspective
Chris Thornhill

Mitigation and Aggravation at Sentencing
Edited by Julian Roberts

Institutional Inequality and the Mobilization of the Family and Medical Leave Act: Rights on Leave
Catherine R. Albiston

Authoritarian Rule of Law: Legislation, Discourse and Legitimacy in Singapore
Jothie Rajah

Law and Development and the Global Discourses of Legal Transfers
Edited by John Gillespie and Pip Nicholson

Law against the State: Ethnographic Forays into Law's Transformations
Edited by Julia Eckert, Brian Donahoe, Christian Strümpell, and Zerrin Özlem Biner

Transnational Legal Process and State Change
Edited by Gregory C. Shaffer

Legal Mobilization under Authoritarianism: The Case of Post-Colonial Hong Kong
Edited by Waikeung Tam

Environmental Litigation in China: A Study in Political Ambivalence
Rachel E. Stern

Law's Fragile State: Colonial, Authoritarian, and Humanitarian Legacies in Sudan
Mark Fathi Massoud

CPSIA information can be obtained at www.ICGtesting.com
Printed in the USA
LVOW04s0706181114

414142LV00004B/6/P

9 781107 440050